4/1/09

FUNDING
FATHERS

To Jeffrey Zabner —
A friend of Ted Smyth,
is a friend of our cause!
You will find kindred
spirits to Ted in This
book.
Enjoy!

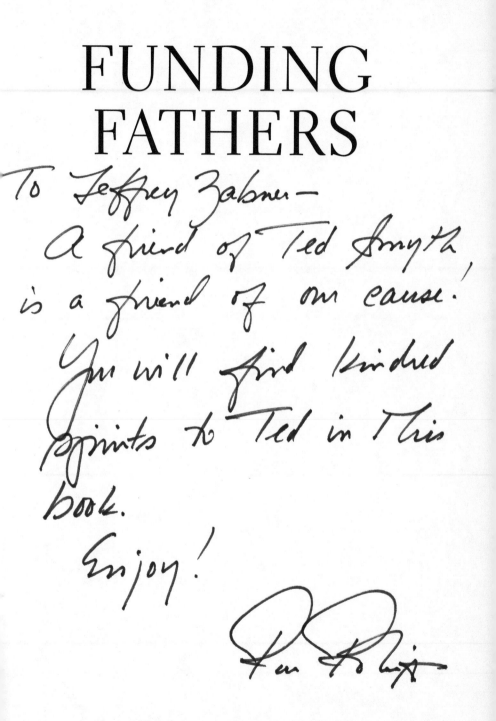

FUNDING FATHERS

★

The Unsung Heroes of the Conservative Movement

Nicole Hoplin and Ron Robinson

Since 1947
REGNERY
PUBLISHING, INC.
An Eagle Publishing Company • Washington, DC

Cataloging-in-Publication data on file with the Library of Congress

ISBN 9781-59698-562-9

Published in the United States by
Regnery Publishing, Inc.
One Massachusetts Avenue, NW
Washington, DC 20001
www.regnery.com

Manufactured in the United States of America

10   9   8   7   6   5   4   3   2   1

Books are available in quantity for promotional or premium use. Write to Director of Special Sales, Regnery Publishing, Inc., One Massachusetts Avenue NW, Washington, DC 20001, for information on discounts and terms or call (202) 216-0600.

Dedication

This effort to acknowledge those who made our Movement possible would not have been even imagined without the commitment and dedication of those determined souls who gave the gifts in the first place. To them, their families, and their causes, we dedicate this book.

And to the members of the Young America's Foundation Board of Directors, individuals who have committed decades to advancing the Conservative Movement and whose gifts of time and effort will never be forgotten: Ronald Pearson, Frank Donatelli, T. Kenneth Cribb, Kate Obenshain, Thomas Phillips, Peter Schweizer, James B. Taylor, and Kirby Wilbur.

Contents

---- ★ ----

Introduction

*"There is little hope for democracy if the hearts of
men and women in democratic societies cannot be
touched by a call to something greater than themselves."*[1]

—MARGARET THATCHER

Conservatives have emerged as an intellectual force by putting the ideas that America's Founders intended to ingrain in her very soul—limited government, traditional values, and free enterprise—at the forefront of national debate. Barry Goldwater united conservatives when he talked about small government and anti-Communism. William F. Buckley's *National Review* gave conservatives a platform to debate, perfect, and communicate their ideas on a weekly or biweekly basis. Ronald Reagan led the United States from despair to win the Cold War using conservative values and ideas. These are the tales of struggles that conservatives hear at large gatherings and conferences and frequently come across on the Internet, in conservative journals, and in books. It would be an anomaly to find a written history of the Conservative Movement without learning about the 1964 election, *National Review*, or Ronald Reagan's transformation from movie star to American president.

Unfortunately, these histories of the Conservative Movement most often lack an intimate review of these success stories' backgrounds and how they came to be in the first place. Favorite publications, admired leaders, and the organizations that help advance important ideas are discussed at length in the writings of both conservative and liberal scholars and authors. With few exceptions, rarely are the individuals who made those books possible, who supported those leaders, and who built those organizations identified. These individuals are the Conservative Movement's "Funding Fathers." History would have been profoundly altered had those people not been there at the right time and acted. The Movement's documented past lacks an important component when it fails to recognize the work or sacrifice of an individual, or in some cases colleagues, families, or friends, who expended tremendous effort and passion to convey their ideas to a broader audience. The stories of the "Funding Fathers," who invested their time, talent, and treasure to build conservatism into an intellectual force, are curiously missing from nearly every written account of philanthropy and more specifically the Conservative Movement. If conservatives intend to build on past successes, it is critical to learn from those who made decisions at crucial times, took risks, sacrificed, and selflessly promoted their ideas. When omitted from its history, the Movement misses a key opportunity to inspire and teach its believers to endow its future.

Contained in the pages of this book are the stories that have rarely been told by the media, the Conservative Movement's best historians, or the recipient institutions themselves. They are the stories of the vibrant lives of people who stood behind some of the Conservative Movement's brightest moments, and who received little recognition or gratitude from the Movement or the country they shaped over the years. More importantly, they are stories of how the most important books, institutions, and leaders came to be.

The Left already effectively pursued and achieved conservative speech restraints through the Federal Election Commission, state regulations, and campus speech codes. Similarly, the Left is attempting to suppress conservative funding and philanthropy which it knows has been equally effective.

Conservatives have neglected to cover the full history of their successes and should not expect that the mainstream media or those on the Left will pursue it justly for them. The mainstream press can be held responsible for one of three actions when it comes to stories (or lack thereof) about conservative philanthropy. It either: (a) ignores a great gift given altogether, (b) vilifies the gift and its significance, or (c) misinterprets and misreports the gift in a way a donor would not intend for it to be remembered. If conservatives rely solely on the media for gift-giving reinforcement, they will seldom take the steps necessary to propel the Movement forward.

Over the years, conservatives' reliance on mainstream media for their inspiration to give gifts has hampered the Movement's progress. Rarely will a mainstream publication highlight a conservative organization's mission and giving opportunities. Yet conservatives don't have to go far to find a full spread on how giving to National Public Radio or the United Nations or a public university or even a small human services organization makes a major difference in our country.

The story of Oseola McCarty best illustrates the media's fascination with liberal philanthropy. In 1995, Miss McCarty gave her life savings of $150,000 to the University of Southern Mississippi to fund black scholarships. She had quit school after the sixth grade and worked as a washerwoman, saving a small sum every week. When she gave the gift in her eighties, the media rallied around her in lockstep. Stories ran in newspapers across the country, including a fifteen-hundred-word, front-page cover story in the *New York Times* on August 13, 1995, that pontificated on its significance. According to the paper, the gift "piqued interest around the nation."[2] Between 1995 and 1999, the *New York Times* ran twenty-six articles, including two front-page stories, in which it featured or mentioned Oseola McCarty. Papers nationwide included stories evaluating the gift and its giver. "This is an amazing gift," they said. She is "a symbol of selfless giving."[3]

Honors and awards showered on Miss McCarty following her gift. She dined with President Clinton at the White House and received a Certificate of Commendation. The Cleveland NAACP honored her at its Freedom

Fund celebration. She flipped the switch on the 1996–97 New Year's Eve ball drop in New York City. Roberta Flack and Patti LaBelle sang to her. Harvard gave her an honorary degree. Whoopi Goldberg knelt in front of her. People called her "holy."[4] She earned a place on Barbara Walters's "10 Most Fascinating People of 1995" list for ABC.[5] The United Nations honored her actions.

When she passed away in 1999, newspapers from the *Des Moines Register* to the *Los Angeles Times*, from the *Washington Post* to the *Tampa Tribune* ran stories on her life and gift. President Clinton issued a statement upon her death. In total, since her gift, more than 612 stories in newspapers across the country have mentioned her name! It was a selfless act of giving for student scholarships to be sure, but conservatives cannot expect to receive such royal, favorable treatment by the media following gifts of similar magnitude.

When conservatives and their philanthropy are included in the pages of the mainstream newspapers and newsmagazines, they are not covered in a way which would encourage further benevolence. A quick browse through articles about conservatism's generous benefactors uncovers a host of labels and derogatory connotations about its patrons as compared to their liberal counterparts. George Soros and a man who he admitted to be his "right-wing version," Richard Mellon Scaife, serve as excellent examples of this dichotomy.[6]

George Soros, whose foundations have given away nearly half a billion dollars, is named in more than five hundred headlines in prominent news publications. Soros has supported untold liberal causes both in the United States and abroad, including MoveOn.org, the Center for American Progress, and America Coming Together. For his efforts, he's described as a "mover of markets," a "guru," and a "philosopher."[7] Another paper calls him a "very concerned citizen."[8] Still another refers to him as a "missionary."[9] One headline features the phrase, "the Essential George Soros."[10] And one even calls him "The Man Who Would Mend the World."[11] Yet French courts convicted George Soros in 2002 of insider trading (because of a deal he made to acquire a French bank in 1988). The ruling was reaffirmed by a 2006 appeals court, and Soros's fine will top $2.8 million for his illegal activity.

On the other hand, Richard Scaife, for his efforts to fund many successful conservative institutions, led the headlines for months in 1998, becoming the mastermind behind what Hillary Clinton dubbed the "vast right-wing conspiracy." When mainline news media stayed silent during the Clinton investigation, Scaife funded early research efforts that looked into the behavior of President Clinton and led to Clinton's impeachment in the U.S. House of Representatives. Yet the media did not stay silent on Richard Scaife's efforts. "Scaife Has Good Reason to Hide," said one headline.[12] "Implausible Dick Scaife," said another.[13] One purported him to be the "sugardaddy of the New Right."[14] "The Right's Daddy Morebucks," wrote still another.[15] "Extremist," one described him;[16] "reclusive heir," yet another.[17]

Richard Scaife has given more than $200 million to conservative and libertarian causes, including the *American Spectator* magazine, the Heritage Foundation, the American Enterprise Institute for Public Policy Research, the Cato Institute, the Washington Legal Foundation, the Manhattan Institute, Newt Gingrich's GOPAC, National Taxpayers Union, the Free Congress Foundation, the Hoover Institution, and dozens of other important groups.[18] Perhaps most important, he has not been convicted of a crime—unlike his counterpart, George Soros. Yet his character is besmirched across the headlines of the country's most read newspapers and newsmagazines. The *Milwaukee Journal Sentinel* correctly identified how the media's treatment of Scaife and his philanthropy did little to strengthen the possibility that others might follow his lead: "For his generosity, Scaife has earned a string of profiles in newspapers and magazines, few of them favorable. The stories generally paint Scaife as a right-wing nut...."[19]

A damaging blow is dealt by the media when other conservatives considering a donation witness how Scaife and others are treated. They are left wondering why they would take a chance in investing in a conservative cause. Potential donors realize they risk being described as "implausible," "extremist," or even "nutty," forcing both themselves and their families to endure tumultuous attacks and ad hominems.

If news agencies or other media outlets report on conservative giving, a predictable storyline generally emerges; conservatives give less than liberals, and this is so because they are selfish. Arthur C. Brooks, author of the groundbreaking book *Who Really Cares*, described this common misconception when he commented on an article that appeared in *Slate* magazine. He summarized the article as claiming that red state conservatives are "irredeemably uncharitable" while blue state liberals are "good and compassionate."[20] Brooks argues the contrary in his book: "[P]olitical conservatives are *not* personally less charitable than political liberals—they are more so."[21] He goes on to report,

> In 2000, households headed by a conservative gave, on average, 30 percent more money to charity than households headed by a liberal ($1,600 to $1,227). This discrepancy is not simply an artifact of income differences; on the contrary, liberal families earned an average of 6 percent *more* per year than conservative families, and conservative families gave more than liberal families within every income class, from poor to middle class to rich.[22]

Even conservatives buy into the stereotype that liberals are more generous. Publisher Henry Regnery once wrote, "If the people on our side would drive Buicks instead of Cadillacs, and use the difference to support the battle of ideas, there might be a chance to save our society...."[23] Brooks recalls the 2000 election as evidence: "Some conservatives often embrace [the stereotype] as well. For example, in 2000, George W. Bush, then running for the presidency, used the label 'compassionate conservative' to describe his proposed approach to governance. He proposed this as an innovation— as if he were going against the grain of conservative tradition."[24] Where does the notion that conservatives are greedy, selfish, and ungenerous come from? Brooks contends the misconception is fueled by politicians and the media's attempts to "milk these stereotypes for everything they are worth."[25]

Examples in the media abound. One report in the *Virginian-Pilot* (Norfolk) discusses a 2004 "Generosity Index" which concludes that conservatives give more than liberals. But the publication doesn't leave the story there. The *Virginian-Pilot* goes on to postulate about conservatives' values: "Certainly, in theory, liberals are more generous than conservatives. After all, liberals created the New Deal, Fair Deal, New Frontier and Great Society—America's best-known public policies to help the less fortunate."[26]

The media often threads a secondary theme through its writing. It argues conservative ideas—patriotism, free enterprise, traditional values—have nothing to do with the rise of conservatism. Instead, conservatism emerged because of "sinister" philanthropists. James Piereson, formerly of the John M. Olin Foundation, uncovers this deception:

> Addressing the rise of conservatism, the Left resorts to explanations that stress manipulation and trickery, with corporate payoffs to politicians looming large in the story. Conservative ideas play but a minor role in the account...A particularly sinister role is ascribed to those conservative philanthropies that have helped fund thinkers, magazines, and research institutions—on the assumption that no one would advance such self-evidently meretricious ideas unless paid to do so.[27]

Ideas are important. They fueled the Movement's brightest times. Russell Kirk said it best in *The American Cause*, "The success or failure of any human society depends upon how sound and true its ideas are." The fact that the Conservative Movement has been so successful over the years is a testimony to the fortitude of the ideas philanthropic efforts have promoted.

Conservatives by nature often do not help promote philanthropy. They are inherently inclined to keep to themselves, raising their families and building their businesses. Conservative donors tend to protect their

philanthropy and their privacy to avoid negative attacks and endless solici-
tations. This creates a classic Catch-22. Afraid of being attacked or labeled,
so many conservatives avoid the media by requesting anonymity in
exchange for a gift, but this only reinforces the left-leaning media's omis-
sions. When conservative organizations don't celebrate a gift, the media
cannot be expected to know about it in the first place. Of course, knowing
about a gift doesn't mean it will be promoted in a positive way by the media
anyway. The point still remains. Gifts given by conservatives often remain
in secrecy, and this deprives the giver of feedback—positive or negative. It
ensures future gifts are given without the benefit of hindsight, reflection,
or full appraisal. By the very nature of a gift, a donor provides legitimacy to
the recipient institution or cause. Without recognition or public attribute
of this gift, legitimacy is slower to become established, and causes are challenged to make the next appeal. This is especially so with newly emerging
groups and efforts. Secrecy and anonymity are not beneficial to a cause
deeply rooted in its history, yet dependent upon future initiative.

Conservative organizations all too often are leery of competition. They
assume the realm of available resources in the world to be a zero-sum situation where limited dollars inhibit every organization from obtaining all
that it needs to operate and thrive. Thus, groups must compete for every
gift, even if that means shutting others out by undermining another group's
reputation. Certainly, this perception is flawed. There are so many potential givers in the world who need a little inspiration and positive encouragement to make a sizeable contribution for a cause or ideas they strongly
believe. When conservative organizations highlight and promote their significant gifts and the wonderful work of others, they provide valuable motivation to those who are considering a sacrificial gift.

Conservatives face unexpected challenges when giving to establishment
organizations such as institutions of higher learning. Gifts are not always
used as donors originally intended. The clearest example can be found in
regards to free enterprise programs. Millions of dollars have been poured
into the public university system to support free enterprise and Western civ-

ilization programs, with disappointing consequences. The *Wall Street Journal* reports, "Capitalism's largest investment in the collegiate marketplace of ideas has yielded returns lower than the shakiest grade of junk bond."[28] It goes on to suggest, "That's because much of the money has been donated to universities to establish chairs of free enterprise and entrepreneurship–and despite the wealth of their endowments, these chairs are remarkably ineffective."[29] Milton Friedman, Nobel Laureate in economics, prior to his passing, warned conservatives against endowing chairs in the public university system, because the gifts rarely have the intended impacts. He advised, "There is essentially no way of guaranteeing that a chair established as a pro-free enterprise chair will remain one."[30] In a response to an individual seeking to establish a chair of free enterprise, he said, "I personally believe it is a great mistake to establish a Chair of Free Enterprise. I do not believe that that is the way to promote the cause that I believe so fervently in, the cause of freedom and of a competitive capitalist system."[31]

In another instance, Lee Bass gave Yale University $20 million in 1991 to start a permanent program on Western civilization and to endow professorships, a gift which the university accepted. Five years later, when the university had "trouble" finding professors to teach the courses, the university decided it didn't want such a program and returned the gift. One may defend Yale's actions by using the fact that Yale once turned down a gift to establish a full-time gay-studies professor, too. Yet Yale has since "expanded its gay studies course offerings and established a rotating professorship."[32] The school also *reversed* its original declination of the gift and accepted $1 million from Larry Kramer's older brother, Arthur, to hire a coordinator for the Larry Kramer Initiative for Lesbian and Gay Studies; now students have their choice of thirty-two courses in gay and lesbian studies. This is one such example of a university which has decided against Western civilization values in favor of alternative programming.

Princeton University has also been at the center of disputes arising from donor intent. It has been alleged by one of Princeton's own employees who investigated a claim that the university did not properly allocate a $1 million gift given in 1959 (now estimated at $18.5 million) from conservative senator John Danforth's family foundation, intended to promote religious life on campus.[33] The income from the gift in 2002, $736,000, was intended for religious scholarships, but purportedly only $6,000 was allocated to the Office of Religious Life and the rest went to general funds.[34] Similarly, Lois Thompson provided $5,000 to maintain the university's chapel pipe organ in 1988. Shortly thereafter, the university's treasurer received a note from a fund-raising official directing the gift to be used for "general funds," and the "Dept is not to know."[35] One Princeton University development analyst, Jessie Washington, believes there have been "many problems with the management of the university's endowed funds," which have "serious legal implications."[36] This practice, whereby universities accept gifts and use them for purposes other than those requested by the donor, happens all too often for a gift to be secure in a university account.

Universities use endowed funds as they desire with little accountability. More than 60 percent of all gifts over $10 million are given to academic institutions. Universities receive more than $25 billion annually.[37] Virtually no protection exists to ensure the ideas the gift intended to promote are upheld. An individual donor is challenged in these situations to guarantee that the college will fulfill their endowment's intent. A donor also cannot direct where the school's potential excess funds may be spent. If a donor endows a professor who already happens to be a tenured faculty member, the school often is not obligated to keep those funds once provided for the salary designated toward that free-market program. Rather, the school can divert the funds as it wishes. Martin Morse Wooster asks in the *Wall Street Journal*, "Of what use is it, for example, to pay a tenured economics professor's salary if a college can use the money saved to pay for socialist speakers?"[38] He goes on to suggest, "For the price of a free-enterprise chair, a donor could pay for a year's budget of a first-rate research organization...."[39]

Conservative organizations themselves compound problems with universities when they highlight and market the failure of establishment charities, universities in particular, to honor donor intent. Inevitably, making the case for giving to conservative causes by focusing on the scandals that have occurred in another sector weakens conservative donors' confidence in philanthropy altogether. According to a Charles Schwab & Co. study, more than half of older, affluent Americans will leave nothing to nonprofit organizations or universities. Nearly one in five of those cited a loss of confidence that their gifts will be used as they intended postmortem.[40] Conservative organizations must do a better job at differentiating the results of gifts given to conservative-run institutions to ensure they don't undermine overall donor confidence in giving. The stories included in this book intend to do just that; they demonstrate the dramatic impact a gift can have on a conservative institution or idea. These gifts exceeded all expectations.

"Money changes everything," the *New York Times* once reported, and when it comes to conservative philanthropy, it has a point. Money does change everything. Yet the amount of funding, whether large or small, often doesn't predict its impact. Some of the most important gifts from conservatives involved modest sums, yet their consequences are dramatic.

The Left dominates the universities, the media, and most of the major philanthropic organizations, but it seldom matches the Conservative Movement's effectiveness. Conservatives can be confident in the returns they receive from two bottom lines—the return on shared values and the return on sound financial practices. Stephen Moore of the *Wall Street Journal* reports, "It is still safe to say that the institutions of the Left—which include liberal foundations, the media, unions, and government itself—have outspent the Right by many multiples. It is a sad irony that the foes of free enterprise are lavishly funded, while advocates of capitalism remain comparatively undercapitalized. The good news is that conservative foundations and individual donors have given their money more efficiently to bring about change."[41] Conservatives should be comforted knowing that their resources are managed efficiently and effectively. They receive more bang for the buck, as the old adage goes.

One key piece of evidence that indicates the Conservative Movement's success is the Left's attempts to emulate its strategies. "Feeling unmatched in the war of ideas, liberal groups have spent years studying conservative foundations the way Pepsi studies Coke, searching for trade secrets," the *New York Times* reported.[42] In 2005, Democracy Alliance, a group supported by George Soros, announced a $200 million fund-raising drive to build new think tanks and grassroots operations to counter conservatism fashioned after the Movement's most effective groups. Democracy Alliance aims "to foster the growth of liberal or left-leaning institutions equipped to take on prominent think tanks on the right, including the Heritage Foundation, the Hoover Institution, the American Enterprise Institute and the Cato Institute, as well as such training centers as the Leadership Institute and the Young America's Foundation."[43] Conservative groups focus on ensuring that every gift made has impact beyond the dollar value of the gift and is efficiently put to use to achieve the desired consequence—a practice leftist organizations cannot duplicate.

Gifts have consequences, and they can be huge. James Piereson, formerly of the Olin Foundation, believes that "wealthy donors who write checks directly to their favorite causes will become a stronger influence."[44] Their ideas will be preserved in the missions and success of the efforts they sponsor and will be embedded forever in our country's future. The Conservative Movement would never be a force today if not for the individuals who stepped forward and invested in its own emerging ideas over the years. The stories of those individuals' lives and the gifts they gave demonstrate that gifts directed to a specific purpose can accomplish immeasurable strides lasting decades. They are all the more remarkable since little or no public acclaim was expected or received.

Great gifts, those that have remained anonymous for so long, once revealed are lures drawing others to make similar commitments. Kay Sprinkel Grace and Alan Wendroff keenly noted in their book, *High Impact Philanthropy*, "[Donors'] transformational gifts can be and almost always are used as magnets to draw other donor-investors to the recipient agencies."[45] Keeping the most important gifts made in obscurity hinders the Movement's ability to create a magnetic field for its future. These tremendous Funding Fathers and their stories to follow are the Movement's magnets, attracting those who aren't sure about making a major sacrifice to provide an investment on behalf of their values and America's future.

Remember Oseola McCarty's surprise gift to the University of Southern Mississippi? Her $150,000 gave opportunities to students who may not have otherwise had them. It has provided seventeen young people with a college education free of charge and has served as a permanent endowed fund which attracts additional donors through the publicity McCarty received upon giving the gift.[46]

But Oseola McCarty's gift of $150,000 made a staggering impact beyond the scholarship assistance. It became a *magnet* for additional givers. When this washerwoman gave her gift, Ted Turner was quoted as saying, "If that little woman can give away everything she has, then I can give a billion."[47] Ted Turner, a multibillionaire who in 1997 pledged $1 billion over ten years to the United Nations to alleviate world poverty and disease, was inspired by McCarty's actions. People from across the nation wrote to the university to share the inspiration they received upon learning of McCarty's gift. Untold others have been motivated as well. The power of one gift goes much further than meets the immediate eye. Until now, a conservative story similar in impact to Oseola McCarty has yet to take the mainstream press by storm, inspiring its audience along the way. It is dangerous for conservatives to be isolated from their success stories. Such a separation undermines the very nature of humanity's desire for companionship and reinforcement for life's major decisions. Aleksandr Solzhenitsyn eloquently wrote, "Solitude weakens a man. All it takes to brace him is another living soul at his side."[48] Being a part of a cause greater than oneself brings comfort and strength of conviction.

This book seeks to share just a few of the many important gifts to the Conservative Movement to inspire those who have the inclination to follow a similar path. In this endeavor, the compilation will never be exhaustive. Because conservative donors value privacy, and because the media neglects to report on their actions, we will never be sure of all those individuals who have helped advance a cause. Sometimes the stories may not be complete, and questions may remain about the gift's intricacies or who actually may have given a particular gift. But with this first step, perhaps we will come to know the others as time and the cause press forward.

The life stories of the individuals and the contributions they made were not just ordinary bequests upon deserving causes; they were investments in America's future. You will be surprised by some of them, enlightened by the "real" story in others, thankful for the sacrifices found in their commitments, and inspired by their deep-seated beliefs in America. Hopefully you, too, will wonder what you can do to change the course of America's future.*[49]

---

* Some reviewers or journalists will surely note that the authors of this book cite news accounts of conservative philanthropy, the action thereby suggesting in itself that underreporting of conservative philanthropy is a moot issue. The authors are acutely aware of how such conservative or freedom-oriented stories are scattered, obscured, and often unpublished. This comparison of gifts to liberal and conservative causes featured in the endnotes bears witness throughout.

———— ★ ————

Chapter One

William Volker and His Nephew Harold Luhnow

"When we give without sacrifice, we haven't given anything."[1]

—WILLIAM VOLKER

T o Harry Wood: $1.00 to replace broken glasses. To Clarence Won-
setler: $3.00 for rent. To County Tax Collector: $24.87 on behalf of
Laura Winn. To Nancy Boswell: $115.00 to obtain hearing aids. To
University of Kansas City: $42.00 for tuition on behalf of Harold Hein. To
Bell Memorial Hospital: $100.00 for James Case's operation.

Scratched on three-by-five pieces of yellowing scrap paper, these notes
reminded William Volker who would receive a check that day. They were
not relatives, nor were they acquaintances. In fact, he had never met the
individuals who lined up at his office door in the wee hours of the morning on a daily basis, but he allowed each to plead his case. He rarely turned
someone away empty-handed.

William Volker was a charitable man and had been giving to those less
fortunate since the age of twelve, inspired to tithe his earnings by his pious

German mother, Dorothea Volker. She taught her children the importance
of charity through the Gospel of Matthew. "So whenever you give alms, do
not sound a trumpet before you . . . . But when you give alms do not let your
left hand know what your right hand is doing, so that your alms may be done
in secret; and your Father who sees in secret will reward you."[2] William
Volker's philanthropy inspired individuals, boosted their capacity to contribute to society, and empowered some of the most accomplished writers,
leaders, and thinkers of the twentieth century's movement toward free enterprise and freedom from intervention. Dubbed "Mr. Anonymous" by those
who knew of his good works, William Volker and his nephew Harold Luhnow changed individuals' lives all around them, one person at a time.

Born on April Fools' Day in 1859 as the fourth child of six, William
Volker grew up on a small farm in Esperke am Neustadt, Germany. His
mother and father gave the children considerable responsibility at a young
age, including tending to the farm's potato and vegetable crops, fruit tree
orchard, and cattle. Each day, after long hours of labor, William returned
home and entered through the doorway adorned with the saying, "Work
and Pray."

Two early experiences left an impact on William Volker's character. In
1871, the Volker family packed their belongings and headed to Chicago to
join William's brother Frederick, who had emigrated two years earlier.
Frederick had made the move to circumvent the draft for Bismarck's
forces.[3] This early episode of fleeing the quickly growing and ever-more
intrusive Bismarck German government resulted in William's skepticism
of a demanding government. The Volkers arrived in Chicago just three days
following the destructive Windy City blaze of 1871. The fire's aftermath
taught William Volker an eye-opening lesson. He witnessed the overwhelming compassion of ordinary Americans who generously assisted those
whose lives and possessions had been destroyed by the fire. They were two
experiences that remained engrained in the heart of a young lad who
became a millionaire in 1906 at the age of forty-seven.[4]

William knew four English words when he arrived in Chicago and began school: "hello," "good-bye," "please," and "thank you." Yet he was still a child, and the language came quickly to the youngster. He recalled, "I was very green when we came to the United States, knew no English, was dressed with ludicrous oddity, self-conscious to a degree and, of course, most unhappy. But I learned."[5] When he turned fourteen, his parents decided it was time for him to earn his keep apart from the family chores. He swept, dusted, and ran errands twelve hours a day to earn $1 per week at a dry-goods business. Soon, his diligence paid off, and the company promoted him to junior clerk where he pulled in $5 per week.

William recognized his own talents and entrepreneurial skills, and with the encouragement of his parents, he attended a local Chicago business college to learn the trade. William taught German to students at night to pay his way. Later in school, he went to work for Charles Brachvogel's picture frame company as an assistant bookkeeper and earned $6 per week.[6] Gradually he became a trusted member of Brachvogel's inner circle. When a tragic buggy accident took his employer's life, William assumed sole responsibility for the store.

William remained a Chicago resident for eleven years, working and saving every penny he earned. His desire to start his own company eventually drove him to leave his position running the picture frame business in Chicago. In 1882, after significant market research and intense study, William settled on building a company in Kansas City, Missouri, home to a significant population of walnut groves along the Missouri River. He started with $1,500 in savings and a $3,000 loan acquired from a mortgage placed on the family home.[7] With two partners, the twenty-three-year-old incorporated William Volker and Company in 1882. He intended to manufacture picture frames and molding since he had experience in making and selling those home goods already. Volker quickly transitioned into wholesaling these products and window shades when the financial loss of the business during the first year forced him to reevaluate its operations.

William Volker worked hard. He put in ninety-hour workweeks, open-ing and closing the shop personally, often sleeping on a cot in the back room.[8] The local folks who stopped in weren't accustomed to a young busi-ness owner—his thin, small build and his grayish, stoic eyes made him appear even younger than he really was. Locals seemed to question his abil-ity to run the company based on his age alone. Frustrated and anxious to expand his company, William Volker grew a mustache and donned a dis-tinguished dark suit and string bow tie to earn the respect of community members. His strategy worked. In 1883, the second year in business, William Volker and Company made a small profit.[9] Profit margins grew steadily from there each year until the Great Depression of the 1930s.

Not only did William Volker work hard, but he prayed diligently, too. His favorite poet, Friedrich Schiller, wrote, "Chance comes from Provi-dence and man must mould it to his own designs."[10] Volker took this line of poetry to heart and believed strongly in divine, yet simple Providence, the significance of God's omnipotence, the importance of his stewardship in the eyes of God, and his Christian heritage engrained in his soul from a young age. He read Scripture everyday; detached, creased pages filled his tattered Bible from its daily use. Scripture guided his actions, and he rec-ognized God's impact on his life: "Providence has been good to me."[11] William Volker did not parade his Christianity, according to his nephew Harold Luhnow. Instead, he lived it in the most humble and modest way possible. He took long rides on his horse, Prince, on Sunday mornings before church and rode his horse to work each day.[12] He enjoyed a simple sandwich at his desk for lunch, personally scurried to and from shops to take care of his own errands, and rarely accepted social invitations. His per-sonality, attire, speech, habits, and lifestyle revealed his simplicity.

Mr. Volker demonstrated his early generosity by the way he treated his employees. He recognized the value of saving and encouraged his employ-ees to deposit a sum per month with him, and he'd personally guarantee a 6 percent return.[13] He purchased insurance plans for some of his employ-ees, funding the premiums for those plans himself. He dreamed of the day when William Volker and Company would be owned entirely by employees, and so he established a trust estate of twenty-four thousand company shares with assets of $2.4 million for employees to buy into a portion of the enterprise.[14] Upon his death, employees owned 55 percent of the company, the Volker Fund held 30 percent, and 15 percent remained on installment contracts.[15] When, in 1931, the company had suffered two straight years of losses, William Volker called all employees together and explained the two options: one-third would lose their jobs, or there would be reduced pay and hours for all employees. Upon the announcement, he left the meeting asking his employees to make the decision that would affect their well-being. They selected the latter option, and while the reduced pay made those two years during the Depression difficult ones for the employees, Mr. Volker refrained from taking any salary whatsoever.[16]

William Volker married Rose Roebke when he was fifty-two years old, in 1911, in front of her family home's fireplace in Holton, Kansas. She was a gentle and kind woman with a large family, a beautiful personality, and a firm demeanor. Each year after their wedding, the couple hosted a Fourth of July picnic for the extended family at their estate, Roselawn, on Bell Street in Kansas City, and the children looked forward to the box of Russell Stover chocolates Rose kept hidden in her cedar trunk. While he had known Rose for twenty years before their wedding, he had spent every moment of his time building his company and had had little time to court potential wives. He rarely spent a day away from the office and had never taken a vacation. The couple's honeymoon to the United States' Pacific Northwest was his first time ever away from the company.[17] In the first year of their marriage, William Volker and Company maintained net assets of $1.3 million and profits of $203,000.[18] As soon as they returned from their honeymoon, William Volker transferred $1 million of his own money into Rose's name. He explained to Rose it was "so that you can take care of me when I grow old," for, he announced, "I intend to give all the rest away."[19]

Giving was a serious business to Mr. Volker, one that he took with caution and sober consideration. Once, when walking down Summit Street on his way home, a bandit pressed the barrel of a gun into his flesh demanding money. Volker hit the man with his fist as hard as he could, turned, and ran away, the trailing gunshot puncturing and knocking his hat from atop his head. He carried only a dime in his pocket that day, but he wouldn't forfeit it to such a lawless individual. That dime could get someone else a hot meal or a bed for a night. Mr. Volker once said, "There remains for every man who has been successful in business the greater success of stretching out a hand to his brothers. I do positively and literally believe that 'I am my brother's keeper,' and a lifetime is all too short to learn that job."[20]

It is estimated that Mr. Volker gave away nearly one-third of his income each year.[21] As his reputation for generosity grew, so, too, did the lines forming outside of his office door each day. Starting from his first year of profit in 1883, he helped nearly every person who knocked on his door, and by 1937, he was scrawling checks to more than one hundred individuals monthly.[22] Volker personally wrote each check so that every transaction would remain a secret.[23]

He also assisted generously with dozens of formal organizations, even those with which he had little experience or knowledge. In those early days, he helped establish a tuberculosis pavilion at Kansas City General Hospital, demonstrated the commerciality of the Missouri River by building a successful steamship enterprise, purchased camels for the Kansas City Zoo, paid for teacher salaries and pensions when he thought more educators were necessary, and bought milk for undernourished children.

The list of causes and charities William Volker supported grew with each passing month. He particularly enjoyed funding the Helping Hands Institute, which provided employment for out-of-work citizens. He gave more than half a million dollars to Research Hospital (now Research Medical Center) making a nurses' residence, research laboratory, and a diagnostic clinic possible. He assisted the state of Missouri with a massive road-building campaign by supplying the city with four hundred thousand barrels of cement each year for five years from his cement plant. He also helped the city acquire the Frederic Nelson Pugsley collection of Chinese art for $50,000, which remains on display at the Nelson-Atkins Museum of Art. He not only gave generously to his own church, but also gave to many others suffering from debt or needing reinvigoration.

The University of Kansas City became one of the most important causes to him. Mr. Volker, more than any other, was responsible for its initial establishment and growth in the Kansas City community. The campus, built in 1930, was constructed on forty acres of land gifted to the university by William Volker. The $100,000 gift was the first of many to the institution: $100,000 for the science building, $75,000 for the library, $10,500 for the president's residence, a cash gift of $200,000 in 1939, a pledge of $1 million over ten years, and a gift of $250,000 in 1944 for general use. Mr. Volker later said, "I am sure the University will pay the biggest dividends to the most people. That is plain logic."[24]

Contrary to Mr. Volker's own intentions, he was responsible for helping create the first tax-supported Department of Public Welfare in America. It stemmed from his experience serving as one of the first volunteers with its predecessor, the Public Welfare Board. Volker witnessed that individuals, with a little guidance and grace, could take responsibility for their actions and turn their lives around. One day in 1910, three boys maliciously threw eggs at passing pedestrians. William Volker, then president of the organization, sentenced the three hooligans to a financial fine in addition to a choice in penalties: attend church every day for six months or break rock for one hundred days. All three chose to attend church. Under his leadership and vision, the board created the Municipal Rock Quarry where unemployed citizens could work for board and lodging. He also established a reformatory for women, purchasing sewing machines and hiring an instructor to teach the women how to use them to make a living. These job opportunities, he felt, gave people the ability to direct their own destinies and rise from destitution. During his tenure, only 9 percent of the parolees committed a further crime.[25] When the public funds for this venture were threatened, he personally supported the job-creation outlet. The volunteer board eventually transitioned into the government sponsored Department of Public Welfare, shifting away from Volker's vision of personal initiative and instead provided handouts to those in need.

William Volker's family also received the fruits of his philanthropy. Having no children of his own, he looked after his nieces and nephews by providing allowances for college and tuition for summer camps and supported his siblings as well.[26] Volker's youngest sister, Emma, had made the journey to Chicago from Germany with her family back in 1871 as a four-year-old. She married William C. Luhnow, a wholesale coal merchant, in 1890, and the couple remained on the west side of Chicago running coal yards. They had six boys altogether. Three of their sons benefited from employment in William Volker's company, and another maintained the Volker residence. When Emma became a widow and developed a cancerous tumor, William Volker built a home next door to his Kansas City estate where he brought her to be close to her sons and cared for her until her death.

One particular nephew became closely involved with Mr. Volker, his business, and his philanthropy. Harold Luhnow, Emma's third child, was born in 1895 in Chicago. One day in 1913, William Volker cancelled his scheduled plans when he heard that his nephew was to begin his journey to the Kansas State College of Agriculture in Manhattan, Kansas. William Volker intended to guarantee that his nephew had adequate housing and spending money at the institution. Volker joined Harold Luhnow on the train ride and questioned the young lad about his ambitions, intentions, and financial needs. Harold assured his uncle that he had sufficient resources to last the school year, but Volker insisted on writing him his first monthly stipend. Again, Harold protested, telling his uncle that his parents had provided him with ample spending money. Volker, rather than acquiesce entirely, instead set up a savings account for his nephew, contributing the same amount to the account monthly through Harold's college career.[27]

After graduating with a bachelor of science degree in agriculture and animal husbandry in 1917, Harold served in the Army as a private during World War I. Upon his return to Kansas City in 1919, he suffered from pneumonia and the flu as a result of his military service, which kept him from pursuing cattle ranching for the time being. When William Volker heard of his nephew's condition, he offered him a position with William Volker and Company as a sales clerk for $15 per week until his health improved. Luhnow accepted with the condition that no favors would be granted on account of their relation, and they would refer to one another as Mr. Volker and Mr. Luhnow. This marked the beginning of a thirty-year professional relationship.

Harold Luhnow climbed his way up the company ranks by working hard and gaining the trust of his uncle over the years. Mr. Volker valued his nephew's judgment and recognized his talent for business. He assigned Harold as the new Dallas, Texas, branch manager in 1921; Luhnow continued to serve in that post until 1928. In Dallas, Harold had the opportunity to raise cattle and farm, one of his lifelong hobbies, but worked diligently to make William Volker and Company successful. He brought the new branch to a status as a healthy competitor in the Dallas market, forcing a move to a larger facility. In 1928, William Volker appointed Luhnow the general sales manager of the Kansas City headquarters and tasked him with overhauling the sales department to improve its operations.

When Harold returned to Kansas City, he arrived in a city overrun with crooks. Tom Pendergast, broad nosed and barrel-chested, led the city with an iron fist. He became "the boss," bribing to fit his political ambitions whenever necessary. At the height of his Kansas City domination, Pendergast's personal operatives, in collusion with the local police, jailed poll watchers who tried to keep illegal voters from casting ballots; he accepted political kickbacks; and in 1935–1936, he paid out $1.1 million more than the revenue he had reported on his income taxes.[28] In addition, Pendergast allowed rate increases by fire insurance companies in exchange for $400,000 in cash.[29] His accumulation of government power and stranglehold on Kansas City's decision-making processes directly threatened the values Harold Luhnow and William Volker held: citizenship, benevolence, and principled character.

Luhnow grew more and more upset with the Pendergast regime and decided to join an initiative to remove Pendergast and his cronies from power. In 1934, he became a director of the National Youth Movement, an organization which sought to destroy the Pendergast grasp over the city. Four years later, he served as the finance chairman for the Independent Voters League, again hoping, yet falling short, to rid the city of Pendergast domination.

When Mr. Volker retired in 1938, Harold Luhnow became president of William Volker and Company. Their long-standing partnership continued as Harold Luhnow, supported by the purse strings of William Volker, continued to work behind the scenes to end the Pendergast corruption. Luhnow demanded financial audits that the Volker-supported Civic Research Institute performed.[30] As an organizer of the United Campaign Committee, a nonpartisan group seeking to influence city government elections, Luhnow helped pass an amendment to the city charter to term-limit city officials, thus throwing the Pendergasts out of government in 1940.[31] While Luhnow labored over the Pendergast situation, William Volker, now eighty-one years old, spent time in the office to keep the company affairs in order.

The Pendergast era in Kansas City caused both Volker and Luhnow to doubt the ability of government to relieve social problems appropriately. In particular, it is clear that Mr. Volker recognized that his personal philanthropy worked much more effectively than government-sponsored welfare. When the Pendergasts maliciously used the Department of Public Welfare, a relief organization Volker helped start, to take hold over Kansas City, Mr. Volker said, "I've learned something about government. Governments must be restricted to those activities which can be entrusted to the worst citizens, not the best."[32] A direct correlation existed in the causes he started to support following this realization; he became less sympathetic to Socialistic schemes and an outspoken advocate for personal initiative.

Influenced by the mounting Pendergast corruption, his disappointment with the welfare project, and his alarm at increasing government involvement, Mr. Volker responded by promoting responsible government.

Through his work with various educational institutions, he began to see how higher education was "furthering the insidious progress toward socialism in this country."[33] The concentration of power in the hands of government and the lackluster interest in civic duties by young people encouraged William Volker to undertake a project to teach effective citizenship. With a gift of $200,000 to Kansas State College, now Kansas State University, students could take a four-year course in citizenship.[34] This Civic Research Institute, the first program of its kind in the United States, was created by William Volker with the help of Loren Miller, a man he had come to admire. Miller devoted himself to principles of freedom, patriotism, and free markets and had a profound impact on many businessmen with whom he was acquainted.[35] Mr. Miller helped Volker achieve many of his philanthropic goals based on this freedom philosophy.

Because of the local government's ineffectiveness and Volker's philanthropic commitment, Mr. Volker, assisted by Loren Miller, established the William Volker Charities Fund in 1932. Volker described his philosophy: "There are two ways of doing this . . . through organized charity or by taxation. Organized charity relieves destitution, but in addition does the utmost to furnish employment, to remove the causes of misfortune, and to restore the individual or family to a basis of independence and productive citizenship. Besides all this, voluntary charity does something for the giver. To depend on taxation would mean that many who are destitute would become used to dependence on others, confirmed paupers who would be a continuous charge of the community."[36] Even more explicit, Volker began to understand that good ideas, more so than government-sponsored improvement projects, could impact and change the future. He placed half of his wealth for eventual distribution in the fund.

The Volker Fund made its giving decisions based on ideas rather than on capital or bricks-and-mortar projects. It supported individuals and their work, but left the individual free to complete his or her work without intervention or restraint. The Volker Fund Statement of Policy conveyed, "Ideas do not originate in monuments but in the minds of creative individuals."[37]

The Volker Fund maintained a relatively small staff dedicated to overseeing each gift and project personally. Three original trustees governed the assets of the trust and its giving decisions: Mr. Volker as president, Rose Volker as secretary, and Harold Luhnow as treasurer.

Volker and Luhnow made most giving decisions together, supporting causes they deemed responsible and necessary. In 1944, Luhnow assumed the role of the president of the William Volker Fund. With the collaboration of Mr. Volker, Luhnow led the Volker Fund's transition to support scholars of liberty and freedom. Already a skeptic of government's power and responsibility resulting from his Pendergast experiences, Harold Luhnow was particularly inspired by Friedrich Hayek's book *The Road to Serfdom*, which persuasively discredited Socialism.[38]

One of the most seemingly insignificant monetary gifts given in the 1940s by the Volker Fund led to the dramatic advancement of free-market and classical liberal ideas worldwide.[39] In 1945, Friedrich Hayek, through his correspondence with Loren Miller, expressed his exasperation over the attack on Western civilization and the full-throttle advance of Socialism. Hayek believed that the best way to combat these dangerous trends involved bringing preeminent scholars of classical liberal ideas together in Mont Pelerin, Switzerland. The successful American debut of his book *The Road to Serfdom* showed that a market existed for the advancement of principles of freedom in the post–World War II era, yet he felt so alone in the Keynes-dominated world.

Hayek thought it particularly important to include Americans in this first gathering of prominent classical liberal thinkers for two reasons. First, his wildly successful book sales and popular lecture tour throughout the United States encouraged him to believe that America could be a leader in the fight against Socialism. Also, Americans were, at the time, perhaps the strongest and largest contingent of classical liberal thinkers in the postwar era. Yet he acknowledged the obstacle of travel expenses. It was Loren Miller who mentioned the plan to his friend Harold Luhnow one day, doubting whether a meeting of this proposed importance would come together without American involvement.

Harold Luhnow, together with William Volker, calmed Hayek's apprehension. The two agreed that critical analysis of governments worldwide and the preservation of Western civilization benefited humanity on an international scale. Hayek's request was reasonable, and they were willing to take a chance on his plan. Volker sketched himself a reminder that day on a piece of scrap paper—*May 7, 1945: Friedrich A. Hayek, $2,000*—and then classified his gift as "educational."[40] The Volker Fund's $2,000 provided for seventeen Americans' travel expenses to Mont Pelerin, Switzerland.

The seventeen selected represented most of the identified American classical liberal thinkers during that time. They have each gone on to achieve great advances through their ideas and their work. The representatives were Herbert Cornuelle, Dr. Floyd "Baldy" Harper, Leonard Reed, and V. Orval Watts of the Foundation for Economic Education; Professors Aaron Director, Milton Friedman, and Frank Knight of the University of Chicago; John Davenport of *Fortune* magazine; Professor Karl Brandt of Stanford University; President Harry Gideonse of Brooklyn College; Professor Frank D. Graham of Princeton University; Henry Hazlitt of *Newsweek*; Professor Fritz Machlup of the University of Buffalo; Loren Miller of Citizens Research Council of Michigan; Felix Morley of *Human Events*; Professor Ludwig von Mises of New York University; and Professor George Stigler of Brown University. It is no irony that Ronald Reagan considered four of the first attendees to be great influences on his intellectual growth. President Reagan said, "Intellectual leaders like Russell Kirk, Friedrich Hayek, Henry Hazlitt, Milton Friedman, James Burnham, [Frank Meyer], Ludwig von Mises—they shaped so much of our thoughts."[41]

That first gathering in 1947 above Lake Geneva set the framework for a voluntary international organization—a worldwide academy called the Mont Pelerin Society—which was committed to principles of liberty and critical analysis of governments. The American representation at that first Mont Pelerin meeting neared 50 percent of the attendance. Indeed, without the commitment by the Volker Fund to cover travel expenses, it can be assumed that those Americans would not have made the arduous trip overseas, potentially threatening the success of the original gathering where the

direction and mission were established. This first organizing meeting set a
strong course for the future, according to attendee John Jewkes, and was "of
very great importance in enabling the liberal social scientists to exchange
views and establish relations. Since that Conference, there has been most
fruitful collaboration among many of the members...."[42] The Mont
Pelerin Society continues today and holds conferences around the world
where prominent professors, thinkers, authors, and businessmen can meet
to discuss and reaffirm their commitment to these principles.

The success of the Mont Pelerin Society can be measured by the individual accomplishments of its members. By 1954, eight hundred publications had been written by members of the Mont Pelerin Society.[43] Between
1974 and 2002, eight members won Nobel Prizes in economics: Friedrich
Hayek in 1974, Milton Friedman in 1976, George Stigler in 1982, James
Buchanan in 1986, Maurice Allais in 1988, Ronald Coase in 1991, Gary
Becker in 1992, and Vernon Smith in 2002.[44] Of these, four attended that
first 1947 meeting in Switzerland. Several members of the Mont Pelerin
Society rose to hold major leadership positions worldwide: Chancellor Lud-
wig Erhard of West Germany, President Luigi Einaudi of Italy, Chairman
Arthur Burns of the U.S. Federal Reserve Board, and President Vaclav
Klaus of the Czech Republic. Martin Anderson of Stanford University
reported that twenty-two of Ronald Reagan's seventy-six economic advisors
on his 1980 campaign were Mont Pelerin Society members.

Nobel Laureate and member Vernon Smith believes that the Mont
Pelerin Society offers members "a forum and an opportunity to meet and
exchange views with people that are similarly constituted."[45] He summa-
rizes its success: the Mont Pelerin Society has "kept alive the idea that cen-
trally managed systems can't work in the long run."[46] Member and Nobel
Laureate the late Milton Friedman believed that his attendance at the first
Mont Pelerin meeting, among other experiences, further stimulated his, at
the time, only casual interest in public policy. "Informal discussions with
colleagues and friends stimulated a greater interest, which was reinforced
by Friedrich Hayek's powerful book *The Road to Serfdom*, by my atten-

dance at the first meeting of the Mont Pelerin Society in 1947, and by discussions with Hayek after he joined the university faculty in 1950."[47] In a
1973 newsletter, Friedrich Hayek conveyed the Mont Pelerin Society's success: "I am perfectly confident that each of us has been enabled to persist
in his effort and to do it with more confidence and more satisfaction,
because we had the comfort of knowing that we could agree about its intellectual justification with some other people."[48]

Perhaps most dramatically, according to author R. M. Hartwell, the
Mont Pelerin Society's achievements played an important role in the
revival of classical liberalism. The general discussion and economic solution shifted in the decades since its inception from promoting more government control and regulation, to embracing less government and more
privatization. Mont Pelerin Society members witnessed the dramatic collapse of Eastern Europe's Communist stranglehold. This promoted classical liberal ideas, created a network for the dissemination of those ideas, and
spawned the establishment of several institutions across the world to
advance these purposes. Several members directly influenced public policy through their roles in high office or as advisors to various administrations.

The success of an organization can also be observed by the comments
of its critics. In this case, one detractor referred to the group as a "semi-
secret, international, political-economic, intelligence service" for the
Right.[49] Scott Thompson and Nancy Spannaus reinforced this perspective
when they wrote, "It is at secret Mont Pelerin Society meetings that many
of the economic policies of the international financial oligarchy get dis-
seminated to the bankers and government bureaucrats who will carry them
out."[50]

Through all their experiences, Volker and Luhnow recognized that the
most effective efforts to impact the future took place at the level where ideas
germinated and proliferated. In the years following the Mont Pelerin Society's initial meeting, the Volker Fund went further to coordinate opportunities for these ideas to advance. It instigated the creation of organizations

which promoted these concepts. The Volker Fund published a series of
books which found homes in nearly every university and college library
across the country. [51] Finally, and perhaps most importantly, the Volker
Fund began to identify and support talented, young individuals who were
certain to become prominent advocates of classical liberal principles.

The Volker Fund assisted in building formal institutions, including the
Intercollegiate Society of Individualists (later named the Intercollegiate
Studies Institute), the Foundation for Economic Education (FEE), and the
Institute for Humane Studies (IHS). It was, at one time, the top contributor to the Foundation for Economic Education and had given the organization $170,000 in the years since its 1946 beginning. FEE became one of
the "principal architects of the libertarian reconstruction."[52] It subsidized
the 1950 translation of Frédéric Bastiat's *The Law* as an antidote to inter-
ventionism.[53] The book became the Foundation for Economic Education's
all-time best seller — twenty years later, more than half a million copies have
been sold.[54]

The Volker Fund underwrote individual authors and their literary works,
including Murray Rothbard's economics text *Man, Economy, & State* and
Richard Weaver's *Visions of Order*.[55] It promoted American pride through
H. G. Weaver's production and distribution of *The Mainspring of Human
Progress*.[56] The Volker Fund purchased fifteen hundred copies of Felix Mor-
ley's *The Foreign Policy of the United States*, fifteen hundred copies of Her-
rymon Maurer's *Collision of East and West*, and one thousand copies of
Bertrand de Jouvenel's *America in Europe* to distribute to college and uni-
versity libraries, among many other texts.[57] It sponsored lectures by Milton
Friedman which eventually formed the basis of his book *Capitalism and
Freedom*.[58]

The Volker Fund supported individuals in unconventional ways. It
funded a $25,000 per year fellowship for Friedrich Hayek at the University
of Chicago for quite some time, without which the scholar would not have
become a member of its faculty.[59] It provided the same type of support to
Ludwig von Mises — $8,500 per year for lecture fees at New York Univer-

sity's graduate school of business.[60] The Volker Fund gave a $200 monthly stipend to Felix Morley for secretarial and research assistance, and a monthly sum to Murray N. Rothbard to write *Man, Economy, & State* (1962).[61, 62] The Volker Fund provided Bertrand de Jouvenel with $2,500 to underwrite his American lecture tour and for appropriate clothing to wear on the tour.[63] The fund also gave Henry Regnery $200,000 to relieve a long-term debenture.[64] The list of the scholars, writers, and liberty-oriented projects the Volker Fund supported is a Who's Who of the freedom movement.

These writings and the thinkers who penned them may not have formed the basis of a burgeoning movement were it not for William Volker and his nephew Harold Luhnow. The ideas received the benefaction of the Volker Fund, and as a result, the brilliant minds who advocated them had the financial means to make a dramatic impact on the philosophical shift that occurred throughout the latter half of the twentieth century.

During the days of 1947, Harold Luhnow visited his uncle at the family estate each evening after work. A heart condition and a large hernia forced William Volker to remain in bed almost constantly, yet his eagerness to hear about the business persisted until he could no longer concentrate on affairs during those last months. Mr. Volker passed away during the afternoon of November 4, 1947, under the constant care and tending of his wife, Rose.

While William Volker wasn't alive to see many of his most important gifts to fruition, the people of Kansas City celebrated his legacy by appending his name on some of the city's prominent institutions and thoroughfares, including Volker Elementary School, Volker Boulevard, Volker Memorial Fountain, and the University of Missouri–Kansas City Volker Campus. City residents also named a local home association after him, Volker Neighborhood Association, and even established a date on the calendar to celebrate his life, Volker Day. While his good intentions of remaining anonymous are important to understand his character, this Kansas City success suggests that a commitment to philanthropy and its results endure long past the giver's lifetime.

The Volker Fund represented the two-pronged legacy of William Volker. On the one hand, he left behind a considerable sum of money generated from his successful business. On the other hand, his established tradition of philanthropic activity remained. There were some lessons that Mr. Volker conveyed to the Volker Fund which guided its future practices. William Volker carefully monitored his philanthropy. He scrutinized giving decisions, but seldom avoided risk. He hoped the fund and its trustees would take the same chances in the future, using their freedom to make bold decisions. Volker also followed gifts and their progress to ensure results. When he recognized his shortcomings related to his knowledge of a particular subject, he sought expert opinions. Mr. Volker also advised future leaders of the Volker Fund, "These Trustees cannot spend any of the Volker funds for perpetuating the Volker name."[65] Operating in the years following his death, the Volker Fund avoided media and rarely published materials except those required by law.

Finally, the trust's rules Volker outlined originally stipulated that the fund would be liquidated thirty years following his death. This decision meant that the fund's leadership would almost surely stay in the hands of those he personally entrusted to carry out his intentions. Examples abound of private institutions whose missions strayed following the passing of their founders, including the Ford Foundation, Rockefeller Foundation, and the Pew Charitable Trusts. Those institutions and their missions barely resemble the values their originators embraced. Just prior to his death, William Volker conveyed to Harold Luhnow, "[A]dapt the Fund to the changing needs of changing times."[66] He recommended that the fund be terminated ten years following his death, rather than thirty as originally planned, because he was disheartened by expanding government and feared what the future may hold if drastic measures were not sought soon.[67] Mr. Luhnow strictly followed four guiding principles of William Volker's philanthropy: "anonymous," "venturesome," "vital and aggressive," and "highly personal."[68]

What freedom's ideas needed most in the 1940s and 1950s was a sense of collaboration and momentum. Perhaps more than any others, William Volker and Harold Luhnow contributed to that cooperation by sponsoring the founding of the Mont Pelerin Society and by hosting conferences and seminars for emerging scholars into the 1950s. Milton Friedman, in his book *Capitalism and Freedom*, said that one Volker Fund conference in particular stood out as "among the most stimulating intellectual experiences of my life."[69] As time went on, the Volker-sponsored scholars left our country with a valuable set of resources in the writings they produced, resources that eventually led to the changing pattern of government's response to social ills and foreign policy. William Volker, also known in his time as "Mr. Anonymous," contributed to this change with his hard work and determined philanthropic spirit that created a pool of resources for these purposes. Rather than remain anonymous, these mystery men, Mr. Volker and his nephew, should be applauded for their commitment, perseverance, and risk-taking. For without them, freedom and liberty would not have the respected position they do today.[70]

———————— ★ ————————

Chapter Two

Henry Regnery

*"I'm not in the business to see how much money I can make
but to see that every significant book which can contribute
to the highest values sees the light of day."*[1]

—HENRY REGNERY

I t is not often that a man enters the business world convinced he will
lose money all in the name of a particular cause. Most entrepreneurs
hope to sell a profitable product or service or, failing to move into the
black, move on to other businesses. Not so with Henry Regnery. He sacrificed his own personal wealth to publish books he believed his fellow citizens needed to read.

Henry Regnery's early contributions to *Human Events* and the Henry
Regnery Company created a conservative communications breakthrough.
In the years to come, other publishing enterprises produced and marketed
similar writings. Free Press, Encounter, ISI Books, and Spence Publishing
joined Regnery as sources of important public policy oriented books.

Henry Regnery gave the Conservative Movement a name, a public relations strategy, and a launching pad for those who would inevitably shift the

tide of American thought to the Right over the later decades of the twentieth century. His talents ran far past having an eye for a good book, yet this
was the skill that impacted the future of America the most. Without his
determination, foresight, indebted company, and personal sacrifice, the
American Conservative Movement wouldn't be a successful, cohesive network toiling toward a common goal.

Henry Regnery, a man who felt impassioned by conservative ideas
before they were even labeled "conservative," lived a typical Midwestern
life. He grew up in Illinois as the fourth child of five. Henry's father,
William Regnery, went to work in Kansas City for Ebenezer White as a grocery boy when he was just fifteen years old.

While sweeping off the front stoop early one morning in the winter of
1892, William Regnery saw a dim light in a building across the street. Wanting a better job, Regnery sauntered straight into the office of William
Volker, president of William Volker and Company. He politely asked
Volker to consider him for a position. After reflecting upon the young Regnery's early morning work habits, Volker hired him in the window shade
department. It wasn't long before Mr. Volker gained trust in William Regnery, soon a twenty-year-old, hard-working, committed, and loyal employee.
Volker asked Regnery to move to Chicago to run his newly acquired company: the Western Shade Cloth Company. William Regnery eventually
purchased the company from Volker and renamed it Joanna Western Mills
Company. The company flourished for many years under the care of Regnery family members. Its financial success also paved the way for future
business and philanthropic endeavors.

Henry Regnery himself wrote of his father as a "modest, unassuming, and
generous" man—traits that would inevitably shape his own life, career, and
personality.[2] His father always offered help when asked, requiring nothing
in return, as was the case with his philanthropic work through the America
First Committee and American Friends Service Committee. The American
Friends Service Committee donated funds to provide food for hungry children in Germany after World War I. The support of this organization first

signaled the family's commitment to generosity and duty, and Henry Regnery continued his involvement, donating $10,000 to it in 1947 and more in years to come. William Regnery, along with Sears, Roebuck and Co. chairman General Robert E. Wood, established the America First Committee. America First, originally named the Emergency Committee to Defend America First, focused on promoting a noninterventionist American foreign policy. It published a statement of goals after its start in 1940, including:

1. The United States must build an impregnable defense for America.
2. No foreign power, nor group of powers, can successfully attack a prepared America.
3. American democracy can be preserved only by keeping out of the European war.
4. "Aid short of war" weakens national defense at home and threatens to involve America in war abroad.[3]

There's no doubt that Regnery saw promoting these ideas as an obligation even as the family worked to achieve business success. *Washington Post* editor, Haverford College president, and author of *Freedom and Federalism* Felix Morley once wrote to Henry telling him, "You, too, I think, tend to be a little over-generous in extending the helping hand. . . ."[4]

Henry Regnery was a brilliant man, a voracious reader, an accomplished cellist, a studied mathematician, an exacting woodworker, a superior gardener, and a keen discerner for quality literature and its impact on the future of our country. He spent any spare moment in time (or spare cent for that matter) with a good book or with his family, and this was the case as far back as he could remember. After he completed high school at Hinsdale High, Regnery went on to the Armour Institute of Technology in 1929 to study mechanical engineering, eventually transferring to MIT for mathematics. The opportunity to explore courses other than math piqued his interest in different subjects, including English, French, German, and philosophy.[5]

One profound influence on his life was a college pianist friend named Hermann, who encouraged Regnery to appreciate his family's German heritage. Hermann, an exchange student, took it upon himself to teach Regnery about those topics of which he knew little, including art and music. His prodding to read texts in their original German helped Regnery to grasp the language quickly.[6]

Henry went on to study abroad in Bonn, Germany, which also enabled him to read German authors with near fluency, understanding even the occasional, subtle wit and sarcasm within the books' pages. As a young American in Germany between the world wars, Regnery built lasting friendships abroad by bowling, biking, and boating in and around Mosel, a grape-growing, wine-producing land.[7]

Regnery had a knack for developing close personal relationships with individuals all over the world, and he excelled at keeping in touch through the years by writing letters and visiting whenever possible. World War II made it difficult to keep in close contact with many of the friends he had made while in Germany. Some were killed; others went missing. Regnery reproved the Nazism and Communism that led to so many horrors, including his loss of close confidants. He remained committed to telling the truth about these repressive ideologies throughout his life.

Upon his return to the United States in 1936, Henry enrolled at Harvard's graduate school where he received a master's degree in economics. Regnery didn't complete the required thesis to receive his PhD even though the coursework had been finished. In the beginning of his studies, he was a supporter of Franklin Roosevelt and his New Deal. Soon, a top-heavy class of Socialist students and bureaucrats at Harvard and a job in Roosevelt's Resettlement Administration led him to question the growing role of public subsidies and government in FDR's America.[8] It was in this period that Henry formulated many of his long-held principles.

Henry's humble spirit cannot be overstated. He was, by nature, skeptical of his own talents, often appearing as unpracticed, unrefined, and uneducated. On the other hand, he was quick to compliment. It was a disarming and charming quality extending through the course of his written letters over the years. Lines of this correspondence portrayed his personal humility: "good counterbalance to my impetuousness"; "Please forgive this rather rambling and badly typed letter—those I get from you are much better organized"; "I don't have much talent for music, I must admit, but it has meant much to me to be able to play with people who do"; "I always have a slight, sometimes more than slight, inferiority complex when I answer one of your letters—yours are always beautifully expressed, with never a wrong word, and equally neatly typed; mine never come out so well, but I will do my best"; and "especially for such a half-educated person as I, unfortunately, am."[9] A concert-level musician and a graduate of both MIT and Harvard humbly concealed his qualifications.

Henry displayed a rather keen sense of humor. In a letter regarding an upcoming trip to Europe, he wrote, "I look forward to the Mt. Pelerin meeting [in Turin, Italy] with great pleasure and to a few quiet talks with you. The beer will probably not be so good, but I am sure that there will be plenty of wine and spaghetti, which will be fine for a while. It will make the first meal in Zurich taste all the better."[10] Perhaps it was his humor that lightened the spirit during years of business and financial turmoil.

Regnery met Eleanor Scattergood, the woman he married and the mother of his four children, in Philadelphia at an American Friends Service Committee dinner. He and Eleanor, after marrying in Philadelphia in 1938, soon helped establish a knitting mill in West Virginia to provide economic vitality and employment during the Depression to former miners of Fayette County. The county at that time suffered from greater than 50 percent unemployment.[11] Eventually, the pair left this enterprise to a skilled knitting businessman from Vienna and headed back home to Chicago to help with his father's textile manufacturing business, Joanna Western Mills.

In 1944, shortly after returning to Chicago, Henry Regnery met Frank Hanighen. Frank had worked with the well-regarded Felix Morley to establish a publication—a small newsletter called *Human Events*, limited both in circulation and financial backing.[12] Hanighen's Washington, D.C., apartment housed the newsletter's headquarters during its infancy. *Human Events*, its first issue dated February 2, 1944, was delivered to only a couple hundred subscribers, though many of those early readers were thought to be high-caliber intellectuals and decision makers.

Regnery entered the picture during that first year as an already accomplished and practiced businessman. He had worked for his father's firm as well as at the knitting plant. Regnery helped put the struggling newsletter in order by incorporating it in 1945. Morley became president, Hanighen acted as vice president, and Regnery served as treasurer. Each man gave $1,000 of his own money to this process, and in return each controlled one-third of the company's stock.

The early issues of *Human Events* took the form of a newsletter mostly because the trio had trouble tracking down adequate funding to publish a magazine. Even still, Regnery took the responsibility for "producing, distributing, and financing" the early series, using a meager office space in Chicago from which to house the operation. He also started producing a series of pamphlets geared to highlight the issues he felt important. The pamphlet business brought ideas and perspectives to the public that Regnery believed were missing from the conversation in those days. They were ideas ignored by the usual publications but were, in his eyes, critical for people to consider.[13]

Soon thereafter, Hanighen and Morley ceded the lead in producing and promoting the pamphlets to Regnery. Regnery hired a small staff to supplement his own efforts. It was at this point that Henry, with his father's full support and approval, bowed out of the textile business altogether to focus his time and energy on an endeavor he perceived to be more important. He began to recognize the existence of "a very influential group in this country which, consciously or unconsciously, is exerting a high degree of control over the communication of ideas."[14] While working on *Human Events*, he noticed "that it was easy for left-wing writers to find publishers for their efforts, while conservative authors were being stifled and having great difficulty finding a publisher." Henry Regnery had built a substantial nest egg while working for his father's company and owned a personal stake in Central National Bank which was started by his father, William, in 1936, not far from the window shade factory. By 1972, the bank had total assets of $100 million.[15] While he committed to his own career path, Henry always remained thankful for the opportunity to lead Joanna Western, because it enabled him to build his publishing enterprise.

He often contemplated what life would have been like had he stayed with Joanna Western Mills. In a letter to a young William F. Buckley Jr., Henry wrote, "I woke up very early this morning, and couldn't help wondering if it was worth it—I was thinking how much simpler life would have been if I had stayed in my father's business, instead of trying to save the world...."[16] His jump into communicating ideas full-time became a lifelong commitment to publishing—a turn that no doubt directed the most significant years of his life.[17]

Henry published his first three books during his time with *Human Events*. They included *Blueprint for World Conquest*, with an introduction by William Henry Chamberlain, and two books featuring collections of essays from previous issues of *Human Events*. While the newsletter, pamphlet, and books' audiences were increasing (nearly five thousand people subscribed to *Human Events* alone), geographic limitations hindered Morley and Hanighen's ability to exert influence on the newsletter. Therefore, Regnery gave up responsibility for *Human Events* and transferred its publication back to Washington, D.C. Years later, Regnery credited Felix Morley with helping him get into the publishing business: "I will always remember that it was largely because of my association with you [Felix Morley] that I went into publishing, a step I have never regretted."[18] Regnery stayed involved with *Human Events* over the years as time permitted and retained control over the pamphlet series as well as the three published books. He used these publications as the initial distributions of what soon became his company: the Human Events Associates not-for-profit corporation of Illinois.

Human Events Associates retained part of the original name, yet Morley and Hanighen exercised little to no editorial control, thus leading Regnery to change the name in September 1947 to the Henry Regnery

Company. Though the name may not, at first glance, portray modesty, he believed that the type of books he desired to publish would be controversial; readers deserved to know who made their publication possible. Thus, the company bore his name and continues to do so today.[19] It was the Porta Nigra Roman gate at the entrance of Trier, Germany, a symbol of the strength and emergence of Western civilization, that Regnery used as a crest of the company; it appeared on each published book. His publishing business was, after all, an undertaking driven by personal motivations, and preserving Western civilization and all it stood for fit with the venture's goals.

His experiences with *Human Events* indicated that profit would be elusive to an infant conservative-oriented publisher, and that a nonprofit entity would suit the realities of the endeavor. He hoped to operate similarly to a college publishing press, aiming to break even, but recognizing the likelihood of deficits. The Internal Revenue Service did not agree, and it forced Henry Regnery to incorporate his enterprise as a "for profit" organization. It was not an easy course, because his position was "in direct opposition to the dominant current of the time."[20] And yet Regnery strongly advocated, "The books that are most needed are often precisely those that will have only a modest sale."[21] This commitment was further reinforced by his father's observation: "If you ever begin to make any money in that business you are going into, you can be pretty sure that you are publishing the wrong kind of books."[22] It indeed was prophetic commentary on his fate in the business.

Under the motto "It is our purpose to publish good books where we find them," the Henry Regnery Company produced its first catalogue of books in 1948. Someone in the book business once told him, "There is always a place for a good book.... The problem is to determine what is good...."[23] The venture offered virtually no financial rewards, but it did provide the rallying point to those who disagreed with the direction American leaders were taking our country. No longer would Americans need to rely solely on liberal media outlets.

The first books he brought to the market under the Henry Regnery Company logo included *In Darkest Germany, Our Threatened Values*, and

Hitler in Our Selves. Our Threatened Values received a five-hundred-word review in the March 1, 1948, edition of *Time* magazine. The $2.50 book was described in the review: "This eloquent if frequently disorganized diatribe is a significant indication of how more thoughtful leftists, repelled by Russian tyranny, now question their old power-centered assumptions. Strands of the Western tradition they had once blithely ignored—its respect for individuality and defense of freedom for dissident minorities—now seem terribly precious...."[24] All three books included information on Germany and the values and standards of civilization, issues quite unpopular following World War II. Regnery believed, "No one else was anxious to take it up, and it seemed to me that if I felt strongly about it and had the means to do something, I had a moral obligation to publish the books...."[25] Moral obligation tended to direct his business decisions and strategies while he was a publisher.

In the 1940s, with few organizations or cohesive ideas to bind them together, conservatives were yet to form a movement. Henry Regnery knew most fellow conservatives through his father, close association with the University of Chicago, and membership in the international association of the Mont Pelerin Society, which brought together accomplished individuals committed to free markets and the advancement of classical liberalism. According to his son Alfred, Henry Regnery wrote letters constantly with these individuals and traveled often throughout his life to visit close friends and colleagues in countries across Europe. He used these important relationships to recruit scholars, writers, and academics to write books on topics he thought significant. Regnery solicited acquaintances to write about the Bricker Amendment (which sought to limit the impact foreign treaties have on our Constitutional rights), international economic development, the law and the Supreme Court, and central control of education.

Henry financed the Henry Regnery Company by giving cash whenever warranted. The first three years the Henry Regnery Company published books, Henry lost $100,000. He had invested $275,000 of his own wealth (that is about $2.1 million today) and refrained from taking a salary or expense reimbursements.[26] He sold personal property in West Virginia in the early 1950s to help fund his publishing efforts.[27] In its first twelve years of operating, the Henry Regnery Company lost money each year but two.[28] Regnery heartily asserted, "[T]he effort to publish good books is out of all proportion to the tangible results, but eternal optimist as I am, I keep on going nevertheless."[29] Even still, while the immediate market seemed to suggest a lack of interest, Henry knew the dissemination of conservative ideas had to be done, and he was willing to do it at great personal sacrifice.

Recognizing that the books he published would rarely receive favorable reviews in newspapers and magazines because of the subject matter (if they appeared at all), he needed a reliable backlist for income. In an effort to establish this backlist to improve finances, the Henry Regnery Company partnered with the Great Books Foundation to supply books, including Aristotle's *Ethics*, Plato's *Republic*, and Smith's *The Wealth of Nations*, to various Great Books chapters. The contract, while initially a financial burden on Henry Regnery, provided a revenue stream that guaranteed income each month. He acknowledged the importance of building a prominent base of books and successfully completed a few business acquisitions toward this end.

Henry Regnery Company first hit the bestseller list in 1951, just four years after the company's introduction into book publishing. Freda Utley's *The China Story* appeared on the market during a time of extreme concern over the emergence of Communist China. Utley, an experienced scholar on matters related to the Far East, wrote about the "loss of China." Utley's candor worried those who had, only a decade earlier, witnessed a destructive World War II. The *New York Times* printed a favorable review on the book, and sales skyrocketed. Bill Casey, a prominent New York City attorney and later Ronald Reagan's CIA chief, asserted that a mistaken American foreign policy assured and essentially armed Chinese revolutionaries, thus bringing them to power. These Chinese were the men killing American soldiers in Korea; the impact of Utley's book may have prevented this had it been published earlier. Casey wrote,

Henry Regnery Company published the first accurate account of this whole sordid [China] story, and got the facts about China and our policy there in true perspective. I dare say that if Henry Regnery Company had been around early enough to publish Freda Utley's "The China Story"... in 1947, or even early in 1948... the American public would have been sufficiently awakened and stirred so that the huge propaganda hoax about the character of the force we are now fighting in Korea could not have been put across. That hoax, sabotaging our wartime ally, handed countless millions of fighting manpower over to our Communist enemy and reversed the century-old American policy of not permitting a potential enemy to control the coast of the China Sea.[30]

In May 1951, Henry Regnery read a manuscript by an energetic young man who had recently graduated from Yale University. William F. Buckley Jr. wrote about his experiences at Connecticut's Ivy League institution, and Regnery loved it. Buckley's style of writing, his insight, and his way with words attracted Henry Regnery to his prose. Yet the Henry Regnery Company had been losing money rapidly, and he knew that this book might jeopardize a critical publishing and distribution contract held with the Great Books Foundation. Henry Regnery wrote to Buckley and said, "I have finished reading your manuscript. I find it excellent, and am convinced that we ought to publish it."[31] In October 1951, the Henry Regnery Company published *God and Man at Yale*.

Regnery knew that the book addressed a critical issue facing the country at the time—the suffocation of conservative ideas in the classroom. Rather than balance, there was a lopsided lineup of liberal professors, liberal classes, and liberal administrators. Buckley's book informed the public about this trend, and it faced scrutiny like no other. Regnery said, "As I think... of the reaction of Yale to your position and to your book, and of many other similar incidents, I cannot help but believe that it all fits into a sort of pattern. It may not be concisely organized, there is certainly not only an orthodoxy of the Left, but an inquisition, and much of it is centered in the Universities."[32]

God and Man at Yale became one of the most popular and controversial books of the day. The left-wing bias at universities had long been ignored, and Buckley, with his eloquent writing, attracted national attention to the topic. Yale University adamantly denied the book's assertions. At a meeting of college presidents and deans at the Pentagon, the Yale representative "violently attacked it," but later had to admit that he hadn't even read it. Another professor of history at Yale called the book a "typical, Fascist, Trotskyite book."[33] A Yale alumni publication spent an entire issue assailing the book. Yale appointed a commission to study whether its contents described the truthful state of Yale's education (unsurprisingly for a liberal administrative body, the commission ruled it was not a realistic account). Hundreds of opinion pieces, letters to the editor, and reviews flooded newspapers and magazines across the country.[34] Henry Regnery aspired to sell five thousand copies. By mid-1953, twenty-five thousand copies had left the warehouse shelves, and the book continued to sell for decades despite the Left's constant attacks.[35]

The primary importance of *God and Man at Yale* did not rest with the book's contents alone. Its success also introduced William F. Buckley Jr. to nationwide audiences. Regnery believed, "When I first wrote to Buckley, at Frank Hanighen's suggestion, to ask if I might have a look at the manuscript I had heard he was working on, I had no idea of what I was helping to launch."[36] William F. Buckley Jr.'s career provided an alternative to the liberal press of the day with the advent of *National Review.* Buckley's numerous books on topics ranging from McCarthyism to academic freedom to faith infused a popular intellectualism to a previously underestimated Movement. Even President Ronald Reagan in 1985 acknowledged Regnery's responsibility for Buckley when he wrote in a letter to the publisher, "*God and Man at Yale,* a volume by a recent Yale graduate [launched] a brilliant career for the man—Bill Buckley—whom many call the godfather of the conservative movement."[37]

While the book informed the American public on a critical issue—by attacking a prominent university—it ultimately led to the severance of the Great Books Foundation contract. When the contract ended, Henry Regnery decided he needed to continue building a backlist on his own to help replace the lost income. He started a new venture called Gateway Editions. This collection of paperbacks featured quality introductions and new translations. Karl Marx and Frederick Engels' *Communist Manifesto* became one such Gateway Edition, with an introduction explaining its importance as lengthy as the book itself. By 1962, Gateway Editions had become accepted as "one of the standard academic series" and provided much needed operating capital throughout the years for Henry Regnery Company.[38]

Shortly after the success of *God and Man at Yale*, Henry Regnery requested a manuscript by an obscure Michigan State instructor in the history of civilization. The manuscript, recently rejected by powerful New York City publisher Knopf, seemed impeccably researched, insightful, and important. It inspired Regnery with its rich themes. Henry Regnery immediately put plans in place to publish *The Conservative Rout*, as it was known. After "much deliberation," its author and Henry Regnery settled on a new title, *The Conservative Mind*. The book, written by Russell Kirk, had an instantaneous appeal, receiving reviews in publications across the country. *Time* magazine, under the editorial direction of Whittaker Chambers, devoted its book review section to *The Conservative Mind* on July 4, 1954. Of all the books Henry Regnery published, this, he believed, was the high point of his career.

The Kirk find, following soon after publishing Buckley, was a breakthrough event. It would inspire other writers, publishers, and even grassroots conservatives. *The Conservative Mind* won accolades from many, coalescing conservatives who previously had not sensed that they belonged to a common intellectual heritage. In fact, *Human Events* called the book "perhaps the most important book to appear in this country since World War II."[39] Indeed, *The Conservative Mind*, according to Henry Regnery, named and gave an identity to the Conservative Movement. Up until that time, conservatives presented few alternatives to the pervasive liberal ortho-doxy. "It was this book which gave the growing movement of protest to the liberal domination not only a name, but intellectual respectability and a positive position."[40]

The 1950s therefore became the decade of the "unexpected appear-ance...of what promised to be a rational, viable alternative to liberalism."[41] College professors assigned *The Conservative Mind* as reading and discus-sion material. Regnery Publishing executive editor Harry Crocker believes the book described "conservatism as a disposition, as a set of prejudices, as a belief in certain traditions.... If you believe that human nature is not entirely malleable, that there are certain eternal truths...you can't be snuffed out by a degraded culture. There will always be the light of faith, a flickering flame that can be fanned to blossom again."[42] Up until its publi-cation, conservatives often regretted the term "conservative," but the book removed that reservation and thus defined a movement.

Henry Regnery Company continued to publish books with meaningful impact. Some credit the publisher with allowing authors opposed to the New Deal to avoid the New York City publishers' cold shoulder. At that time "any writer who had a message which did not entirely swallow the eco-nomic fallacies of the New Deal-Fair Deal crowd could expect that his manuscript would be banished as 'unsound,' not 'forward thinking,' 'reac-tionary,' or even 'fascist.'"[43]

Henry Regnery is described as a renaissance man by Crocker. He thor-oughly enjoyed and was educated in various disciplines, including culture and religion. Regnery recognized the need to "work on all fronts in which values are involved—politics, education, philosophy, literature, religion, art, etc."[44] It was not surprising then that he acquired another publishing enterprise called Reilly & Lee. This venture gave Henry Regnery an addi-tional backlist, which included the famous Oz children's books as well as books of poetry by Edgar Guest and Roy Cook. Regnery also began pub-lishing textbooks for the Catholic Archdiocese of Chicago, intended for children who attended government schools whose parents wanted to provide them with some religious instruction. His Catholic textbook list provided 10 percent of the company's volume.[45]

Henry Regnery recognized that mainline textbook publishers did not always report the American story accurately. In the early 1960s, he developed a plan to establish his own college textbook press in order to distribute textbooks of truth to college and high school classrooms. He said, "The more I see of textbooks and the educational apparatus, the more convinced I become that really drastic overhaul is necessary."[46] He later wrote to J. Howard Pew:

> When one considers the harm that has been done by bad school books, or that China was lost largely through the influence of not more than six or eight writers, one or two small magazines and a cooperative editor in an established publishing firm, you can imagine what could be accomplished in a positive direction with a vigorous and intelligently directed publishing firm.[47]

Regnery spearheaded a plan to contact leaders of the philanthropic community to pitch the idea, including Dr. Donald Cowling in Minneapolis, Pierre Goodrich with the Indiana-based Liberty Fund, and Harold Luhnow of the Volker Fund. Through his own personal initiative and modest financial support, he began publishing Latin books and economic texts for college students, an American history textbook for high school students, and a two-part series to teach elementary-aged children how to read.[48]

The Henry Regnery Company was still losing money nearly two decades after its creation in a competitive environment that required substantial capital. It really was no surprise even to Regnery himself. *Time* magazine had not reviewed a Regnery-published book in years, and only a couple were reviewed by the *New York Times*. In a 1967 letter, Henry Regnery said, "Swimming against the stream has its exhilarating moments, but it cannot be continued indefinitely."[49] Yet it was during this year when Henry Regnery gained control of the paperback rights to Whittaker Chambers's landmark memoir, *Witness*. He built partnerships with conservative student organizations in order to distribute thousands of copies of the book.[50]

The Henry Regnery Company over the years was truly a family enterprise. Henry's father, brothers, and sister contributed financially to its formation, as did his wife and children. Henry's wife, Eleanor, was a steadying hand for her husband. It once was said, "Without Eleanor Regnery, loving, quietly judgmental, generous and practical, Henry would have been half a man."[51] She became an attentive hostess over the years, entertaining hundreds of authors at the dinner table with her children. Henry and Eleanor Regnery had four children: Susan, Alfred S., Henry F., and Margaret. Susan followed in her father's footsteps by studying in Germany and later helping edit manuscripts for the family business. Alfred graduated from the University of Wisconsin Law School, served in the United States Coast Guard, worked for Senator Paul Laxalt on the Senate Judiciary Committee, held a position with the U.S. Department of Justice, and then led the publishing firm in the 1980s. Henry F. achieved a master of arts degree in history from the University of St. Andrews (Scotland) and spent some years farming in New York before leading an arm of the publishing company in the 1970s from his South Bend, Indiana home. As the youngest child, Margaret traveled often with her parents all over the world, meeting authors and experiencing the publishing business even while not being directly involved with the enterprise. It is clear that the Henry Regnery Company was a family endeavor from the beginning and continued to remain so with the involvement of the Regnery children.

Henry Regnery named his son-in-law Harvey Plotnik president of the Henry Regnery Company in 1967. Plotnik's wife, Susan Regnery, knew the business well, as she had spent time copyediting manuscripts for her father years before. Shortly after a serious medical operation performed on Henry Regnery, the Henry Regnery Company acquired the publisher Cowles in 1971, and Henry Regnery sold a substantial portion of his interest in the firm, thus forfeiting editorial jurisdiction.[52] A Chicago publisher later purchased the entire company including Henry Regnery Company which assumed the name Contemporary Books. Contemporary Books transitioned into publishing trade books including sports almanacs and auto repair manuals, thus shedding any resemblance of the former publisher.

Henry Regnery did not feel satisfied at the conclusion of his publishing career. He wanted more and felt an obligation to continue contributing to the communication of ideas. That thought had never left him. Upon his retirement, Regnery retained control of his Gateway Books paperback series, the name "Gateway," and a select few of his hardbacks. In 1973, he attempted to raise money to fund a college press at Hillsdale College. In return for raising the funds necessary, Henry Regnery would run the non-profit and would give the press control of his Gateway series paperbacks. Unfortunately, in meeting after meeting, Henry Regnery was turned down by those who could potentially fund the project.

After Henry Regnery seemingly gave up a career that had meant so much, he devoted himself to gardening, harvesting strawberries, blueberries, pears, apples, peaches, and apricots. But spending time without the responsibilities of sorting through manuscripts ate away at his conscience. His free time encouraged him to ponder his contributions to the production of conservative ideas and all that he could accomplish with his talents for scouting for books with long-term impact.

In 1977, he made a decision. He wrote to California oil entrepreneur Henry Salvatori, "I have made up my mind that there is a need and a place for such publishing as I was doing, and knowing something about it as I do, I have an obligation to get back into it."[53] To raise the necessary capital, Henry again sacrificed his personal wealth and sold his shares of the suburban Central National Bank. He incorporated under the name Regnery Gateway Editions, Ltd. and began publishing books in the fall of 1977, using his retained Gateway Editions paperbacks and portions of the Henry Regnery Company backlist as inventory.

The community of conservative authors and thinkers could not have been more thrilled. Felix Morley wrote to his friend, "The coming year could bring no happier portent than your decision to return to publishing. You have a moral purpose, and an artistic sense, which the profession has lost in its pathetic slide towards conglomeracy."[54] Distinguished manuscripts inundated Gateway's offices, thus further encouraging its efforts and reinforcing Henry's belief that a void existed. *God and Man at Yale* even continued to sell more than a quarter century after its debut.

Henry installed his son Henry F. Regnery (or "Junior," as he was sometimes called) as the president and chief operating officer of Gateway Editions, Ltd., while Henry himself remained involved financially and editorially. They shared common principles, which made the relationship ideal in getting the publishing firm back on its feet. And yet, some things still hadn't changed. In a letter to Russell Kirk, Regnery wrote, "The financial results of our first two years in business have been very disappointing—disastrous, would probably be a better description—but I have by no means given up hope."[55]

In a freak airplane accident, son Henry F. Regnery died on May 25, 1979. American Airlines Flight 191 crashed on takeoff from Chicago's O'Hare airport due to the separation of an engine from the wing. It was a crushing loss to the family, but Henry remained the ever-optimistic personality, concentrating on the happy memories and grateful for the times he shared with his son. Less than a year later, Henry lost a sister and a brother, his last remaining siblings. These losses catapulted him back into the family business, becoming chairman of the board of Joanna Western Mills and settling family affairs with Central National Bank. Publishing books of importance also continued undeterred.

So many Regnery publications brought facts and ideas into the forefront of American consciousness. Ronald Reagan required each member of his cabinet to read the Regnery book *Fat City*, by Donald Lambro, which suggested cutting wasteful and ineffective government programs. Other books linked to policy shifts include *The China Story*, *What Price Israel*, *Roosevelt's Road to Russia*, and *Back Door to War*.

Alfred Regnery, Henry's only son now, took over the firm in 1986. Al served in President Reagan's Department of Justice and was adept at highlighting issues of interest to Washington's emerging conservative leadership. For example, *Red Horizons*, a book written by Romanian defector and former head of foreign intelligence Ion Mihai Pacepa, gave shocking testimony to the horrors of Communist Romania. Radio Free Europe broadcast the book into Romanian homes. *Red Horizons* has been cited as the impetus for the Romanian liberation from Communism. Death threats, phone taps, and FBI surveillance followed the publication of this book. It was a small price to pay considering the twenty-two million people now living in greater freedom.

In 1993, Thomas Phillips brought Gateway Editions under Phillips Publishing International, Inc. and Eagle Publishing, which included *Human Events* (the publication Henry Regnery helped establish in the 1940s), and the Conservative Book Club among other publications. The name changed to simply Regnery Publishing. Since that time, Regnery Publishing has flourished with best-selling books including John O'Neill's *Unfit for Command*, Ann Coulter's *High Crimes and Misdemeanors*, Bernard Goldberg's *Bias*, and Ted Nugent's *God, Guns & Rock 'n' Roll*, among countless others. By 2002, it boasted annual sales of $15 million, making it the leader among publishers of the *New York Times* best-selling books per titles published.

Henry Regnery's gifts to the American Conservative Movement—advancement of freedom and preservation of Western civilization through the publication of important books—did not go unnoticed. At a 1985 tribute dinner honoring Henry Regnery, Michelle Easton, who became deputy undersecretary for the Department of Education in the Reagan administration, asserted that his subsidization of the publishing of conservative books was "quite a gift to the movement."[56] Easton now heads the Clare Boothe Luce Policy Institute, an organization with a unique and important mission: preparing young women for future conservative leadership.

Henry Regnery's gifts did not end there. He remained committed to assisting almost any conservative organization that approached him. Henry, along with his father, established the Foundation for Foreign Affairs in 1945 to focus on influencing America's foreign policy strategy. It provided grants to authors for research purposes, such as a gift to Freda Utley to go to Germany, hosted conferences on topics including "The Berlin Problem and the Future of Eastern Europe," and published a quarterly periodical near and dear to Henry's heart called *Modern Age: A Conservative Review*. Henry Regnery's family foundation, the Marquette Charitable Organization, funded the venture over many years providing $50,000 annually for its first four years and thousands more each year thereafter.[57] Marquette funded nearly half of the organization's budget each year.

Regnery, his father, and his siblings controlled the assets of the foundation, but many of its resources went to support burgeoning conservative-related causes. Once the Foundation for Foreign Affairs could no longer support *Modern Age* financially in 1976 (it required $60,000 to operate annually), Henry Regnery approached the Intercollegiate Studies Institute (ISI) to take over the magazine. Henry had been involved with the organization since its inception as the Intercollegiate Society of Individualists, Inc., donating funds from the Marquette Charitable Organization annually since at least 1960. The Marquette Charitable Organization became dependable for providing ISI with operating resources, giving more than $150,000 over fifteen years.

Henry also assisted ISI in other ways. He hosted a luncheon featuring Milton Friedman in 1964 to introduce Chicago businessmen to ISI's president, E. Victor Milione. He provided books at a drastically reduced rate for ISI's student and professor networks and paid for the postage himself. Regnery took a leadership position with the organization in 1967 and assumed the role of chairman of the board of ISI in 1971. When faced with financial problems threatening the closure of two regional offices and cuts on their summer school program, Regnery sent a letter to ISI's major contributors requesting funds as a personal favor to him. His commitment to this organization no doubt helped the conservative group survive to the point where it now includes its own publishing arm and supports a network of well-regarded independent student newspapers.

Henry Regnery's generosity reached far too many people to list within these pages. Some of the most noteworthy, however, are important to document. In 1944 and 1946, Regnery gave handsomely to the Friends Committee on National Legislation. He and his father contributed financially to the group America's Future each year from 1950 until 1967. Henry bought back $25,000 worth of shares in his company from William F. Buckley Sr. so that William F. Buckley Jr. could start his magazine, *National Review*. He gave books to the Foundation for Economic Education at reduced prices for its students and gave the organization a substantial portion of his personal economics book collection in 1965 to help expand its library. Henry became a founder of the Freedom Studies Center with a gift of $10,000. He assisted Americans for Conservative Action with a grant for books in 1965. He contributed proceeds of a Russell Kirk book in 1966 to the American Conservative Union. Regnery's support of Young Americans for Freedom earned him the group's award of merit in 1967. He also drafted language for his will as early as 1949, leaving substantial portions to the conservative causes most important to him upon his passing.

If this weren't enough, he helped establish the Philadelphia Society, contributing to its annual meetings and working to schedule accomplished lecturers for its events. This organization, established in 1964, operates under the mission, "To sponsor the interchange of ideas through discussion and writing, in the interest of deepening the intellectual foundation of a free and ordered society and of broadening the understanding of its basic principles and traditions. In pursuit of this end we shall examine a wide range of issues: economic, political, cultural, religious, and philosophic. We shall seek understanding, not conformity."[58]

Henry Regnery accidentally fell in June 1996, and he required major surgery. He spent an extended period of time in a coma but eventually lost his battle, leaving behind a legacy of literature that has enriched the Movement.

America is a country where benevolence can make dramatic change. In this case, Henry Regnery's philanthropic spirit urged him to continue publishing books of such importance, and in so doing, he helped build a Conservative Movement. He once said, "We are not going to save the world with books or even magazines, but a start has to be made some where, and books are still the chief means by which ideas are put into circulation."[59] While the company did have a hand in changing American policies and defeating Communism, its real success rests in the millions of individuals inspired by the ideas weaved in the pages of a Regnery book. America may never know who all these individuals are, but the success of the Movement is a sure sign of their inspiration. At his start in the 1940s, there was no movement, but to look at its success today in so many facets of our culture requires due credit to Henry Regnery and his family. Henry Regnery fondly admitted, "Armour Institute of Technology convinced me that I would never become an engineer, M.I.T. that I would never become a mathematician, Harvard Graduate School that I would never become a scholar, my father's business that I would never become a businessman. Because of my good fortune in being the son of a successful and wise father, I did become a publisher."[60] And what a gift it was.[61]

★

Chapter Three

William F. Buckley Jr.

*"And before there was Ronald Reagan there was Barry Goldwater,
and before there was Barry Goldwater there was* NATIONAL REVIEW,
and before there was NATIONAL REVIEW, *there was Bill Buckley
with a spark in his mind ..."*[1]

—GEORGE WILL

B
y the time William F. Buckley Jr. was seven years old, conservatism
had already developed in the lad. During a 1932 day at a London
Catholic school, a precocious Buckley wrote to King George insisting that Great Britain relieve its war debts.[2] In his tenth year, Buckley
appealed to the president of his British prep school to provide him with a
list of the school's insufficiencies.[3] When he reached twenty-five, he had
written an important and best-selling indictment of higher education, *God
and Man at Yale*. At thirty, Buckley founded *National Review*. By the time
he was forty, he had his own television show, *Firing Line*, which went on
to win an Emmy award. And when he became fifty years old, the country
recognized him as a frequent national lecturer and one of its "best-known
intellectuals, a Renaissance man of the right."[4] William F. Buckley's personal story is that of a man who sowed the seeds for conservatism over

decades, personally weathering stormy seasons to protect the Movement's seedlings. The Conservative Movement he helped develop continues to admire his work today.

While the story of William F. Buckley Jr. is perhaps one of the few well-documented histories of our Movement, the writing on his accomplishments and celebrity alone does not reflect the acute sacrifices he and his family endured. While journalists admired, but sometimes poked fun at, his debate savvy, vocabulary repertoire, and refined style of speech, there was so much more to the man, his character, and his industry. His lifetime forms the basis of a courageous story of hardship readily endured to entrench traditionalism, patriotism, and capitalism firmly in his homeland.

The story begins back one generation with a father, Will Buckley, who was born in 1881 and raised in San Diego, Texas, by John and Mary Anne Buckley, descendants of Irishmen. When he was young, Will Buckley's own father died, and he took it upon himself to manage the learning of his younger three brothers and two sisters.[5] Brought up with a rich education in subjects including Latin, history, and Catholic doctrine, it was not only necessary, but probably wise for Will to educate his siblings. Will Buckley also possessed superior writing skills. One year, when funding his own university degree, he entered a writing contest and won a $100 prize.[6] Buckley relied on his experience in teaching his siblings when determining how to raise his own ten children appropriately years later.

After graduating from the University of Texas with a bachelor of science degree in 1904 and a law degree in 1905, Will Buckley moved to Mexico City and used his Spanish fluency to set up a law firm with his brothers in 1908.[7] The firm soon became a hub of oil activity; his brothers oversaw the legal aspect of the business, while he explored real estate and oil production. Biographer John Judis believes that by 1914 Mr. Buckley had amassed a $100,000 personal fortune, which included a private island of his own.[8] Because of his success, Mexican political leaders and American public servants—including three secretaries of state—often looked to Mr. Buckley for advice and recommendations.[9]

Will Buckley served as legal counsel to the Huerta government prior to and during the revolution that overthrew the Huerta regime in Mexico. Ironically, U.S. President Woodrow Wilson opposed the Huerta government. Slowly, revolutionaries and rebel armies began demanding tolls from the oil companies Buckley served and classified the Catholic Church in Mexico as a "cancerous tumor."[10] When Huerta lost control of the state, Buckley joined an underground movement to protect priests, the church's belongings, and religious liberty. Eventually, the new Mexican leader, General Álvaro Obregón, forced Buckley out of the country and seized his properties and much of his fortune in November 1921.

The rise of the revolutionaries in Mexico mirrored Lenin grasping control in Russia; it was Communism crushing the church and capitalism. When Mr. Buckley returned to the United States, he was vehemently opposed to revolution and strongly in favor of a conservative America. Rather than continue to fight the Mexican problem, Mr. Buckley turned to his family and business, hoping to regain some of his lost wealth and make a lasting impact on his children. According to close friend Nemesio Garcia Naranjo, Buckley "believed sincerely in his Catholic faith, and he also believed in the United States of America, of which he was very proud. He rejoiced in his country's wealth and beauty. He gloried in American initiative, in American know-how and in the competitive spirit of the American people."[11] Buckley recognized the American system would triumph when hardworking people built their companies free of regulation. According to son John, "his faith in unfettered free enterprise was 'an emotional feeling verging on the quasi-religious.'"[12]

Will Buckley met Vivian Steiner through her banker uncle during the 1916 Christmas season in Mexico City. When Mr. Buckley later traveled to New Orleans to visit her, she had already become engaged. That didn't deter Will Buckley. During his stay in New Orleans, he met, proposed to, and married her older sister, Aloise, all within a matter of days that Christmas. Born into a Swiss banking family in 1895, Aloise spent two years in school at Sophie Newcomb College, becoming a distinguished writer and editor both of poems and short stories that newspapers and magazines later published. She had hoped to serve as a nurse on the front lines of the war but fainted at the sight of blood and was disqualified.[13] Instead, she moved with her husband to Mexico.

Aloise Steiner Buckley gave birth to William Jr. (Bill) on November 24, 1925, the sixth child behind Aloise, John, Priscilla, James, and Jane. Patricia, Reid, Maureen, and Carol would come later. As a mother of ten, the petite, cheerful woman leaned heavily on her husband to support the family and complemented her husband's career, politics, and vision for the future with a calm kindness and a Southern belle's charm. Bill Buckley spent his first year of childhood on board ocean liners to and from Venezuela, a transitional time for the Buckley family. The Buckleys next moved to a Sharon, Connecticut, estate. It was a beautiful home built in 1763, at one time occupied by a Connecticut governor, and the state's largest elm tree grew there.

Erudition was valued above all else in the household. A close friend wrote about Mr. Buckley Sr., "His scholarship lacked the academic pedantry that so often accompanies the wisdom of even very learned professors, and makes them dull and tiresome. He read and studied during his 77 years thousands of books, and the erudition derived was never for the purpose of showing off, but to better his strong spirit and—later in life— competently to advise his numerous descendants."[14] In time, Mr. Buckley personally designed an education program outside of the local schools specifically for his children. Bill received training from personal tutors in the typical subjects of math, science, and reading, but also in athletics, social skills, languages, rhetoric, and music. A cadre of skilled teachers (two at a time) taught the Buckley children, gave them tests and marks, and set requirements for graduation.

Mr. Buckley used dinners for family time to confirm that his children were advancing in their studies at school, teach them about his political views, and, above all, improve their skills of persuasion and public speaking. Biographer John Judis noted, "What education did not take place in the classroom took place at the dining table.... Will's dinner-table examinations encouraged a certain kind of performing intelligence among his children. They succeeded or failed not simply by saying the right thing, but by saying it well—with wit and with style."[15] While his brothers adored sports, hunting, and fishing, Bill Buckley preferred to perfect his oratorical skills. As the sixth child of ten, Bill Buckley became extremely competitive, especially for his parents' affection and approval. Friend William Coley once observed, "Exhibitionism rather than intimacy was the way you came to the attention of the father."[16] Rarely did Bill Buckley lose an argument, and he was never afraid to take on his older siblings when he disagreed.

Mr. and Mrs. Buckley also instilled a strong commitment to appropriate use of language—be it English or any other—in Bill. His grasp of vocabulary and proper grammar perhaps came from his mother's inconsistency and his father's perfection:

> She [Aloise Buckley] spoke fluent French and Spanish with undiluted inaccuracy. My father, who loved her more even than he loved to tease her, and whose knowledge of Spanish was flawless, once remarked that in forty years she had never once placed a masculine article in front of a masculine noun, or a feminine article in front of a feminine noun, except on one occasion when she accidentally stumbled upon the correct sequence, whereupon she stopped— unheard of in her case, so fluently did she aggress against the language—and corrected herself by changing the article: the result being that she spoke, in Spanish, of the latest encyclical of Pius XII, the Potato of Rome ("Pio XII, la Papa de Roma").[17]

All the children by the time they reached thirteen could speak French, Spanish, and English fluently.[18] In fact, when the children were still quite young, Jane, Bill, and Patricia only spoke Spanish, a little French, and no English![19] Bill Buckley didn't acquire English until he reached seven years and his father sent him to study at a school in England.

Bill Buckley's parents also imparted a strong base in religious faith, a constant source of strength for Buckley as he faced life's difficulties. Mr. Buckley, even though he demanded intellectual strength and strong academic performances, valued conviction and solid character above all, according to daughter Priscilla Buckley. She said, "If his children ended up as captains of their college football teams (they didn't), or editors of the school year book or presidents of the class (they occasionally did), it was all well and good, and he was very proud. But it was far more important to Mr. Buckley that his children be courteous, industrious and God-fearing."[20] When he was just five and six years old, members of the family would occasionally find the young Bill Buckley praying on his own in a cathedral. He later wrote to his mother about the joy he had in what she had taught him: "Probably the greatest contribution you have given me is your faith. I can now rely on God in almost any matter."[21] And, in fact, after he went to college and beyond, he was known to credit God with all of his successes along the way.

Except for a four-year stay in Paris, France, the family split its time between Sharon, Connecticut, and Camden, South Carolina, during Buckley's preteen years. The whole clan of siblings felt like outsiders no matter where they were. Neighbors saw the family as extravagant and attention-seeking. That didn't bother Mr. Buckley. Instead he continued the children's educations at the dinner table, during public outings, and whenever he found a spare moment; he did not stop encouraging their talents. The children later wrote, "There was nothing complicated about Father's theory of childrearing: he brought up his sons and daughters with the quite simple objective that they become absolutely perfect."[22]

Bill Buckley, while mastering the art of debate, piano, reading, writing, and horseback riding, wasn't always perfect as his father intended. Bill Buckley loved to sail. On the sea, he seemed to relax, but his grasp of the art appeared to be rather clumsy. A sister and a classmate nearly drowned while sailing with him; one of his boats sank in a boatyard; and he crashed into rocks during one race and nearly landed in a station on the St. John's

River. Even still, sailing was a hobby Buckley continued throughout his adulthood.

In 1938 when Bill was thirteen years old, Mr. Buckley sent him, Jane, Reid, and Patricia on a ship for the second time to England where they entered St. John's Beaumont private school just before the war. By the spring of 1939, Mr. Buckley took the children out of school and on a trip through Italy before returning to Connecticut. Bill then started attending the Protestant prep school Millbrook. By the time he entered Millbrook, Bill Buckley had far surpassed his classmates on an intellectual level, so the headmaster allowed him to skip one grade and gave him the only A he had ever given in English class.

When Bill Buckley turned fourteen years old, his siblings started their own newspaper, the *Spectator*, to deal with issues related to involvement in what became World War II, Catholicism, and anti-Communism—the roots of Mr. Buckley's political persuasion. At first, the older children refused to let Bill and his sister Patricia help, but when they mastered touch-typing in less than two weeks, they earned bigger responsibilities and were allowed to proofread the publication. The *Spectator* became the outreach mechanism for the local America First organization.

Mr. Buckley took his son Bill to Mexico in between finishing high school at Millbrook in 1943 and being drafted into the military. He enrolled him at the University of Mexico to improve his son's Spanish language skills even further. In July 1944, Bill Buckley landed at Camp Wheeler in Georgia for his basic infantry training. He applied to and joined the officer training course at Fort Benning in January 1945, barely making it through the program because his personality—bold and sometimes even undiplomatic—aggravated the officers who decided whether or not to pass him forward. They felt he was obnoxious, opinionated, and didn't take his military duties seriously.[23] A friend who was with Buckley in the military, Charles Ault, described Buckley's behavior: "'He was very vocal about his feelings about the Democrats in general and Roosevelt in particular... He would express those feelings very vociferously.' These political views were also 'not well received by the commanding authorities.'"[24] In another instance, Buckley stopped to pick a flower in the middle of leading a training-exercise competition which cost his team victory.[25] Buckley believed that his officers didn't value intelligence, nor did they appreciate his raucous debates. He was right; rather they sought discipline and quiet deference to leadership. Nevertheless, he passed out of the school and became an infantry training officer at Fort Gordon in Georgia. Because of his Spanish language skills, he quickly transferred to a base in San Antonio where he worked on counterintelligence.

Lieutenant Buckley entered Yale University as a freshman with the class of 1950, following the roots established by his older brother James, who had graduated in 1943. Buckley excelled at Yale. Reportedly, he and National Intelligence Director John Negroponte were the only two students to achieve an A in Wilmoore Kendall's political science course at Yale.[26] Kendall also had a lasting impact on Buckley's enunciation and inflection. As a native Oklahoman, Kendall studied at Oxford in England and improved his speaking skills through a doctoral program in Romance languages.[27] Kendall's accent was, in no uncertain terms, unique, and the time Buckley spent with him reflected on his own speaking style.

Buckley became passionately involved in the Yale community. He entered the famous Fence fraternity contingent upon the acceptance of his roommate, a Jew, by taking a courageous stand during a time when Yale's social climate lacked religious tolerance.[28] Buckley joined the Yale debate squad as a freshman, one of only three selected (the other two were Arthur Hadley, a tank commander, and L. Brent Bozell, a man who would later marry Buckley's sister). The Buckley-Bozell duo was the best the Yale debate coach had had in twenty years.[29]

Buckley worked diligently to become the chair of the *Yale Daily News* which, due to the lack of a student government in those days, essentially served as class leader. He succeeded as a freshman by writing more stories than all the others (his knowledge of touch-typing from work on the family paper, the *Spectator*, surely helped) and became chair for 1949–1950.

Involvement in writing and the dissemination of his ideas through editorials was a natural extension for Buckley who had been practicing for years with the *Spectator*. For his achievements and involvement in the Yale community, Buckley was tapped to join the prestigious secret society Skull and Bones, to which three presidents (William Howard Taft, George H. W. Bush, and George W. Bush) and countless government leaders are said to have belonged.

During his time in college, Bill Buckley's family helped connect him with his future wife. Buckley met Patricia Taylor because of his sister Pat, who roomed across the hall in a dormitory at Vassar. Patricia came from a wealthy Canadian family that stood farther to the right than the Buckleys. She had a beautiful, lean figure, and her wit and charm affectionately attracted the ambitious and bold Buckley. After one date, the two exchanged letters, but gradually lost touch when Patricia didn't return to Vassar because of a back injury she sustained from a horseback riding accident.

One summer later, when Buckley and friend L. Brent Bozell worked for Mr. Buckley's new oil holding in Canada, the two decided to visit Pat Buckley over Independence Day weekend in 1949 at Patricia Taylor's Vancouver home. After four days with Patricia, Bill Buckley interrupted her from a game of cards and asked, "Patricia, would you consider marriage with me?" She tersely replied, "Bill, I've been asked this question many times. To the others I've said no. To you I say yes. Now may I please get back and finish my hand?"[30] Ironically, Bill Buckley and Patricia Taylor's wedding wasn't the only one coming out of that Vancouver weekend. L. Brent Bozell married Pat Buckley following that weekend reprieve, too.

Before their marriage, Patricia visited Buckley on occasion throughout the next year as he finished his degree at Yale, and she earned the affection of his peers. According to Francis Donahue, faculty advisor of the *Yale Daily News*, "She came into Buckley's room with a mink coat on, and she just let it fall off her shoulders onto the floor. All the students were in love with her."[31] One weekend prior to their marriage in spring 1950, Evan

Galbraith, a friend of Buckley's at Yale and later a U.S. Department of Defense representative to Europe and an advisor to the U.S. mission to NATO, invited the pair to dinner at his fraternity, DEKE. He wrote, "Pat had an *Animal House* view of fraternities, and once seated she looked around and audibly said: 'I hear everyone around here is drunk half the time.' I demurred: 'Oh now, we drink twice that much.' She roared with laughter and grabbed my hand and said: 'We'll get along just fine!' Pat Taylor Buckley was humor."[32]

Bill Buckley and Patricia Taylor married in July 1950 in a Vancouver church. The wedding was quite the affair; more than one thousand guests gathered on the Taylor front lawn to celebrate the union. According to Buckley friend Evan Galbraith, Patricia was nervous that some of the Yale ushers might show up intoxicated. She and her mother issued a rule to the ushers: "No Nips before Nups." According to Galbraith, "Violators would be seized and pressed into the Canadian army and sent to Korea. Pat's father was a very big wheel and we all believed he could do it. We all laughed for years, on land and at sea over 'No Nips before Nups.'"[33] During their first year of marriage, the newlyweds lived in a New Haven, Connecticut suburb, close to the Bozells and Yale where Buckley taught Spanish in the mornings and spent time writing an important exposé in the afternoons.

It had been a rebuff by Yale's administration that provoked Bill Buckley to uncloak his alma mater by describing his experiences as a student. During his time heading *Yale Daily News*, Buckley acquired a positive and praiseworthy reputation from most faculty members and students. As the student invited to give the Alumni Day speech, Buckley could not have been more pleased for an opportunity to share his perspective with the large gathering. Two days before the event, Yale Secretary Carl Lohmann requested that Buckley practice his speech before him in advance, suspecting that Buckley's sometimes critical views might be present in the speech. Buckley refused to practice the speech, but he did submit a written copy for review. In it, Buckley unveiled Yale's liberal faculty members by name. Yale's president, secretary, and alumni director all disapproved of the speech and asked him to revise the copy. When he did—only slightly—and offered to withdraw the speech as a token gesture, believing it was too close to the event to find a replacement, the college president accepted his offer, much to Buckley's disbelief. Buckley immediately felt rebuked for his ideas and became convinced that word about the faculty's intolerance needed to get out now more than ever.

William F. Buckley penned *God and Man at Yale* based almost exclusively on his experiences with the liberal academe at Yale University during the late 1940s. His thesis purported that, while Yale University claimed to be a premier educational institution which protects and upholds the values of American society, including individualism and Christianity, reality demonstrated its intolerance for those ideas. He hoped to dispel the myth suggested by *Time* magazine that Yale epitomized a college "triumphant of conservatism."[34] In the preface to the book, Buckley outlined his intentions: "I propose, simply, to expose what I regard as an extraordinarily irresponsible educational attitude that, under the protective label 'academic freedom,' has produced one of the most extraordinary incongruities of our time: the institution that derives its moral and financial support from Christian individualists and then addresses itself to the task of persuading the sons of these supporters to be atheistic socialists."[35] Buckley asserted that the economics department was devoid of free enterprise advocates; instead, collectivists comprised its core. He lamented that atheists and agnostics rather than Christians filled the religion and philosophy departments. It was one of the first attacks on America's institutions of higher education at the time.

God and Man at Yale triggered a backlash among Yale professors, trustees, and students. Frank Ashburn, Yale University trustee, wrote a piece for the *Saturday Review of Literature* in which he stated, "The book is one which has the glow and appeal of a fiery cross on a hillside at night. There will undoubtedly be robed figures who gather to it, but the hoods will not be academic. They will cover the face."[36] Herbert Liebert, employed by Yale's library, complained in the *St. Louis Post-Dispatch*, "The book is a series of fanatically emotional attacks on a few professors who dare to approach religion and politics objectively."[37] McGeorge Bundy, associate professor of government at Harvard (and a Yale graduate), described the book for the *Atlantic Monthly* as "dishonest in its use of facts, false in its theory, and a discredit to its author" and later referred to Buckley as "twisted and ignorant."[38] These scathing reviews served to fortify Buckley's confidence in individualism, traditionalism, freedom, and capitalism. Through all the criticism, Bill Buckley became, as brother Reid Buckley conveyed, "a tough polemicist, like the young Cassius Clay."[39]

The attacks also spurred book sales dramatically. *God and Man at Yale*, produced by Regnery Publishing, appeared on bookshelves in October 1951. By November, Regnery Publishing sold more than twelve thousand copies, and the book climbed to number sixteen on the *New York Times* best-seller list. *Time, Newsweek, Life,* and *New England Quarterly* all ran stories on the book. Publisher Henry Regnery described the ease with which the book promoted itself:

> No book in the past generation has aroused more discussion and controversy, been more passionately condemned or more widely reviewed and commented on, than *God and Man at Yale*. It was an instant success, appeared on the best-seller list for weeks, and went through many printings. We had planned an extensive advertising and promotional campaign, and to help get the book noticed in New York had hired a bright and efficient lady, amusingly enough from the socialist *New Leader*. But all that was unnecessary—the vehemence from the response of the liberal establishment assured the book's success, and in William F. Buckley, Jr., we had an author whose talents for debate and for provoking his antagonists were of inestimable value.[40]

By the time spring arrived, more than thirty-five thousand copies had sold, and it continued to sell for decades, with new anniversary editions pro-

duced through the years. The book was the first time an insider took a critical look at higher education and called its bias what it was: indoctrination
of America's future leaders.

Following the publication of his first book and encouraged by his Yale
mentor, Wilmoore Kendall, William F. Buckley Jr. joined the Central
Intelligence Agency for several months in 1952. His Spanish fluency, tow-
ering intelligence, and commitment to America's ideal of freedom helped
him acquire the job through James Burnham and E. Howard Hunt. He
worked directly under E. Howard Hunt, the novelist who had won a
Guggenheim fellowship in 1943 for his work, *East of Farewell*, against competition including authors Gore Vidal and Truman Capote. As a covert
operator, Buckley funneled thousands of dollars to politicians, the very ones
his father worked with in Mexico. When after eight months Buckley
decided that the CIA no longer fit his career plans, Buckley quit and
returned to the States, but not before telling Hunt he intended to purchase
a magazine.

Upon his return to America, he and Patricia resided in New York City
in an apartment complex also occupied by tenant Marilyn Monroe. Buckley took a job as an associate editor with *American Mercury*, a somewhat
floundering national publication, but he also found time to coauthor
McCarthy and His Enemies with friend and brother-in-law L. Brent Bozell
in 1954. *McCarthy and His Enemies* appeared on the shelves of bookstores
at a precise moment in time, just one month before the Army-McCarthy
hearings. Senator McCarthy publicly blamed the shortcomings of American foreign policy square on Communists who had successfully infiltrated
U.S. government at all levels. Liberals and detractors went wild with criticism and attacks on the senator. Buckley and Bozell set out to write a cred-
ible account of the situation and defend "McCarthyism," or "the
maintenance of a steady flow of criticism . . . calculated to pressure the President, Cabinet members, high officials, and above all the political party in
power, to get on with the elimination of security risks in government."[41] The
pair argued that Soviet penetration of the American government threatened

the balance of power on a worldwide scale. While the senator's exaggerations in implying General George C. Marshall was guilty of treason were an "egregious blunder," the duo became loyalists to a crusade against Communists, especially those in government.[42] At a celebration of the book's publication, McCarthy told members of the press, "It is the only book ever written about me not written by an enemy or by McCarthy."[43]

While books shared Buckley's ideas with a nationwide audience, the time they took to produce didn't allow for the quick dissemination of his current thinking. He had contemplated starting a magazine, and the time seemed appropriate to undertake this project, considering his growing stature as a conservative spokesman. Buckley tried to buy *Human Events*, but the owners at that time did not want to sell. In 1955, he attempted to purchase the *Freeman*, but again, the directors hesitated to sell the publication. Around that same time, a good friend and an advisor to Henry Luce on foreign policy at *Time* magazine, William Schlamm, also had wanted to start a weekly magazine. He had sought help from Henry Regnery and Henry Luce with no success. When Schlamm became aware of Buckley's similar interests, he turned to him to collaborate. Bill Buckley had the resources, Schlamm had the experience, and they both had the inclination to start such a publication. Before long, the two had joined together in this endeavor.

With a $100,000 investment commitment from his father and Bill Buckley at the helm as editor-in-chief, Buckley chose the name *National Weekly* for his publication. He then discovered *National Liquor Weekly* had already copyrighted that particular name. Working through then attorney Bill Casey, who later became CIA chief under Ronald Reagan, Buckley decided on the name *National Review*, and Casey processed the papers.

Two classes of stock formed the basic corporation. The first, Class A common stock with full voting rights but no par value, would be owned solely by Bill Buckley, and Class B would be sold to the public as nonvoting stock with a value of $1.[44] Buckley then embarked on a year-long campaign to raise funds to supplement the magazine, succeeding in coming up with $300,000 in capital for the project from more than 120 individual investors.[45] Among the early significant contributors to the untested magazine were California oil entrepreneur Henry Salvatori and South Carolina textile manufacturer Roger Milliken.

It was a difficult undertaking during the inhospitable political climate of the 1950s. Conservative stalwart, Ohio Senator Robert Taft, had died in 1953. One of the only publications dedicated to freedom and capitalism, the *Freeman*, virtually collapsed in 1954. The Left had eight weekly journals at the time to express its ideas, including the *New Republic*, *Nation*, *Commonweal*, and *New Leader* among others, while the Right had only one: *Human Events*.[46] President Eisenhower's middle-of-the-road approach to governing caused *U.S. News & World Report* to suggest both political parties nominate him for president in 1956.[47] George Will describes that time period in American political thought as "conformity in the nation's intellectual life."[48] The first *National Review* editors recognized their uphill challenge in this cable to Henry Regnery: "They [the coeditors] fully recognize the implications of presenting conservative ideas in a period when so-called forces of liberalism still exercise a strong influence on the principal informational media."[49] It was hardly an opportune period to start a contemporary publication for conservative readers, yet its owner and editors embraced the occasion.

The first issue of *National Review*, debuting November 19, 1955, featured thirty-two pages to rally conservatives. Seventy-five-hundred copies came off the press and arrived to readers that November week. In the inaugural issue, Bill Buckley wrote an introductory piece that described his intentions with *National Review*. He said, above all, *National Review* will stand "athwart history yelling Stop."[50] The blue-bordered cover article focused on foreign policy; Senator William Knowland, a California conservative who many touted as an opponent to Richard Nixon in 1960 for president, warned against Soviet disarmament proposals. The rest of the new magazine promoted freedom and chastised Communism, as was the case with Aloise Buckley Heath's article about her travails to expose

Communists in the faculty at Smith College. The back cover of the first issue highlighted endorsements from some prominent policy makers and businessmen, including Spruille Braden, Governor Charles Edison, J. Bracken Lee, Admiral Ben Moreell, and J. Howard Pew.

The initial capital raised by Bill Buckley lasted for eighteen months, and in that time *National Review* gave conservatives and their ideas a weekly outlet. To set *National Review* apart from its contemporaries, Buckley sought to make the magazine "biting and witty as well as serious."[51] Various contests poked fun at the magazine's mission; one offered a gift subscription of *National Review* to the U.N. secretary-general, Dag Hammarskjöld, in honor of the first subscriber to send in $7. Each issue contained pieces by prominent conservative thinkers of the day. From the beginning, L. Brent Bozell wrote a weekly column on legislation and policy; William Schlamm wrote on foreign policy; F. A. Voigt on matters behind the Iron Curtain in Europe; Morrie Ryskind on arts once a month; James Burnham on the Cold War and balance of power; Karl Hess on the liberal media; John Chamberlain on new books of the day; and Russell Kirk and Bill Buckley on education.[52] In addition, books published by Henry Regnery attracted growing readership when reviews appeared in the pages of *National Review*.

Buckley spent all of his time and energy in the magazine's early years to keep it alive. He worked tirelessly to hire and fire staff, watch the finances, and write his weekly columns. He gave up precious time at home with his son, Christopher, in order to keep the magazine afloat. He changed the magazine from a weekly publication to a biweekly one. By June 1957, the staunch defender of American free enterprise and conservative principles was losing $2,400 on each issue.[53] This overlooks the fact that Buckley often personally donated his speaking fees and hosted annual fund-raisers to keep the publication in circulation.

William Schlamm encouraged Buckley: "If *National Review* ever actually began publishing and went on to acquire 25,000 readers (!) they would not let us go out of business."[54] In 1958, its subscribers hovered at 25,000.[55]

And Schlamm was right; they didn't let the magazine wither away. In that year when the finances of the magazine were so dire, Buckley wrote a long personal letter to his subscribers and requested they give a donation to the magazine over and above the subscription cost. The subscribers listened intently to his plea. Year after year, subscribers chipped in to keep the magazine in business. This is what makes *National Review* unique. As an opinion magazine, its readers value the content so much that they contribute to its operations over their monthly subscription fees. These are rare contributions according to present-day editor Rich Lowry, who speculates the same is not true for other magazines, such as *Vogue* or *Vanity Fair*.

In the fifty years since its inception, *National Review* has lost more than $25 million, which equates to nearly $500,000 annually.[56] Those figures still didn't stop *Time* magazine from admitting the prominence of *National Review* by suggesting it was "easy to read" and "entertaining."[57] Rich Lowry, in a piece appearing on *National Review Online*, appealed, "We Need Your Help" and went on to document *National Review*'s chronic financial shortage:

> If your business needs advice on how to develop a loss leader, come to us. We have it down. I assure you we can help you start to lose money almost immediately. It's our specialty. We have been doing it for 50 years and hope to keep doing it for many more.
>
>   That last bit isn't quite right. We'd prefer not to lose money. But there is something to the opinion journalism business that makes it inherently unprofitable...As WFB [William F. Buckley Jr.] said long ago, NR exists to make a point, not a profit....We exist to advance a worldview not to rake in money.[58]

Despite its financial losses, those on the Left found the writing within its pages worthy of dissection in their own journals and magazines. Accused by Dwight Macdonald in *Commentary* of "opacity," "brutality," "banality," and "vulgarity," and called names such as "Scrambled Eggheads on the

Right," "half-educated," and "half-successful provincials," Macdonald went on to mention that the Right definitely needed its own publication, but "[t]his is not it."[59] Another publication asserted, "This country needs a conservative magazine, and having read *National Review*, we *still* say what this country needs is a conservative magazine."[60] The Left seemed to know precisely what the Right "needed." Buckley and his conservative team paid no heed to the attacks and dug in their heels for the long-term.[61]

Perhaps *National Review*'s most enduring acclamation came from a man who had a hand in bringing the Conservative Movement to the forefront of the policy agenda. When Ronald Reagan won the presidency in 1980, Buckley mused on the pages of *National Review*: "With the election of Ronald Reagan, *National Review* assumes a new importance in American life. We become, as it were, an establishment organ; and we feel it only appropriate to alter our demeanor accordingly. This is therefore the last issue in which we shall indulge in levity. Connoisseurs of humor will have to get their yuks elsewhere. We have a nation to run."[62]

The *Right Nation* called *National Review* "the most important platform for conservative ideas."[63] For one reason, *National Review* played an important role in gathering support for many of Ronald Reagan's policy initiatives. Magazine contributors wrote favorably about "Reaganomics"—the combination of tax cuts and spending restraints that led to America's economic recovery. Writer James Burnham's controversial suggestion recommending the buildup of the American military to counter the Soviet Union played out almost immediately in the Reagan administration.[64] Upon the thirtieth anniversary of *National Review*, the founder held a celebratory party in its honor featuring President Ronald Reagan, who confirmed the impact *National Review* had on him since his days as a Democrat. Ronald Reagan, speaking from the presidential dais, playfully announced,

> If any of you doubt the impact of *National Review*'s verve and attractiveness, take a look around you this evening. The man standing before you was a Democrat when he picked up his first issue [of

National Review] in a plain brown wrapper; and even now, as an occupant of public housing, he awaits as anxiously as ever his biweekly edition—without the wrapper. Over here is the Director of the Central Intelligence Agency [Bill Casey], who, besides running a successful presidential campaign in 1980, is the same New York lawyer who drew up the incorporation papers for *National Review*. Or ask any of the young leaders in the media, academia, or government here tonight to name the principal intellectual influence in their formative years. On this point, I can assure you: *National Review* is to the offices of the West Wing of the White House what *People* is to your dentist's waiting room. . . . I want to assure you tonight: you didn't just part the Red Sea—you rolled it back, dried it up, and left exposed, for all the world to see, the naked desert that is statism. And then, as if that weren't enough, you gave to the world something different, something in its weariness it desperately needed, the sound of laughter and the sight of the rich, green uplands of freedom.[65]

National Review is said to be "America's only surviving journal of conservative opinion" and a "truly seminal contribution" to the Conservative Movement.[66] Bill Buckley recognized that for conservatism firmly to take root, it needed a new generation of believers, which is why he frequently hired emerging writers out of college, provided internships, and proactively gave students a dose of his conservatism and advice. Even today, *National Review* continues to uphold the values of a free society by inspiring future generations of leaders by supplying free annual subscriptions of the magazine to thousands of conservative young people.

Editor Rich Lowry believes it was a "knack" of Buckley's to identify emerging thinkers and writers and give them rich experiences to build their confidence. It was an effort that Buckley spent significant time and energy undertaking. *National Review* recruited budding talents who wrote within its pages and later went on to other written achievements, including John Leonard (book reviewer for *Harper's*), Joan Didion (award winning author),

David Brooks (the *New York Times*), columnist Maggie Gallagher, columnist Mona Charen, Arlene Croce (a writer for the *New Yorker*), George Will (Ronald Reagan's favorite columnist according to the *Washington Post*'s Lou Cannon), Richard Brookhiser (senior editor at *National Review* and author of *Founding Father: Rediscovering George Washington*), Tony Dolan (Ronald Reagan's chief speech writer), Charles Kesler (editor of the *Claremont Review of Books* and frequent *Los Angeles Times* and *Wall Street Journal* contributor), and Paul Gigot (*Wall Street Journal* editorial page editor).[67]

The publication itself also attracted a young following of individuals who would go on to make great strides for the Movement. An ad in *National Review* in 1961 encouraged a young Richard Viguerie to seek a job as a political organizer. Young Americans for Freedom subsequently hired him as its executive secretary.[68] Viguerie's efforts in direct mail communications jump-started and sustained numerous conservative organizations by getting their ideas and messages heard by millions of Americans. Pat Buchanan, columnist, television pundit, and aide to both Ronald Reagan and Richard Nixon, picked up his issue of *National Review* while a student at Georgetown University and said it was "the first magazine [that] expressed, with a sense of humor and intelligence and wit, exactly the things I believed."[69] And, as Ronald Reagan verified at *National Review*'s thirtieth anniversary gala, countless other public officials and leaders credit the magazine with sparking their involvement and beginning their conservative educations.

William F. Buckley Jr. spent much of his time relentlessly lecturing at college campuses across the country, sponsored by Young America's Foundation, to meet with and encourage young people. But he also made sure his efforts were channeled appropriately to keep these new recruits inspired and active. His commitment ran deeper than simply attracting new readers and writers to his magazine; rather, it was a faithfulness to cultivate the Movement from its deepest roots to ensure its resilience and momentum in decades to come.

A new generation of conservatives sprouted at Buckley's home, Great Elm, during the September 9–11, 1960, weekend. Buckley had attended the July 1960 Republican convention in Chicago, Illinois, with public-relations expert Marvin Liebman. The pair met two student leaders of the Youth for Goldwater organization at the convention and took the youngsters under their tutelage. David Franke began an internship at *National Review*, while Doug Caddy worked for Liebman at his firm. Buckley and Liebman suggested that Franke and Caddy, in their spare time, organize a new youth-related conservative organization. The two diligently began preparing for what became the first meeting of Young Americans for Freedom (YAF) at Buckley's home. Ninety-three college students traversed the Connecticut countryside and arrived at Buckley's Sharon estate for a weekend retreat.

The meeting produced the Sharon Statement, a "conservative manifesto" as liberal publication the *Nation* called it.[70] Succinctly written by the group's young founders, the four-hundred-word Sharon Statement outlined its conservative credo:

> In this time of moral and political crisis, it is the responsibility of the youth of America to affirm certain eternal truths.
>
> We as young conservatives believe:
>
> That foremost among the transcendent values is the individual's use of his God-given free will, whence derives his right to be free from the restrictions of arbitrary force;
>
> That liberty is indivisible, and that political freedom cannot long exist without economic freedom;
>
> That the purposes of government are to protect these freedoms through the preservation of internal order, the provision of national defense, and the administration of justice;
>
> That when government ventures beyond these rightful functions, it accumulates power which tends to diminish order and liberty;
>
> That the Constitution of the United States is the best arrangement yet devised for empowering government to fulfill its proper role, while restraining it from the concentration and abuse of power;

That the genius of the Constitution—the division of powers—is summed up in the clause which reserves primacy to the several states, or to the people, in those spheres not specifically delegated to the federal government;

That the market economy, allocating resources by the free play of supply and demand, is the single economic system compatible with the requirements of personal freedom and constitutional government, and that it is at the same time the most productive supplier of human needs;

That when government interferes with the work of the market economy, it tends to reduce the moral and physical strength of the nation; that when it takes from one man to bestow on another, it diminishes the incentive of the first, the integrity of the second, and the moral autonomy of both;

That we will be free only so long as the national sovereignty of the United States is secure; that history shows periods of freedom are rare, and can exist only when free citizens concertedly defend their rights against all enemies;

That the forces of international Communism are, at present, the greatest single threat to these liberties;

That the United States should stress victory over, rather than coexistence with, this menace; and

That American foreign policy must be judged by this criterion: does it serve the just interests of the United States?[71]

The Sharon Statement established the platform for Young Americans for Freedom (YAF), a group which would be inspired by Barry Goldwater and united behind Ronald Reagan. Lee Edwards, aspiring journalist, said of Buckley's role in the event, "His presence, having it at his family home, lent a flavor of glamour to the event...I was particularly under his spell because I wanted to be like this brilliant young writer, editor, speaker, orator, debater, thinker."[72] Buckley became the "paternalistic" figure of YAF, an invaluable resource for the group's leaders over the years.[73]

Buckley assisted YAF chapters and their members for decades whenever he could with publicity, financial support, encouragement, and advice. Once, when the New York YAF chapter was looking for a place to host its headquarters, Buckley ran an ad at no cost in *National Review*, advertising the group's need for an office. A gentleman in Greenwich Village stepped forward with free office space which he provided for ten years for the burgeoning group. YAF member Herb Stupp remembers when Buckley lectured at St. John's University and Pace University in 1971, organized by the schools' YAF chapters. Following the events, Buckley gave the individual YAF chapters the honorarium he received for his speeches. When Buckley found out Stupp was interested in a career in journalism, Buckley interviewed him on his show, *Firing Line*, to give him some television experience; published his pieces in *National Review*, sending a note back saying *Nice Job!*; and provided tips and encouragement to the emerging talent.[74]

Each year, Buckley addressed YAF's national convention. At the 1964 YAF meeting, he outlined how YAF should proceed through the Goldwater election and beyond and offered prophetic advice. He said, "The point of the present occasion is to win recruits whose attention we might never have attracted but for Barry Goldwater; to win them not only for November the third, but for future Novembers; to infuse the conservative spirit in enough people to entitle us to look about us, on November fourth, not at the ashes of defeat, but at the well-planted seeds of hope, which will flower on a great November day in the future, if there is a future."[75] Buckley stunned many in the audience with his prediction of defeat in 1964, but his message remained in the hearts of so many of the young leaders that year, enough so that it carried the group forward to 1980 when Ronald Reagan carried the banner once again. Buckley also plugged the group in *National Review* after each of its national conventions to help raise funds for the organization.

YAF's success emerges in three distinct areas: the activities it undertook, its members who went on to great achievements, and its use as a model organization. During its early years, YAF took major responsibility for organizing Goldwater rallies and building support for the candidate across the country. Six months after its start, in March 1961, YAF held a rally at the Manhattan Center. Three thousand young conservatives showed up at the auditorium; three thousand others organizers turned away at the door.[76] Greeted with a roaring ovation, Barry Goldwater addressed the crowd with a moving message of freedom and liberty. Both *Time* magazine and the *New York Times* took notice of the event, and stories appeared within their pages describing the excitement. By 1964, the year Barry Goldwater ran for president of the United States, YAF boasted a membership of twenty-eight thousand students on more than one hundred campuses, while the leftist counter group, Students for a Democratic Society, had merely two thousand members.[77]

In 1965, YAF successfully fought against Firestone Tires' intention to build a rubber manufacturing plant in Communist Romania. YAF thought Firestone's decision, blessed by the United States' government, to do business with Communists was against America's founding principles. After boycotts and letter-writing campaigns, Firestone backed off its plans, much to the chagrin of Senator Fulbright, who denounced YAF for voicing its opposition. The organization had set an important precedent for standing behind freedom and opposing tyranny on all levels.

In 1974, under the leadership of Frank Donatelli (who later became Ronald Reagan's assistant for political affairs), YAF created the largest conference specifically dedicated to the growth of conservative ideas. The Conservative Political Action Conference (CPAC) is the preeminent gathering of young conservatives still today, an event which draws more than seven thousand people for a single weekend event annually and provides them with training and motivation to become active in the political process. CPAC has hosted Presidents Reagan and Bush, Vice Presidents Quayle and Cheney, and scores of other distinguished leaders and practitioners.

Many successful conservatives emerged through the YAF channel. Dan Quayle, vice president of the United States, was involved in YAF as a student. Lee Edwards, prominent author, historian, and distinguished fellow at Heritage Foundation, edited the group's successful magazine, *New Guard*. Alan Keyes, presidential candidate, diplomat, and Reagan administration official, came up through the YAF experience while in college at Harvard. Thomas L. Phillips, a key conservative publisher, was the YAF leader at Dartmouth College.

YAF served as the prototype for so many organizations that sprouted as a result of the efforts of its members in subsequent years. Young America's Foundation, the Fund for American Studies, the American Conservative Union, and the Committee for Responsible Youth Politics all got their starts because of young YAF leaders who put their activism skills to use in building new conservative outlets. YAF was the first action-oriented group of its kind, a hybrid of policy and activism.

Not only did Buckley help spearhead YAF, but he also helped other youth-related causes, including an institution and the collegiate atmosphere in general. He agreed to serve as the Intercollegiate Studies Institute's (ISI, originally named Intercollegiate Society of Individualists) first president. ISI identifies young conservatives on campuses and sends them literature on individualism and capitalism. In addition, ISI promotes philosophical growth for emerging scholars through historical, classical liberal thinkers, including Edmund Burke and Ludwig von Mises.

Buckley earned a reputation as a campus celebrity along with Barry Goldwater and Ronald Reagan.[78] Greeted like a rock star at many schools, Buckley perfected his speaking style, seeking to capture the attention of young people. At Rutgers University in 1967, three thousand students packed the gymnasium to hear him speak on "The Responsibility of Students," during which he called Communists "barbarians" and a liberal think tank a "zoo."[79] Publisher Henry Regnery summed up Buckley's importance for young people: "[B]y his manner and personality, he came to symbolize the conservative movement.... [I]t would be difficult to conceive of the conservative movement without Bill Buckley. He has not only served ever since as an inspiration and a rallying point, particularly to student generations; he has given it a style and rhetoric of its own, and has done more than anyone else to reconcile potentially conflicting viewpoints into a coherent intellectual force."[80]

While he continued to build the Movement among America's youth, Buckley also stayed involved in *National Review* and public policy in particular. In 1965, William F. Buckley Jr. decided to run for mayor of New York City as a conservative party candidate. The decision was precipitated by Buckley's repulsion with the media over its coverage of a speech he gave to New York City policemen where the paper misquoted and misrepresented the event, claiming the policemen laughed and cheered at his mention of a civil rights activist's death. In reality, the crowd had done neither. When Buckley considered the surging New York City crime rates, soaring deficits, and disappointing candidates in the race already, he felt compelled to compete for the job. While he didn't anticipate winning, he did intend to call attention to some issues, speaking his mind to help his city. When asked by a reporter what he would do if he were elected, he responded with his characteristic wit: "Demand a recount."[81]

The 1965 mayoral race made Buckley a television phenomenon. According to personal assistant Neal Freeman, "It made him a star, and the transformation was quite electric . . . In 1964, you would travel anywhere in the country with Bill Buckley and both of you were anonymous. By 1965, you couldn't walk twenty-five feet in an airport without the autograph hunters."[82] He even drew the attention of contemporary culture at the time. A 1966 *Glamour* magazine poll asked movie and drama critics, "Do you prefer (check one) Robert Kennedy or William Buckley?"[83] It is no surprise that the critics' philosophical bent provoked them all, each one, to check Robert Kennedy!

Buckley had been hoping to start a debate show for television before the mayor's race, but no local affiliates would consent to sponsor the program. He used the mayoral debates to draw attention to his debate talent and shined in the process. His classic sarcasm and charm radiated from his demeanor and witty, quick responses. WOR-TV, a private New York City station, agreed to syndicate a show for Buckley. On April 30, 1966, Buckley began as host of *Firing Line*. The intellectual debates each Friday night enlivened Americans who watched.

Firing Line became an overnight sensation. On November 3, 1967, Buckley appeared on the cover of *Time* magazine under the headline, "Conservatism Can Be Fun." In the piece, *Time* magazine asserted that Buckley was "too clever, too humorous, [and] too well read."[84] According to *Time*, Buckley displays "forensic marksmanship" where he "confronts his adversaries with a polysyllabic vocabulary and an arsenal of intimidating grimaces."[85] His Yale advisor, Wilmoore Kendall, said about his performances, "Buckley could do as much with his voice as Laurence Olivier."[86]

By 1968, just two years after its start, *Firing Line* won an Emmy and gave Buckley even more stardom. The *Wall Street Journal* and *Harper's* both carried features on him. In an end-of-the-year special, Woody Allen called on Buckley to appear on his NBC one-hour broadcast to comment on the year 1967. By 1970, *Firing Line* appeared on more than one hundred television stations.[87]

Even still, adversaries attacked him personally time and time again. Jack Paar, host of *The Tonight Show*, publicly proclaimed that Buckley had "no humanity" after Buckley appeared as a guest.[88] David Susskind, producer and talk show host, called Buckley's mannerisms "symptoms of psychotic paranoia" on national television.[89] Larry King in *Harper's* wrote, "His enemies, laid end to end, would reach from here to Southern Purgatory, to which they variously damn him for inciting radical hatred."[90]

These personal attacks run counter to Buckley's way of dealing with opposition. *National Review* editor Rich Lowry admired William F. Buckley Jr., not only because of his beautiful and graceful writing, but also because of his "high intellectual standards" for which "he never portend[ed] into name calling or insulting people."[91] In all the years of public discourse and debate, Buckley refrained from relying on personal derisions

or scornful attacks, except for one occasion. Buckley had been asked by
ABC News to appear in a series of debates during the Democratic and
Republican national conventions in 1968. His adversary had not yet been
chosen, and news officials inquired as to who Buckley would be willing to
debate. He provided a list of eight recommendations, including John
Kenneth Galbraith and Norman Mailer.[92] He also conveyed to the execu-
tives that he did not want to debate a "Communist," nor did he want to
debate Gore Vidal. Buckley had appeared with him on Jack Paar's show
and on *Open End*, David Susskind's talk show. Vidal's previous appearances in debates convinced Buckley that Vidal formulated his own quota-
tions, attributing them to experts, and fabricated facts to win arguments.
Buckley also regretted Vidal's personal attacks on Buckley's family. In addition, Buckley didn't care much for Vidal's outward "flaunting of his bisex-
uality."[93] Against Buckley's recommendations, ABC News hired Gore Vidal
with the intent of making the Vidal-Buckley pair entertainment worthy of
sky-high television ratings. By the time the Miami Republican convention
had closed, Buckley had tired of Vidal's personal derisions and requested
that their appearances alternate on television instead of appearing together
in a live debate; the producer denied the request.[94] It was on to the Democratic convention in Chicago. During one such infamous exchange, Gore
Vidal first called Buckley a "pro- or crypto-Nazi" in front of a national television audience of ten million people.[95] Buckley, shocked at the vitriol
espoused from Vidal, responded defensively with an attack of his own, calling Vidal a "queer" and threatening to "sock" him in the face.[96] It was an
uncharacteristic, but fully provoked, personal attack that came from frustration and never occurred again.

Buckley did, however, aggressively spar on television with some of the
most preeminent leaders of the day. He debated Jimmy Carter, John Kenneth Galbraith, George McGovern, Robert Schrum, and Socialist party
chairman Norman Thomas. Buckley's skill at debate made it increasingly
difficult to attract the most prominent liberals to debate him, but such
unwillingness only highlighted Buckley's adeptness and level of prepara-

tion. When Buckley offered Senator Robert Kennedy $500 and a role in the planning of that show's format, Kennedy declined, and Buckley characteristically responded, "Why does baloney reject the grinder?"[97] Over the years, prominent figures joined the show, both in agreement and opposition to Buckley, including presidents, prime ministers, monarchs, poets, musicians, scientists, and athletes.

On December 14, 1999, after thirty-three years, *Firing Line* taped its final show and ended as the longest-running television program with the same host in history.[98] Its impact, along with Clarence Manion's *Manion Forum*, gave television and radio outlets confidence that a wider audience yearned for conservative commentary. George Will writes, "When *Firing Line* began, it was to television what Israel is to the Middle East—an embattled salient of civilized values in an inhospitable region. . . . The good news is that rising generations of conservatives, looking for instruction on how to make the most of the medium, need only consult the archives of *Firing Line*."[99]

Bill Buckley earned his reputation as the "godfather of the Conservative Movement" and rightfully so. In the words of colleague William Rusher, "Bill Buckley's emergence onto the national stage as a major conservative spokesman and a minor celebrity in the 1950s, and the impact of his striking personality when this began to be brought to bear, caused a lesion in the self-confidence of many liberals that materially influenced the attitudes of both conservatives and liberals thereafter, as well as the ultimate outcome of their long struggle."[100] William F. Buckley Jr.'s legacy defines him as one of the most consequential figures of the twentieth century. He was a man whose industry never lagged, but rather flourished as an inspiration and a call to action for all conservatives. His time and financial sacrifice over the years should not be taken for granted.

Buckley's most important project, his "baby" in the words of editor Rich Lowry, was *National Review*, a publication that has withstood the tests and trials of the free market literary business. Author Dan Flynn, who confirms *National Review*'s positive impact on his life as a teenager, says about its legacy, "Since someone did invent *National Review*, Young Americans for Freedom, the Goldwater campaign, conservative non-profits such as Heritage and Free Congress, Rush Limbaugh, the *Wall Street Journal* editorial page, and so much more followed. Conservatives have more choices than *National Review* in no small part because of *National Review*."[101]

Once referred to as the "aging Boy Wonder of the American Right," William F. Buckley Jr.'s contributions to our country's conservative ascendancy are dramatic.[102] When William F. Buckley Jr. reached eighty years of age, he was still reading and writing, some seventy years after his adventures in conservatism began. He had scribed more than four thousand columns and authored forty-seven books, not to mention all he wrote to keep in touch with friends and foes alike by letter.[103] When he died in 2008, he is said to have been still working on yet another piece at his desk.[104]

Chapter Four

Dean Clarence "Pat" Manion

"We have heard much in our time about 'the common man.'
It is a concept that pays little attention to the history of a nation that
grew through the initiative and ambition of the uncommon man."[1]

—BARRY GOLDWATER

Incensed at the floundering flicker of the American founders' intentions, Dean Clarence "Pat" Manion sought to rekindle the flame for the principles he valiantly imbued. In so doing, he endured personal hardships, suffering defeats for electoral office, giving up an opportunity to hold a seat on the United States Supreme Court, getting fired from the chairmanship of an important federal committee, and weathering brutal campaign losses on behalf of the candidates he admired. His experiences seem to mirror the astounding defeats of so many incinerated victims of political carnage. Yet Clarence Manion persevered, personalized the Conservative cause, and, in his own words, sparked a prairie fire, resulting from "the finest exposition of genuine Americanism since the Federalist Papers."[2] It is rare in the face of setbacks that an individual relies on determination alone to fan the flame. But Clarence Manion was, after all, no common man.

Clarence Emmett was born on July 7, 1896, to Edward and Elizabeth Carroll Manion in a little yellow brick rambler in Henderson, Kentucky. He was the ninth-born in the family. One previous son and four daughters survived before his birth. Three other children didn't mature past childhood according to the family Bible.[3] Clarence's mother, a devoted housewife and parent, never missed Mass a day in her life. Her religious commitments played a major role in Clarence's upbringing and undoubtedly impacted him throughout his life. She was a thrifty woman, never leaving anything to waste, hiding away a few dollars here and there under a mattress or under the carpet for emergencies.[4] Additionally, she skillfully stitched beautiful suits and clothing out of worn-out, discarded articles. Manion's father, a sidewalk contractor, constructed many of the pedestrian aisles through the city; his name is still engraved in the corner of each block he built.

Henderson, Kentucky, resembled a typical American boomtown. Daniel Boone reportedly came across the beautiful, lushly growing plot with one of the first groups of men to explore this area. The town, founded in 1797 on a bluff overlooking the Ohio River, thrived on tobacco, river commerce, and more recently, mining. It was at one time the second richest city in the world per capita. Women went about their daily chores of sewing, washing, and preparing meals while the men engaged in hard labor during daylight. Replete in history and architecture, the blue-eyed, fair-faced youngster spent his days exploring Henderson, often falling into mischief.

Clarence Manion's family was steeped in Irish tradition and Catholic roots. The family originally hailed from County Cork, Ireland, and Clarence's daughter, Carolyn, says that the entire family had "temperaments to prove it."[5] Growing up, his family spoiled young Clarence, and he responded in kind with temper tantrums and an aggressive and independent personality.[6] His aunt recalled times when Clarence would be found eating with neighbors or hitching rides around town with the day laborers.

Against the instruction of the nuns at Holy Name grade school, he once climbed to the top of the church steeple seeking to become the "class hero."[7] Much to his dismay, his classmates, who initially prodded him along from the sidewalk below, disappeared, and Clarence was left waving out the peephole of the steeple to his chagrined mother below. Clarence seemed to forget the reprimands passed to him as quickly as he could find the next bit of excitement.

Even through mischief, the family members maintained close-knit relationships, working together to support their livelihood. Elizabeth Manion kept the home operating under strict rules, and thus Clarence spent most of his free time performing various chores, so, according to his mother, he would not feel compelled to make the usual trouble with the other young boys in town. Even so, Clarence enjoyed the time he spent at home, saying, "Our family was very close, all of us. Too close I guess, because we tended to be introverts and self-sufficient, but in our simple way, we had fun. Regardless of how little you have, it's a great consolation to know that 'all are for one and one for all.'"[8] Throughout grade school, Clarence saved money for his college fund, helping drive a grocery delivery wagon for his brother's convenience store and walking his next-door neighbor's dog.

Clarence wanted to be a lawyer. Rare as it was for a young lad from that area to continue his education, Clarence left home at the age of fifteen for St. Mary's College. In 1911, he paid the $180 for tuition which he had been saving for years, and three years later, Clarence had a BA and a standard education from which to expand his pursuit of knowledge. While at St. Mary's, he caught the baseball bug. He had not been involved with the game before, but Clarence was determined to be a ballplayer. He tried out for the team in the catcher position after never having attempted to squat behind home plate before. Lo and behold, Clarence made the team! He chalked up the experience as his opportunity to turn failure into success: "The boys in Henderson couldn't understand how I did it, but it goes to show that when you go into a new environment with new people, you can start over. You can bury your weaknesses and succeed where you have

formerly failed utterly."[9] It was a pattern that Clarence emulated throughout his life.

After finishing college in three years, he traveled to Washington, D.C.,
under a Knights of Columbus scholarship and spent time at the Catholic
University of America, acquiring a master of arts degree in 1916 and a master of philosophy degree in 1917. Over and above his studies, he took
advantage of the Washington, D.C., hobnobbing lifestyle. A friend lent
him a tuxedo which was "all you needed to get in on the big parties with
loads of food."[10] Washington in those World War I days was a slower paced
yet exciting place for a teenager who came from a rural Kentucky background.

Less than a year after finishing his master of philosophy degree,
Clarence went on to serve in the United States Army as a second lieutenant
in the Transportation Corps, enlisting at twenty-one years old in Septem-
ber 1918. The army described him as a young man of excellent character.
The other men in his camp recalled stories of Clarence's personality.
Vaudeville acts came from the city theaters to entertain the troops.
Clarence would often join the act, becoming a "ham" for the crowds while
he humored the men with his tales.[11] Following his stint in the army,
Clarence debated between going to law school or embracing vaudeville to
become a professional piano player.[12] In the end, inspired by his adoration
for philosophy, he applied and was accepted to Notre Dame Law School
just outside of South Bend, Indiana. Clarence Manion and Notre Dame
began a relationship that would last a lifetime.

Manion taught American history at the prep school there, while completing the courses necessary for his law degree. He graduated from Notre
Dame in 1922 with a JD. Less than two years later, Manion began what
would become a long and distinguished career in law at Notre Dame. In
the interim, a small Evansville, Indiana, firm hired him, so he could gain
some experience. After submitting job applications to several law schools,
he heard back from one: "Dear Clarence: Welcome to Notre Dame."[13]
Manion joined the faculty as a professor of law in 1924. Students adored

the rousing Manion. He became a staple at Notre Dame football pep rallies, leading the charge with voluminous words of encouragement bellowed before audiences each week prior to the big game. Perhaps in no irony for this popular, pep-rally spokesman, he was reported in the *Augusta (GA) Bulletin* to be "one of the most widely known orators of the country."[14] These words applied in particular to his professorship of constitutional law where students considered him highly persuasive and efficient, but were made also true by his pep-rally popularity.[15]

In 1926, he wrote *American History*, a textbook in which he warned, "Where the government is unlimited in its power and authority, no citizen is free." His philosophy on the limited role of government, especially the federal government, became more apparent during the controversial prohibition years. "Wet to Run in Indiana" appeared as a headline in the April 2, 1930, edition of the *New York Times*. Clarence Manion, proponent of states' rights and thus opponent of the 1919 federal Volstead Act prohibiting alcohol sales, manufacturing, and transport, joined the race for Congress in the thirteenth district of Indiana. His efforts, including published pamphlets and other editorials, commended by a key congressional committee, Maryland Governor Albert Ritchie, Anheuser Busch, and others, probably helped propel the Twenty-first Amendment to the Constitution, which voided the Volstead Act and repealed prohibition in 1933.

In 1932, Manion fell short of becoming his Indiana district's Democratic congressional nominee. Two years later, spurred on by faithful friends and admirers, Manion again joined the race and lost his bid on the fourth ballot for the nomination to run as a candidate for the United States Senate against Sherman Minton. These setbacks, while painful initially, served as a lifetime reminder to Manion that electoral politics could be brutal. But more than that, they directed the course his life eventually pursued, a course outside of politics and one which Manion was destined to follow.

One day in March 1936, Clarence Manion felt the urge to send a friendly fan letter to a young movie reporter who had prepared a critique of a movie he viewed days earlier. The intelligent and beautiful twenty-five-year-old Virginia O'Brien had caught the attention of this confirmed bach-elor. Less than six months later, on August 3, 1936, Father Daniel A. Lord married the pair at Boston College.[16] It was a partnership that would last more than forty years. The couple resided on a small farm outside of South Bend, and while Clarence remained committed to his work in law, Gina, as she was affectionately called, took responsibility for the farm, turning it into quite the business enterprise over the years. She built the farm into a 350 acre parcel, with more than twenty Arabian horses which they raised and sold along with more than fifty head of cattle. Together, the couple raised five children in a loving and thoroughly Christian home. Daughter Carolyn once wrote, "Our family is a close one—we laugh and cry together; we pray and play together; we enjoy each other's company to the utmost."[17]

Manion's politics, faith, and family strongly impacted his writing and vision for his country. *Lessons in Liberty*, perhaps Clarence Manion's most well-known piece of writing, came to the educational market in 1939. It was, in his words, "a study of God in government," to describe religion's role in public institutions and our heritage. Effortlessly eloquent through his writing and speaking, one of Manion's most profound and life-abiding lines emerged during a speech he gave in Georgia on the topic of his book. Manion conveyed to the audience, "American laws are not the source of American liberties, but merely the protection for liberties that are etched by God into the birth certificate of every human soul."[18] He used these words as the creed of his life and focused his professional and personal efforts to this end. Recognizing his commitment to faith and America, Boston University bestowed a doctorate of civil and canon law upon him in 1941.

Manion became the dean of Notre Dame School of Law in 1941, and the title became synonymous with his own first name as he became more well-known across the country. In fact, he became so familiar to people around the country as "Dean Manion" that when he'd introduce himself to someone as "Clarence Manion," he was continuously asked if he was related to Dean Manion. After a while, he started introducing himself as "Dean Manion" to reduce the confusion, and that's how he's been known ever since.[19]

Outside of his work at Notre Dame, Manion stayed informed of the country's political environment. When Franklin Roosevelt's administration began mobilizing the military for entry in World War II, Manion rejected the move for American involvement in a conflict he deemed unnecessary. He joined the America First coalition's national committee and served alongside the Sears, Roebuck, and Co. genius, General Robert E. Wood. Opposed generally to policing the world's affairs, Manion hoped America First could prevent Roosevelt and the country from entering the conflict. Pearl Harbor thwarted America First's efforts, but his friendship with General Wood affected his personal philosophy in an important way; he no longer supported Roosevelt and the New Deal. By the end of the war, both Wood and Manion found disappointment in nearly every move Roosevelt made. The experience was, according to author Rick Perlstein, "a dramatic conversion to conservatism."[20]

Even while a Democrat, Manion never wavered from advancing those principles which he found deep within his gut, namely, a strong opposition to what he termed "Godless Communism" and a steep commitment to states' rights. His son Daniel Manion, a Seventh Circuit Court of Appeals judge, indicated that his father's overwhelming allegiance and devoted loyalty to the party he was born into inhibited him from abandoning it in favor of an alternate party organization, even though his convictions were in conflict with many Democrats. Dean Manion believed his party had left him years earlier, yet was wholeheartedly committed to his family history and allegiances to remain a lifelong Democrat. When son Daniel ran for Congress in Indiana as a Republican, Dean Manion didn't vote for him because he wasn't allowed to participate in the primary. Even still, Manion was a widely known orator on conservative ideas throughout the country.

Manion had always been a fervent patriot dedicated to his country, but now he began to articulate his patriotism specifically through his writing and speaking. He began to write articles for the *South Bend Tribune* in 1947 on "Americanism," topics from law and order to private enterprise, which were delivered to the paper's 250,000 subscribers. Manion served as dean of Notre Dame Law School until 1952, when he retired to promote his book *The Key to Peace*, which "hit the jackpot of popularity."[21] He had become so tired with the pace of lectures he was giving and his role with the law school that he just didn't have enough time in the day to do both well. Notre Dame wanted him to stay, but he decided to focus on sharing his ideas through his books. *The Key to Peace* gathered momentum when the American Legion provided the book to high schools across the country. Soon, he was giving three to four speeches every week on the topic.[22]

Alarmed at the expansion of Communism and centralized power, especially within America's own borders, Manion recognized Senator Robert Taft from neighboring Ohio as the one man who loudly and boldly fought this trend. In addition, Taft had an admirable record in the Senate, leading a conservative Congress to cut federal expenditures from $60 billion to $39 billion between 1946 and 1949.[23] Upon his retirement, Manion worked to win Taft's nomination for president, coming close but losing to Eisenhower after hours of contention. Taft turned around immediately and announced his support of Eisenhower for president, and Manion, following Taft's audacious pledge, jumped on the bandwagon as a leader under the banner, "Democrats for Eisenhower."

Eisenhower went on to win the 1952 election, and during his first year in office, he faced a controversial legislative agenda item. The Bricker Amendment divided the country in 1953–1954. Triggered by a fear of Communism and its threats to America, many Americans felt the provision in Article Six of the Constitution that made treaties the "supreme law of the land" endangered American security, and so did Dean Manion. The proposed constitutional amendment sought to ensure that foreign treaties, signed by the American president, didn't restrict the rights of Americans. Rather, legislative action formed the basis for laws and governing powers over the American people. "Section 1. A provision of a treaty which conflicts with this Constitution shall not be of any force or effect; Section 2. A treaty shall become effective as internal law in the United States only through legislation which would be valid in the absence of a treaty; and Section 3. Congress shall have the power to regulate all executive and other agreements with any foreign power or international organization."[24] Announced on January 7, 1953, Senate Joint Resolution One introduced by Senator John Bricker captured the support of sixty-two senators, including forty-four of the forty-seven Republicans; the president of the American Bar Association; the U.S. Chamber of Commerce; the Daughters of the American Revolution; the American Legion; the Veterans of Foreign Wars; and many other groups.[25]

Manion, now chairman of an executive branch committee, spent much of his free time traveling the country making speeches on behalf of the amendment. Manion "was not getting any compensation" for his Bricker Amendment efforts. Rather, he was "propelled solely" by his "vital interest in constitutional law."[26] He sought to influence the legislative process, traveling throughout the country expressing support for its passage. The version he supported included a controversial requirement for referendums in all forty-eight states before a single treaty could be enacted. He used the following description of his views on the Bricker Amendment when speaking across the country:

> For historical reasons the language referring to a treaty in the Constitution is different from the language referring to the laws. In substance the Constitution says this: This Constitution and the laws made in pursuance thereof and the treaties made under the authority of the United States shall be the supreme law of the land. This is torturing language. Why did the Framers of the Constitution do that? They wanted to confirm the validity of the Peace Treaty with England, which had been ratified before the Constitutional Convention was held. But in doing so, they opened up the whole treaty law danger. To become the supreme law of the land, any treaty needs only to

be proposed and ratified by two-thirds of the Senate. The Constitution validates it ipso facto, even if it surrenders our sovereignty or gives away the state of Texas. This made the Bricker Amendment necessary, particularly after we joined the UN, which was grinding out new multilateral treaties every day.[27]

As a Democrat, his support of Eisenhower nearly ensured Manion, who risked his reputation on the hope that Eisenhower would be a leader who fervently supported an anti-Communist, pro-America agenda, of a presidential appointment. Against the recommendation of Robert Taft, who encouraged Eisenhower to appoint Manion as attorney general, and brother Milton Eisenhower, who encouraged the president to appoint Manion head of the Department of Labor, Eisenhower instead appointed Manion to chair the Commission on Intergovernmental Relations in August of 1953.

When President Eisenhower first appointed Manion to his post in 1953, Manion declined the offer saying he didn't have time because of his work giving speeches to boost the Bricker Amendment. Eisenhower responded, "That won't make any difference, everybody tells me that the Bricker Amendment is all right.... I don't know much about it but my brother, Ed, is a lawyer and he is one hundred per cent for it."[28] Upon hearing this affirmative response from Eisenhower, Manion took the job. Eisenhower's views changed dramatically soon thereafter, when the State Department convinced the president that the amendment would limit his ability to make treaties and conduct foreign policy.

President Eisenhower soon came to loathe Dean Manion's support of the Bricker Amendment. The media also chastised Dean Manion for his opposition to the administration's position. Dean Manion described how liberal columnists began to "berate" him because of his divergent views. *Time* magazine accused him of "deserting the Eisenhower 'team'" and even went so far as to demand that Eisenhower fire Manion.[29] In February 1954, Eisenhower called on Manion to try to calm his opposition. According to son Chris Manion, the conversation went like this. Eisenhower sat him down and said, "Look, Dean. I know that you've had trouble with these executive compacts. But, I'm president now." He continued, "If you just stay neutral, I'll put you on the Supreme Court." Dean Manion responded with uncompromising principle and vehemence: "No. Don't even bother."[30] Dean Manion's refusal to surrender his convictions was an example of how he lived by the words he preached to his law students at Notre Dame: "If you take the first bribe you may as well take the rest."[31] Manion's refusal to compromise principle in the face of a lucrative career appointment shows the strength of his character and the moral authority of his convictions. Two years later, another Irish Catholic Democrat, William J. Brennan Jr. of New Jersey, landed the lifetime appointment and replaced Supreme Court Justice Sherman Minton. Eisenhower was clearly incensed at what he saw as Manion's rebuke.

The sentiment worked both ways. Manion was frustrated for so many reasons. Manion's job on the commission was to identify needless programs for the government to abolish, and yet Eisenhower's pace of expanding government overrode Manion's efforts. At one time, Eisenhower boldly announced, "The Federal Government did not create the states in this Republic. The states created the Federal Government. The creation should not supersede the creator, for if the states lose their meaning, our entire system of government loses its meaning and the next step is the rise of the centralized national state in which the seeds of autocracy can take root and grow."[32] Manion had thought, or rather hoped, after this bold statement that Eisenhower, a man who beat "his" Taft, would be a proponent of the limited government needed so desperately after Roosevelt's utter limitless expansion of federal prerogative. And now, not only did Eisenhower enlarge government, but he opposed the Bricker Amendment, too—a provision Manion believed integral to American sovereignty. Manion couldn't have been more disappointed with Eisenhower's leadership.

On February 12, 1954, President Eisenhower's chief assistant requested the resignation of Dean Manion from the commission. Five days later, Manion delivered the conceding letter along with a report on the commission's accomplishments to the president. He wrote,

> It is ironical that the depth of my sympathy for this wise counsel has caused me—and through me this Commission—to be criticized by certain left-wing columnists who recently stated that I would be "fired" from the chairmanship of the Commission on Intergovernmental Relations because of my support of the Bricker Amendment. This advance information was confirmed on last February 12th when Presidential Assistant Sherman Adams requested my resignation.
>
> The Bricker Amendment embodies a principle to which I have long subscribed and which I have openly advocated for years . . . constitutional prohibitions against the concentration of power are our best defenses against every form of despotism. I cannot forfeit this honest conviction, nor will I suppress the frequent expression of it. To forestall possible future embarrassment either to your wise and patriotic administration or to this important Commission, I now ask to withdraw from the Commission on Intergovernmental Relations.[33]

Most news outlets ran the story, confirmed by Manion's letter, that his dismissal resulted directly from his disagreement with Eisenhower over the Bricker Amendment. But Manion believed that his fate was also an ironic consequence of his successful dismantling of the federal bureaucracy by reducing federal aid to states and returning power to tax estates, highways, etc. to the states.[34] Upon his resignation, Manion's colleagues on the commission issued a unanimous statement praising his efforts.

Representatives in Congress opposed to the Bricker Amendment used their parliamentary prowess to keep the amendment in judiciary committee hearings, avoiding a full Senate vote for nearly a year. During the winter of 1953–1954, the amendment went through significant media scrutiny and modifications by senators seeking to find common ground with President Eisenhower. But President Eisenhower was determined to end the debate. He "used all his persuasive powers—in stag dinners, at meetings, in private, in correspondence, even on the golf course—to kill the amendment."[35] In February 1954, the bill failed by one vote to capture two-thirds of the senators' support. If not for Senator McCarran of Nevada, who remained sick in bed under doctor's orders and couldn't get to Washington to vote in favor of the amendment, the Bricker Amendment likely would have gone to the states for ratification and then on to become the Twenty-third Amendment to the U.S. Constitution.[36]

Even though Manion's political reputation seemed smudged, the "ousted federal aide" continued to fight for the principles he knew to be important for this country. Following his forced resignation, it became clear that his opinions were valued in the national discussion, and people wanted to hear what Manion had to say. He was convinced that regular American shopkeepers, farmers, and patriots formed an untapped market. On October 3, 1954, Dean Manion, with the help of Dr. Ross Dog Food, a generous California corporate benefactor interested in promoting a strong America, launched the *Manion Forum of Opinion* radio broadcast with the intention of airing thirteen short, fifteen-minute segments over the next two months. Modeled after the ideas in Manion's book *The Key to Peace*, every Sunday evening Dean Manion's stentorian voice delivered a brief oration over the radio waves, sometimes interviewing a guest and other times speaking on his own volition. His sincerity, genuine appreciation for America, and commitment to thwarting Communism attracted thousands of listeners each week. At the height of his radio broadcasts, 261 radio stations and three television stations carried the *Manion Forum* to forty-four states.[37] The *Forum's* stated goals included waging war against: "(1) the confiscatory, Marxist income tax; (2) wanton foreign aid squandering; (3) Socialistic 'public power'; (4) destruction of states' rights; (5) futile conferences with Kremlin gangsters; (6) ridiculous budgets; (7) Federal aid to education; and (8) unrestrained labor bossism."[38] The radio show brought Dean Manion in tune with Americans with similar principles who sought new leadership. It also earned him the tagline, "a powerhouse of influence helping bring about renewed loyalty and patriotism in contemporary America."[39] The ral-lying point came at a low cost for our country. Manion never personally took a penny or a salary for a single one of his radio broadcasts. He instead raised the funds necessary for the $6,000 a week broadcast from industrial-ists, entrepreneurs, and other colleagues.[40] And he dedicated thousands upon thousands of hours preparing and perfecting his remarks for the broadcast.

The *Manion Forum* provided an outlet for so many conservatives who had no way of connecting with the American people. In the words of son Chris Manion, "Walter Cronkite certainly wasn't going to let them on."[41] Dan Smoot, T. Coleman Andrews, General Bonner Fellers, Willis Stone, and Phyllis Schlafly are just a few of the figures Manion interviewed over the years.

Beyond that, the *Manion Forum* also attracted young talent on the con-servative side to become involved in their country's political system. Both Senator Bob Dole and Congressman Jack Kemp indicated they would never have been in politics if it weren't for Dean Manion.[42] During that first year of the radio show, 1954–55, Manion also scheduled more than one hundred public appearances at locations across the country, planning his calendar on the wall of his basement.[43]

While Manion did all he could to promote patriotism and a strong Amer-ica, he also recognized the importance of having a candidate on the ballot who could invite even more enthusiasm for those ideas. Manion admired Taft's ability in 1952 to bring an anti-Socialist agenda to the forefront and attract conservatives to the polls who were willing to invest financially in the ideas the candidate advocated. It was an episode that Manion wanted to repeat, but he needed a new candidate, because Taft's three electoral losses probably wouldn't generate enough excitement. In a May 25, 1959, letter to C. S. Hallauer, president of Bausch & Lomb Optical, Manion wrote that he had been brainstorming for seven years following the 1952 convention, hop-ing to compile a "conservative action" plan. Manion maintained, "The mid-dle of the road is all right in theory but after six years of Eisenhower and

Nixon, the road itself is now running along the left field fence."[44]

As the chairman of the "For America" committee for political action, Manion completed a study on the laws of states that governed getting a third-party candidate on the ballot. This brief foray into establishing a third party, a States' Rights Party, comprised of disenchanted Southern states' rights Democrats and Midwestern Taft Republicans, didn't meet success. Dean Manion was convinced his candidate needed to win the Republican nomination in a traditional way. It simply would have been impossible to get an independent candidate on the ballot in some states, especially in time for the 1960 election.[45]

Looking around the country at options for a conservative leader, only one seemed logical and principled, but how could he be swayed to run for the presidency in a long-shot bid? It was unusual for a man of ideas to search for a candidate who would best represent those ideas. And it was even more unusual for this same man to believe the candidate's loss of the White House might actually do well and not be just another disastrous disappointment. When Dean Manion sat back one afternoon contemplating how best to impact his country, he could think of only one person to turn to for capable and principled leadership: Barry Morris Goldwater.

Barry Goldwater, Arizona's dear son and senator, had just won his second term in the U.S. Senate in 1958. It was particularly impressive that Barry Goldwater, representing a liberal stronghold at the time, won his second term by 12 percent, a resounding affirmation by his constituents. The same cannot be said for many others in the Republican Party who stood for election. The party suffered brutal defeats that year: a twelve seat loss in the Senate, forty-eight seats in the House, and thirteen of twenty-one gubernatorial elections. Bill Knowland, the Senate Republican leader, lost his bid for the California governorship. John Bricker lost reelection.

The *Manion Forum* convinced its emcee that there were many conservatives out there who were just waiting for the right kind of leader to inspire their involvement. Barry Goldwater might just be his guy, as demonstrated by his Arizona victory. Goldwater could lead the charge to capture the votes of conservatives who were turned off by those "soft and selfish leaders" who failed to inspire and provoke action.[46] As discussions of conservative ideas appeared in books and magazines and over the airwaves, Manion believed the base of those who believed in them had grown substantially, even if the popularity wasn't immediately evident. The "multi-millions of Conservatives" were the folks who stayed home from the polls, neglected to contribute to candidates, and generally disliked the direction America was headed.[47] Through his experiences with the *Manion Forum* and traveling across the country to give speeches, Manion decided, "As a director of the Manion Radio Forum, I get thousands of letters from people in all parts of the country. . . . In these letters and personal contacts, I have encountered a widespread popular sentiment favoring Senator Barry Goldwater of Arizona for President of the U.S."[48] Manion believed in Goldwater because he was the right man—the only man—who could run for president and advocate mutually shared values. He wrote to the senator,

> It is precisely your time-honored honesty, courage and statesmanship that our country now so desperately needs in the White House. You and your valiant, patriotic coterie in Congress may fight on for Constitutional Government as indeed you must, but neither you nor all the Senators put together can possibly change the prevailing Socialist weather in Washington until you change the political climate by putting an unadulterated American in the White House who believes in Constitutional Government. For that important assignment, there is nobody, *literally nobody* to whom the American people can now turn except to Barry Goldwater.[49]

In 1958, Barry Goldwater stood apart from all others in the country. Goldwater didn't hide his conservatism to win his election, nor did he cater to the center moderates. In fact, he purposely countered all those "me, too" candidates by focusing his full efforts on advocating principles of a limited government and the free market. And he won because of it. Manion, highly educated and with a long career in academia, admired Goldwater, a college dropout who considered himself unqualified for the position of president of the United States. Manion believed, above all, that convictions could overcome what some may consider Goldwater's shortfalls. Coming off 1958's devastating Republican defeat, Manion did not believe the alternatives, Richard Nixon or Nelson Rockefeller, could ignite Republicans like a conservative could in order to be victorious over the Democratic opponent.

Not only did Goldwater win his second term convincingly, but he was the foremost elected conservative of the day. Republican Party leadership of the time included Nelson Rockefeller, Dwight Eisenhower, Richard Nixon, and establishment figures. But none of these men represented the ideas Dean Manion wanted to be implemented. For too long Manion had been disillusioned by the broken promises of administration after administration. Now, with the advance of Communism worldwide, Manion felt the threat knocking on America's door and especially feared the future should the establishment claim victory. He warned, "The deadly disease of Communism is ravaging mankind today and sentencing Christian civilization to death precisely because four successive Presidents of the United States and eight successive Congresses have refused to say, and mean it, that Communism is intolerable."[50]

When Barry Goldwater won his second term in 1958, he was one senator of ninety-six in the country. His name lacked recognition in the homes of non-activist voters, especially when compared to the more well-known elected officials of the day, such as Nelson Rockefeller and John F. Kennedy. Even still, Manion had faith in Goldwater's positions and confidence in his ability to work hard to win the votes of his countrymen. In April 1959, Dean Manion wrote to General Robert E. Wood and inquired, "Confidentially, what would you think about a Committee to draft Goldwater for the Republican nomination for president?" He went on to justify, "Such a movement might start a 'prairie fire.'"[51]

Manion, confident in his philosophy, didn't feel out of place as a Democrat pushing Barry Goldwater. He wrote,

I, myself, am a registered Democrat and for many years was active in
the counsels of that party. I was keynoter of the Democratic State
Convention in 1932 and was a candidate for United States Senator
in 1934. If I am comfortable on the Goldwater Nominating Committee, you should certainly feel at home there. In 1952, Taft had a
Pre-Convention Committee composed of Republicans and Democrats headed by General Albert Wedemeyer and I was proud to be a
member of that Committee.[52]

Manion hoped—based on his personal record—that Barry Goldwater
would be viewed not as a fringe candidate, but rather as representative of a
cross-section of pro-American ideas.

Barry Goldwater did not intend to run for the presidency. When Dean
Manion approached him with his proposal to develop a committee, Goldwater hesitated, but agreed to let it move forward. At the time, Goldwater
led the Senate Republican Campaign Committee, an organization that
sought to develop strong candidates for coming elections. He didn't want
to divide the party by beginning a full-scale public pursuit of a higher office.
But he gave Manion and Wood permission to establish a secret Goldwater
Committee of 100 designed to "draft" Barry Goldwater as its presidential
nominee with the specific agreement that the committee would remain
wholly confidential and secretive until such time when he could decide
whether or not to run officially. He did not want party leaders spending the
next year attacking him and his ambitions instead of focusing on the more
important task of finding strong candidates to run side by side with the man
who would run for president.

Hours and hours of Manion's free time went to planning his course of
action to win the nomination for Goldwater. But recruiting for this secret
committee plodded along sluggishly, and Manion spent the early summer

weeks of 1959 contemplating a better strategy. As the days passed, he became convinced that the best way to recruit sympathizers would be through a written declaration, a short book in which Barry Goldwater could plainly outline his philosophy. Manion's own books had attracted a wide audience over the years. It was a simple formula: state what you believe straightforwardly and believe it with your whole heart. If Manion himself could author books that spurred hundreds of speaking requests, so could Barry Goldwater.

The book, if distributed through the network established by the Goldwater Committee of 100, could put Barry Goldwater's name in houses across America quickly and could inspire more uncommitted folks to involvement. In exchange for permission to continue with the committee and explore a potential presidential nomination, Barry Goldwater agreed not to endorse a candidate prior to the 1960 convention, and he consented to write the book if Dean Manion would keep his committee secret. Dean Manion outlined his early efforts in a letter addressed to fellow organizer Frank Brophy:

> The Committee will not be announced until Barry says the word, but will work like Hell in the meantime. Barry will refrain from endorsing *anybody* for the nomination—this in the spirit of his neutrality as Chairman of the Congressional [Senate] Campaign Committee.
>
> We will contrive to expand the Committee which now numbers seventy-five, plus as many more who are "for us 100%," but who cannot *officially* affiliate.
>
> The book is on the way, I hope ... Soon, I must break down the mailing list and give each of a selected half-dozen members of the Committee the responsibility for keeping a segment of the Committee notified of developments. The perimeters are now too wide for me to reach everybody and still earn a living.[53]

The list of members who agreed to be a part of the Goldwater

Committee of 100 included many heavy hitters, such as Chief Justice M. T. Phelps of the Arizona Supreme Court, J. F. Schlafly Jr. of Illinois, publisher Eugene Pulliam, Fred Koch, Brent Bozell, General Wedemeyer, Robert Welch of *American Opinion*, Colonel Archibald Roosevelt of New York, Howard Buffett of Nebraska, Roger Milliken of South Carolina, George Strake of Texas, and Herbert Kohler of Kohler Company in Wisconsin.[54] Still, rejection letters caused him to wonder whether his efforts were in vain. Some of those who refused to join preferred Nixon over Goldwater for the nomination because they believed Goldwater had slim chances to win, others wanted to remain uncommitted until the convention, one declined to serve due to doctor's recommendations, and still others didn't want to hurt their businesses. Even close friends discouraged Manion from pursuing a Goldwater nomination. Manion wrote, "Although friends Buckley and others discourage me from running into this buzz saw, I am more and more inclined to do so."[55] But those who joined formed a network to publicize a book by Goldwater which was to come.

On July 27, 1959, Dean Manion wrote to Barry Goldwater to suggest, "'The Conscience of a Conservative' appeals to me as a title."[56] He then predicted, "It will be a rallying point for millions of old-fashioned Americans who are ready to march and are clamoring for a banner."[57] The book, once completed, would be used as a recruiting mechanism for the Goldwater Committee of 100. It would convey Barry Goldwater's philosophy in a clear, concise, and simple way. Manion firmly believed, "this project will stand or fall on what he *says* in this book."[58] The committee would use it to implant Barry Goldwater's name in the minds of conservative Americans, in hopes that he would emerge as the leading candidate for the Republican nomination for president of the United States. Their first targets needed to be Republican delegates to state conventions—those at the grassroots level who would ultimately choose their standard-bearer. As the conventions across the country slowly approached, Manion knew that the book needed to be in the hands of delegates prior to these nominating events.

Manion had no manuscript—only a commitment—and what publisher would agree to produce a book without a copy to review in hand? Manion, inexperienced but determined to follow through on his plan, still contacted most of the major publishers of the day, including Bobbs Merrill. Suspect of the book's contents and the tight timeline, each publisher he approached denied the book.[59] Manion wanted the book to bear the imprint of a reputable and well-known publisher, but regardless of the book's backing by a prominent name, Manion wanted the book written, vetted, copied, and bound in less than eight months. The fast timeline would ensure that delegates would have copies prior to the conventions.

Manion decided to move forward without a publisher and committed himself to do whatever it took to get the book done on time. He dipped into his personal resources and offered Goldwater an advance of $1,000.[60] Then he personally filed paperwork to start a publishing company of his own, Victor Publishing Company, which would provide the book's initial imprint. He contracted with a printer in Shepherdsville, Kentucky, Publishers Printing Company, which specialized in trade magazines, to get the book printed and bound before the Republican convention in July. The not-for-profit Victor Publishing imprint would enable private companies to take a tax deduction for bulk purchases of the books, a strategy he hoped would encourage the business owners on the Goldwater Committee of 100 to employ.[61] And then, to compensate its author, Manion, through Victor Publishing Company, sent Goldwater a contract offering a 10 percent royalty on all gross sales receipts.[62]

Manion was not a publisher. He could rely only on his experiences with the few books he had written for direction on how to proceed with Goldwater. The publishing business was a risky one. A firm's solvency was often staked on the success or failure of one particular book. Most publishers offered the book on credit to a bookstore which was then able to return the unsold copies. Publishers themselves faced the burden of bookselling rather than the bookstores. In this case, Manion needed to sell more than fifty thousand books to recover the investment Publishers Printing Company made to produce the book.[63] As the average publisher nets five thousand copies sold and loses money on more than 80 percent of its inventory, Manion had just entered a very risky business endeavor, one that afforded him little room for failure.[64]

While Manion worked the behind-the-scenes channels to lay the groundwork for the book's publishing and develop the Goldwater Committee, Barry Goldwater hired ghostwriter and friend L. Brent Bozell to help him pen the manuscript. Together they agreed to split the royalties from the books sold. It was Manion's hope that Bozell would begin writing immediately to meet the book's ideal publishing deadline. Already it was running late.

An event in America preempted work on the book. Nikita Khrushchev, Soviet dictator and Communist party head, announced a two-month sojourn to the United States, accepting the invitation of President Eisenhower himself. This occurred just one year after the Soviet Union tested its first intercontinental ballistic missile. Vice President Richard Nixon also intended to welcome the foreign leader. To conservatives and friends of freedom including Bozell, Goldwater, and Manion, a visit to the land of liberty by the "Butcher of Moscow" was a dangerous signal to the world's other tyrannical regimes. It was Khrushchev, a murderer of political opponents, who was assigned by Stalin to oversee the "The Great Purge" in Ukraine.

While Vice President Richard Nixon publicly defended Khrushchev's visit (in private he told Goldwater the visit was a "mistake"), Goldwater criticized the move openly, thus calling the public and media to question whether Goldwater would support Nixon for the presidential nomination.[65] Until this time, it was widely assumed that Goldwater had indeed already endorsed Nixon, but that was far from the truth. Manion, through the *Manion Forum*, set up a National Committee of Mourning led by Senators Dodd and Bridges of Connecticut and New Hampshire. He aimed to halt Khrushchev's visit, or at the very least turn it into a "continuous display of ill will" by greeting him with public prayers, tolling of bells, and black armbands. The anti-Communist efforts included paid newspaper ads to inform the American public of who Khrushchev really was: the "arch murderer of all recorded history."[66] Congruently, ghostwriter L. Brent Bozell, rather than write the Goldwater book, established a Committee for the Freedom of All Peoples—a tactic to draw attention toward Khrushchev's record against freedom, also hoping to thwart the visit altogether, or at least make it unproductive for the Soviet Union. Bozell admitted to Manion that all other obligations would now become secondary. Manion personally prodded for months by phone and enlisted the help of those mutual friends who could encourage Bozell, including William F. Buckley Jr. and Bonner Fellers. By early December 1959, the delay began to anger Manion, who opined to fellow conservative Hub Russell, "He tells me he is at work on the manuscript but I haven't seen any copy yet. This is maddening to say the least. Either one of us could have written two books like the one we have in mind while we have been waiting for this one."[67]

Manion, while he didn't know it at the time, had Eastern establishment, liberal Republican Nelson Rockefeller to thank for helping to get *The Conscience of a Conservative* published. As Nelson Rockefeller began considering a run for the White House, conservatives believed he would split the moderate vote with Richard Nixon, allowing an opening for Barry Goldwater to snag the nomination. Rockefeller's serious deliberation of running solidified Dean Manion's concern for the future and added to his vision of the book's intent: "This book will serve several important purposes. First of all, it will put Goldwater precisely on record on such subjects as Foreign Policy, States Rights, Communism, the TVA, the Connally Reservation, etc. At the same time, it will be a conservative rallying point which will irritate the Nixon-Rockefeller campaign no end."[68]

Rockefeller's announcement had one more unintended effect; it triggered Brent Bozell's frantic start to write the piece for Goldwater. Bozell felt confident all of a sudden that Goldwater's chances of winning the nomination improved drastically. He spent painstaking time artfully constructing each sentence of his manuscript, passing completed chapters by

Goldwater in person as he finished them. Goldwater, in turn, provided his corrections in the margins or dictated the changes to a voice recorder. Led by Goldwater's honest and no-nonsense assessment of the world, Bozell used an August 1959 memorandum that Goldwater wrote on an airplane while commuting from Washington as the basis for the piece. The two had worked together in years prior, and Goldwater thought Bozell would be just the right person to capture his philosophy, with little input on his part. It took Bozell only six weeks to write the short, 124-page volume once he started. The masterpiece was nearly finished in late December when Rockefeller decided not to run for the presidential nomination. Bozell flew to Arizona over Christmas and showed Goldwater the manuscript. Goldwater endorsed it: "Looks fine to me. Let's go with it."[69] Goldwater biographer Lee Edwards reflected on that moment in history, "With these few words, Goldwater approved a manuscript that would establish him as not just the leader but the *conscience* of a political movement."[70]

In the weeks following the book's first draft, Dean Manion and his family worked diligently to perfect the manuscript for the printer. Manion spent hours peering over the galleys spread across his dining room table making revisions when necessary. His children and wife helped proofread the copy during that time to keep punctuation and grammar errors at a minimum.[71] Manion spent time on the phone conveying these changes to the printer and confirming layout plans.

Publishers Printing Company printed, hand-bound, and jacketed the book in time for the South Carolina Republican convention on April 1, 1960. The cover, decorated in patriotic red, white, and blue, and the back, featuring a photo of Goldwater, protected the pages of a slim piece which would get its first glance from South Carolina convention-goers. Five hundred books were flown overnight to textile manufacturer Roger Milliken just twenty-four hours before Goldwater addressed the delegates. Goldwater agreed to stand for the presidential nomination at that convention and received unanimous support from thirteen South Carolina delegates.

The twenty-thousand-word book, named by Manion, aptly outlined the big ideas that Barry Goldwater's conscience believed. In the book, Goldwater proclaimed, "I have little interest in streamlining government or in making it more efficient, for I mean to reduce its size. I do not undertake to promote welfare, for I propose to extend freedom. My aim is not to pass laws, but to repeal them. It is not to inaugurate new programs, but to cancel old ones that do violence to the Constitution, or that have failed in their purpose, or that impose on the people an unwarranted financial burden."[72] The book distinguished between good and evil, ending with a frank and inspirational battle cry to spur Americans to action on behalf of their country's future:

> The future, as I see it, will unfold along one of two paths. Either the Communists will retain the offensive; will lay down one challenge after another; will invite us in local crisis after local crisis to choose between all-out war and limited retreat; and will force us, ultimately, to surrender or accept war under the most disadvantageous circumstances. Or we will summon the will and the means for taking the initiative, and wage a war of attrition against them—and hope, thereby, to bring about the international disintegration of the Communist empire. One course runs the risk of war, and leads, in any case, to probable defeat. The other runs the risk of war, and holds forth the promise of victory. For Americans who cherish their lives, but their freedom more, the choice cannot be difficult.[73]

In the weeks following its press run, Manion worked to promote the book through whatever means possible. The book sold for $3 a copy. One dollar went for the book's expenses, one went to the Goldwater Committee of 100, and the last one went to print more books.[74] He sent copies to university libraries, stocked bookstores, gave a copy to each member of Congress, placed ads in the *Chicago Tribune* and the *New York Times*, and mailed flyers to Republican county leaders. The committee used the book to build momentum for Goldwater and his positions. Manion asked each member to help distribute the book through whatever means available: by attracting favorable reviews, acquiring praise for the book from prominent leaders who would then call for a Goldwater presidential nomination, and purchasing bulk orders of the book themselves. He hoped to sell a hundred thousand copies of the book to give the committee a profit of $100,000 to jump-start the Goldwater campaign.[75] And so the committee undertook its challenge.

Manion worked tirelessly to get the book completed on time. He dealt with publisher after publisher turning him down. He worried about Bozell's slow approach to writing the book. He endured pessimism from close friends who predicted, "I doubt there's much money to be made by mass sales of a Goldwater manifesto...."[76] With all that said, book-distribution problems following its astounding success proved nearly insolvable. The high demand for books meant nearly doubling the size of orders. Copies at bookstores rarely sat on the shelves. And boxes upon boxes of books were held up at a warehouse in Washington, D.C., because an angry detractor removed the labels. The F.B.I. investigated the delinquency, suspecting labor unions had orchestrated the label removals, but could prove nothing.[77] Regardless, it all took a toll on the Manion family. Dean Manion wrote at one time, "[W]e damn near blew our stacks and hardly slept."[78] After much consternation, the project's success made the struggles seem worth it.

According to Goldwater biographer Lee Edwards,

[T]he committee did change history by publishing a book that began as a pamphlet on Americanism and ended as the most popular polit-ical primer of modern times.... Before *The Conscience of a Conser-vative*, Barry Goldwater was an attractive, forthright, often controversial senator from a small Western state . . . a long-shot vice presidential possibility. After *The Conscience of a Conservative* appeared, Goldwater became the political heir to Taft and McCarthy, the hope of disgruntled Republicans, partyless Independents, and

despairing Democrats, the spokesman of a national political movement destined to change the course of the nation and the world.[79]

Despite its publication by an obscure Indiana publishing house and not
a powerful New York City publisher, *The Conscience of a Conservative*
soared to success. The book earned a place on *Time* magazine's best-seller
list on June 6 and went on to become number four within a matter of
months. It appeared at number fifteen on the *New York Times*' best-seller
list on June 26, despite receiving a negative review within its pages suggesting that Goldwater "suppress" the book. The *New York Times* claimed
Goldwater's "conscientious conservatism contains too many things that not
enough voters like" and called him "as true a conservative as a stage coach
or a buffalo."[80]

Less than two months after its debut, *The Conscience of a Conservative*
sold more than a hundred thousand copies.[81] In August, the book was number three on *Newsweek's* list of the "Week's Top Bestsellers" compiled by
Publishers Weekly Magazine.[82] Harvard's History 169b required the reading.[83] Some conservatives even referenced the book as their "Bible."[84] By
the time the election rolled around in November, more than half a million
copies were in circulation around the country.[85]

Despite the strong book sales, Barry Goldwater lost to Richard Nixon in
his bid for the Republican nomination in 1960. But he left the convention
following a speech during which he called on conservatives to ready themselves for another day, another battle that would surely come. He told the
delegates, "This country is too important for anyone's feelings. This country, and its majesty, is too great for any man, be he conservative or liberal,
to stay home and not work just because he doesn't agree. Let's grow up,
Conservatives. We want to take this party back, and I think some day we
can. Let's get to work."[86]

The Conscience of a Conservative had created an "ever growing popular
wave" for Goldwater to ride into the next election cycle.[87] By the time Goldwater appeared on the cover of *Time* magazine in June 1961, he had

received more than six hundred and fifty speaking invitations in just three months, eight hundred pieces of mail poured in to his office daily, copies of his twelfth-edition paperback book were still flying off the shelves, and his column appeared in one hundred and four papers.[88] *Time* predicted Goldwater's involvement in the next election: "Whether as candidate or merely as Republican conscience, Arizona's Barry Morris Goldwater—GOP salesman supreme and the political phenomenon of 1961—will have plenty to say about the tone and spirit of his party's next platform, and even more to say about who will be standing on it."[89]

By the 1964 election, more than a million copies of *The Conscience of a Conservative* had been sold, and within a few years the number purchased topped three and a half million.[90] William F. Buckley Jr., a prolific author himself, believes that *The Conscience of a Conservative* "had the largest sale of any polemical in American history" but gave it credit for another major accomplishment: "Its popularity contributed to Goldwater's nomination for President in 1964."[91]

Yet even more important than a Goldwater nomination was the Movement it spurred. Those involved, including Dean Manion, recognized that Goldwater may not win, but their efforts served a larger purpose. They sought to stake principles that would gain momentum. It was a keen sense of foresight so rare in politics. As a result of *The Conscience of a Conservative*, Goldwater's run for the presidency became a "conservative crusade," a battle for the "soul of Western civilization" that attracted nearly four million people to work for it.[92] That was twice the number that worked for Lyndon Johnson in 1964.

Barry Goldwater lost to Lyndon Johnson in 1964 following Kennedy's assassination. The loss was devastating to conservatives, but looking back, it had an ever-important consequence. Bill Rusher, longtime *National Review* publisher, describes 1964 as a "watershed year":

> It is a commonplace to say that 1964 was a year of disaster for American conservatism, and of course, in one sense it was: Lyndon John-

son defeated Barry Goldwater that November by 43,126,506 votes to 27,176,799, or 61 percent to 39 percent. Goldwater carried only six states (Alabama, Arizona, Georgia, Louisiana, Mississippi, and South Carolina) with a total of fifty-two electoral votes. It was indeed, as the media proclaimed, "a landslide."

But to say that, and stop there, is to overlook almost entirely the real political significance of 1964. On any serious accounting, 1964 was the most important and truly seminal year for American conservatism since the founding of *National Review* in 1955. It laid the foundations for everything that followed. Before 1964, conservatism was at best a political theory in the process of becoming a political movement; after 1964, and directly as a result of it, conservatism increasingly became the acknowledged political alternative to the regnant liberalism—almost fated, in fact, to replace it sooner or later.[93]

Reagan's 1980 victory occurred partly because of 1964. And 1964 happened because of a book called *The Conscience of a Conservative*. And the book was just an idea that came one day to Dean Manion.

George Will best counts the tally. Goldwater "lost 44 states but won the future."[94] Manion knew from the very beginning that Goldwater's popularity would soar if his ideas were communicated to young people, so he funded the distribution of one copy of *The Conscience of a Conservative* for each new member of Young Americans for Freedom.[95] And it worked. The 1964 campaign itself inspired so many of our nation's brightest talents. Both Senator Trent Lott and Representative Dick Armey credit that 1964 race with drawing them into politics.[96] And, of course, it was the year Ronald Reagan stumped for Barry Goldwater, a year in which Barry Goldwater passed the torch to the Conservative Movement's rising star.

An inscription scribbled by Barry Goldwater in Dean Manion's copy of *The Conscience of a Conservative* says it clearly: *To Pat Manion, The Daddy of all of this.* In the 1950s, conservatives had few leaders to propel their ideas forward. Still fewer individuals recognized the need to recruit their own conservative leaders and were willing to take personal risk to make it happen. Manion possessed unparalleled foresight and also acted on his insights. It wasn't until later that poll results confirmed his prediction. The Dunn Survey, an organization that studies public opinion, reported in November 1959 that "[c]onservatives are on top, but don't know it." It went on to indicate, "[This] conservative majority is without leadership or a vehicle thru which to seek the reins of government." Rogers Dunn then recommended, "Unless conservatives gain leaders and a vehicle, the present state of socialism will be the plateau from which the next 'liberal' advances will be made."[97] Certainly, Manion's undercover efforts to publish a Goldwater book and assemble a Goldwater for president committee reveal his recognition of the conservative agenda's lack of leadership before any other, and his personal initiative reflects sacrifice and trail-blazing.

After a lifetime of providing America moral authority, Dean Manion succumbed to a stroke on July 28, 1979, while the battle for America's future was still in doubt. Manion worked up until the day he died. His last broadcast of the *Manion Forum* taped three days before his stroke and aired posthumously. In fact, well into his seventies, Dean Manion swam a half mile every morning, practiced law, and gave lectures in addition to running the *Manion Forum* broadcasts. Upon his passing, his children contacted Milton Friedman, Paul Weyrich, and M. Stanton Evans to inquire as to whether the program should continue without their father at the helm. They wondered if guest hosts could rotate each week. Friedman, Weyrich, and Evans all agreed the *Manion Forum* should end with the loss of its only host. After all, "Dean Manion *was* the Manion Forum."[98]

Author Rick Perlstein believes that Dean Manion is "a figure that's been obscured by history."[99] The time has come for conservatives to remember Dean Manion for what he was: "the Daddy of all of this." Acknowledgment of his personal efforts grows in importance with each passing year. Too few conservatives act on their convictions with such determined consciences. Barry Goldwater knew that our country benefited from the sacrifices of the few: "We have heard much in our time about 'the common man.' It is a concept that pays little attention to the history of a nation that grew through the initiative and ambition of the uncommon man."[100] Dean Manion was no common man, and our Movement will benefit because of his uncommon efforts.[101]

Chapter Five

★

The Kitchen Cabinet's Original Three

"That speech was one of the most important milestones in my life—
another one of those unexpected turns in the road that led me
onto a path I never expected to take."[1]

— RONALD REAGAN

Cocoanut Grove, a tropical night club at the glitzy Ambassador Hotel in Los Angeles, served as the host hotspot for campaign fund-raising dinners, among other star-studded events. It was an ordinary evening in the heat of a political season during the late summer of 1964. Palm trees with stuffed monkeys dangling from their branches and a blue painted starlit sky formed the backdrop for the event. Men and women gathered to pledge their support and their dollars in exchange for assurances that their platform would prevail come Election Day. The wait-staff served an ordinary dinner to the crowd, while speeches meant to inspire those present to dig deeper in their pockets did the trick. The candidate's team went home that evening with some important cash to get him through the next week of campaign jet-setting.

In 1964, as in most elections, a lack of funds limited the Goldwater campaign's activities nationwide. Three successful California businessmen wanted to do their part and volunteered to host this Cocoanut Grove dinner in Barry Goldwater's honor in Los Angeles. Holmes Tuttle, owner of a successful Ford dealership in Los Angeles; Henry Salvatori, founder of Western Geophysical Company; and A. C. "Cy" Rubel of Union Oil Company recruited attendees and organized an evening that would alter the course of the Conservative Movement for decades.[2]* The $1,000-a-plate dinner was a rarity in the country at that time. Most dinners asked $100 per person, some $200, but a dinner at that level was nearly unprecedented, especially considering it had no confirmed speaker until shortly before the event.[3] One of the hosts, Holmes Tuttle, resorted to calling his friend Ronald Reagan, since Goldwater himself was unavailable to speak. Holmes Tuttle had known Ronald Reagan since 1946, the day he sold him a Ford coupe, and his telephone call asking for a quick twenty-minute speech convinced Ronald Reagan to attend as the fund-raisers' keynote speaker.[4] With a speaker confirmed, the three men recruited four hundred guests and raised $400,000 for Barry Goldwater. While Barry Goldwater carried the conservative banner as the Republican Party's presidential candidate in that year of 1964, it was his California campaign cochairman, Ronald Reagan, who stole the show that evening at the Cocoanut Grove. Before that, it's important to understand who organized this important event in the first place.

Holmes Tuttle

Born in 1905 into an Indian Territory cattle ranching family, Holmes Tuttle knew the value of hard work and struggle. During the Civil War, his family lived in Texas but later moved to a small town on the South Canadian River in what is now Tuttle, Oklahoma. The town, shortly after being

---

* Edward Mills also indicated his involvement in planning and hosting the dinner at the Cocoanut Grove nightclub when interviewed by Lawrence de Graaf of California State University-Fullerton. At the time, he helped recruit attendees and later worked for Tuttle at Holmes Tuttle Enterprises (Mills, 64). There is little evidence to suggest, however, that he was part of the original group of men that suggested Ronald Reagan's speech be televised, nor was he a part of the initial group that approached Ronald Reagan later to run for governor.

William Volker became a millionaire at the age of 47 and a philanthropist as a child.

As a nephew of William Volker, Luhnow helped run William Volker & Co. and took over Volker's philanthropic activities following his passing.

ABOVE: William Volker & Co., a home furnishings and window shade company, began with $1,500 from Volker's savings and a $3,000 loan.

LEFT: Volker rode his horse, Prince, for hours before Sunday church and to work every day.

RIGHT: William Rappard (an influential Swiss diplomat), Karl Popper (founder of the Department of Philosophy, Logic, & Scientific Method at the London School of Economics), and Ludwig Von Mises (notable economist and social philosopher) participate in the first Mont Pelerin Society meeting in 1947.

BELOW: In the audience of the 1947 Mont Pelerin Society meeting, Milton Friedman can be seen on the left, a man who went on to win the Novel Prize in 1976 and credited the Mont Pelerin Society with stimulating his interest in public policy.

ABOVE: Friedrich Hayek won the Nobel Prize in Economics in 1974, a feat made possible by the "comfort" and "intellectual justification" he received during Mont Pelerin Society gatherings.

LEFT: On May 7, 1945, on a piece of yellowing scratch paper, Volker decided to give $2,000 to Friedrich Hayek for educational activities, a gift that would jumpstart the Mont Pelerin Society.

Photo courtesy of Alfred Regnery.

Henry Regnery believed in the importance of reaching young people, and his generosity reached far and wide as he spoke to young audiences, including this Intercollegiate Studies Institute event. For his efforts, he earned the "Award of Merit" from Young Americans for Freedom in 1967.

Photo courtesy of the Young America's Foundation records.

At a dinner honoring Regnery's accomplishments in 1985, Intercollegiate Studies Institute President E. Victor Milione, Congressman Jack Kemp, publisher Henry Regnery, son Al Regnery, and Young America's Foundation President Ron Robinson participate in the ceremony.

In his book, *Memoirs of a Dissident Publisher*, Henry Regnery relayed his father's advice: "If you ever begin to make any money in that business you are going into, you can be pretty sure that you are publishing the wrong kind of books."

CIA Director William Casey and Eleanor and Henry Regnery meet during a 1985 dinner honoring Regnery. In 1951, Casey acknowledged the importance of Regnery's first bestselling book, Freda Utley's *The China Story*. He said, "Henry Regnery Company published the first accurate account of this whole sordid [China] story, and got the facts about China and our policy there in true perspective. I dare say that if Henry Regnery Company had been around early enough to publish Freda Utley's *The China Story*…in 1947, or even early in 1948…the American public would have been sufficiently awakened and stirred so that the huge propaganda hoax about the character of the force we are now fighting in Korea could not have been put across."

Photo courtesy of the Associated Press.

Photo courtesy of Twin Lens Photo.

ABOVE: William F. Buckley Jr., mayoral candidate for the Conservative Party in New York City, addresses a National Press Club briefing on August 4, 1965.

LEFT: William F. Buckley Jr., dedicated to advancing conservatism among our country's youth, addresses an audience of Young America's Foundation students during a 1992 luncheon.

LEFT: A major public showing of support for Barry Goldwater occurred at Madison Square Garden in New York City, an event planned by a group of young conservatives Buckley helped organize called Young Americans for Freedom.

BELOW: Buckley predicted in 1964 that Goldwater would not win the presidency, but he recognized the importance of young people, "the planted seeds of hope," those who would propel conservative ideas forward.

RIGHT: Clarence Manion started the Manion Forum radio broadcast in 1954 to share his ideas with the American people directly.

BELOW: Clarence Manion, in addition to helping Barry Goldwater with *The Conscience of a Conservative*, wrote his own books, including *The Conservative American*.

ABOVE: Barry Goldwater becomes the presidential nominee following the popularity of his book, *The Conscience of a Conservative*, an idea brought to fruition by Clarence Manion.

LEFT: Clarence Manion was one of many pro-America democrats who deeply opposed "Godless communism" and advocated states' rights, positions that Barry Goldwater also held.

At the urging of Holmes Tuttle, Henry Salvatori, and A.C. Rubel, Ronald Reagan ran for governor of California and won in a landslide.

On July 15, 1964, Ronald Reagan led a rally outside of the Cow Palace in San Francisco, shortly before Barry Goldwater became the Republican Party's presidential candidate.

Ronald Reagan drew accolades for his public speeches in support of Barry Goldwater during the 1964 election.

Henry Salvatori, Nancy and Ronald Reagan, and Grace Salvatori were friends in
California. Henry Salvatori used his wealth to support Ronald Reagan's "Time
for Choosing" speech on NBC.

Holmes Tuttle, owner of several car dealerships in California, met with Ronald
Reagan in the Oval Office after his election. As a member of the Kitchen
Cabinet, Tuttle encouraged Ronald Reagan to run for governor of California.

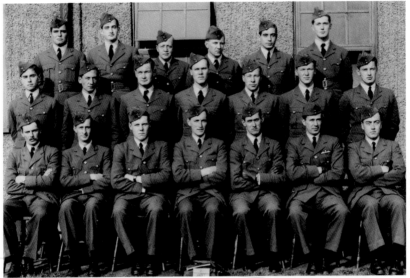

The Fisher brothers joined the Royal Air Force's 111 Hurricane Squadron in 1939. Antony Fisher is pictured third from the right in the front row.

By 1965, Antony Fisher's company, Buxted Chicken, produced 500,000 oven-ready birds. His educational Institute of Economic Affairs had been operating for ten years to provide a free enterprise perspective in Britain.

Antony Fisher addresses IEA's 25th anniversary in 1980 with then chancellor Margaret Thatcher recognizing its importance and success in Britain's transition in leadership and movement toward free market policies.

Gerald "Spike"
Hennessy helped
Hillsdale College
through difficult
financial and legal
times.

The 1957 Prudential Committee of the Hillsdale College Board of Trustees included Spike
Hennessy. Pictured from left to right are: Wayne Gray (administrative assistant), President J.
Donald Phillips, M. G. Van Buskirk, B. Freeman, Gerald Hennessy, F. Andom, Doris Mauck
Friedrichs, Ray Knight (secretary), Ralph Rosecrance (chairman), John Stoner, E. C. Hayhow,
and B. Scott Edwards (business manager and treasurer).

Helen Hennessy served Hillsdale College as an associated professor of economics and volunteered her time with the Hillsdale Board of Women Commissioners.

Photo courtesy of Hillsdale College.

Spike Hennessy served on The Hillsdale College Board of Trustees for thirty years. The 1963 Board included from left to right: Shirley T. Johnson, F.I. Goodrich, Gerald D. Hennessy, Richard Knight, B. Scott Edwards, Dr. Ralph C. Rosecrance, President J. Donald Phillips, Nelson B. Beaman, Donal Jenkins, and E.A. Dibble.

Joseph Coors meets with President Reagan in the White House to discuss the Strategic Defense Initiative.

Photo courtesy of the Ronald Reagan Library.

Ronald Reagan credits the breakthroughs that occurred with the Soviet-U.S. relationship to have resulted from the SDI.

Photo courtesy of the Associated Press/Jim Cooper.

Roger Ailes, once a TVN news director for Joseph Coors, now is the CEO of FOX News. September 29, 2006.

Russian prince Jean Engalitcheff arrived in the United States in 1924 as a "non-quota immigrant student" and began studies at Johns Hopkins University.

On November 15, 1981, John Engalitcheff suffered a stroke at the White House. President Reagan comforted Engalitcheff in his last days, while Engalitcheff's bequest enabled Young America's Foundation to save Rancho del Cielo, a comfort to the Reagans during the president's last days.

Engineer John Engalitcheff held 47 patents building his company, Baltimore Aircoil Company, from the ground with hard work and a patriotic spirit.

Ronald Reagan boldly faced communism, a leadership quality John Engalitcheff admired.

awarded a stop along the Frisco Railroad Company tracks in the early 1900s, had yet to be named, even though it already had stockyards and a depot. The settlers who flocked to the growing community chose the name "Tuttle" after the prominent rancher, James H. Tuttle, Holmes's father, who rode a white horse across the fields. The town of Tuttle served as home to ranchers and homesteaders resulting from Western expansion.[5] Tuttle's mother, Carrie, was a member of the Chickasaw tribe of Oklahoma by blood, and in 1906 Holmes was enrolled as a member, too.[6] He grew up as the seventh child of ten, a wild bunch with several thousand acres of romping space on the ranch property. Because there was no local country school close to the ranch for the children, James donated a ten acre parcel from his ranch acreage in order for a school to be built. Holmes and his siblings attended the little eight grade schoolhouse for a time. In 1916, Holmes transitioned to a private boarding school in Minco until the family moved into Tuttle, Oklahoma, in 1918, where he attended high school.

In 1920, the family packed up again and moved twenty miles northeast to Oklahoma City where Holmes completed high school, but not without family strife. His father, who had built a modest fortune in the ranching business, lost it all shortly following World War I—a period of time when many cattle ranchers faced the same fate. He passed away not long after in 1922. Holmes, at the age of eighteen, necessarily went to work for the Ford Motor Company's assembly plant as a stock boy for $5 a day in 1923, a year in which a new Model T Ford sold for $450.[7] Three years later, Tuttle's good friend Bob Scott lost his job with the company and wanted to make a fresh start in California, a place brimming with possibilities. With little more than a couple of dollars in his pocket, Tuttle left for California, hitching rides the entire way and even spending some time in a freight train boxcar.[8] The two friends arrived in California at the home of Bob Scott's brother more than two weeks later.

Through a friend of this brother, Holmes met Charlie Cook, a gentleman who owned a Ford dealership and the Community Bank in Los Angeles. Tired of factory work, Tuttle decided to make a living in the retail business. Cook's dealership in Whittier hired him first to be a clerk and then the parts manager, followed by sales manager at another dealership. These employs began a career partnership and friendship lasting decades. Holmes even lived with Cook's mother and sister during those early California years. In 1930, the Cook dealership, managed by Tuttle, was the only one in the area not to fall victim to insolvency, mostly because Tuttle worked hard, but also because a heavy-duty equipment business joined the dealership.

After World War II, the Ford Motor Company sought to build a dealership on the west side of town, and Holmes Tuttle was the logical candidate to oversee this facility. It would become the first Ford dealership opened following the war.[9] Located near several movie and television studios, the salesmen at the dealership frequently sold cars to movie starlets.[10] Construction was completed on the Ford enterprise in 1946, and by 1958, Holmes owned two Ford and two Lincoln-Mercury dealerships. He had one in Beverly Hills, another in Irvine, and the other two were located out of state in Tucson, Arizona, and Spokane, Washington. His business skills earned his enterprise the reputation of being one of the best and most lucrative car dealerships in the country.

The tall, lean Tuttle married schoolteacher Virginia Harris on August 7, 1934. She was an ambitious and friendly woman who kept a watchful eye over her husband and his welfare and that of their two children, Robert and Sally. The two became heavily involved in Los Angeles. Virginia became a founder of the Los Angeles County Museum of Art and the Music Center, and Holmes became a director of the Chamber of Commerce and a member of the California Club and the LA Country Club.[11] The pair socialized with the other conservatives around town, involved in a circle similar to those of the Salvatoris, Wilsons, Bloomingdales, and Reagans.

Tuttle had always been interested in politics. His father, a progressive Theodore Roosevelt "Bull-Mooser," impacted the youngster's emerging philosophy if only in confidence. He later recollected a high school experience in Minco—the first political memory he had. Late on election night in 1916, Holmes celebrated the perceived victory of conservative supreme court associate justice Charles Evans Hughes of New York just before bedtime, gloating to a friend that Democrat Woodrow Wilson had lost.[12] Much to his consternation, he awoke in the morning to the opposite news. It was his first foray into tracking the political process.

In 1930 while living in Pasadena, Tuttle began raising funds for political campaigns and encouraging the local citizens to vote. This continued through the presidential elections of 1948 and 1952. In 1956, Justin Dart, finance chairman for the Eisenhower presidential campaign and head of Rexall Drug Company, ventured down the street from his company's headquarters to visit Tuttle in his Ford dealership office. Dart said quite emphatically, "Holmes, I want a $5,000 contribution." Holmes initially replied, "You've lost your cotton-pickin' mind!"[13] Dart walked out with his contribution and with a new volunteer fund-raiser for the campaign team. It was Holmes Tuttle's first political donation.

As a successful businessman, Tuttle felt a responsibility to be involved in public affairs. In particular, he recognized the strengths of the capitalist system and the importance of free-market economics, especially for business. It was more common at the time for business leaders to stay away from politics. Tuttle recognized this shortcoming: "We in business who had more to be concerned about than anybody else would say, 'Well, we don't want to get mixed up in politics.'"[14] But Holmes reacted differently than his peers and took responsibility with utmost diligence to give future generations a similar chance at being successful entrepreneurs, the hallmark of America's own success.

Holmes had no personal interest in running for office. Instead, what started as a quick visit to solicit a campaign contribution turned into a passion that imbued Holmes for the rest of his life. Rather than only writing out a check for the next candidate, Holmes chose also to raise resources from those around him, reaching out to bring more people, business leaders in particular, within the fold of active conservatism.[15] Upon reflection as to his motives, Holmes Tuttle said, "I began to be concerned about the direction of our country—that our giant bureaucracy has been so centralized in Washington, the difficulty our country has with so many people sitting back. I wanted to lead a crusade to get the people of California interested."[16] Bill and Nancy Boyarsky, *Los Angeles Times* writers, considered Holmes Tuttle to be "the single most influential Republican contributor and money-raiser in the state."[17]

Henry Salvatori

Henry Salvatori grew up in Pennsylvania with immigrant parents. He had been born outside of Rome, Italy, on March 28, 1901, and moved to Pittsburgh when he was five years old. His father built a successful wholesale grocery business in Philadelphia in 1903, three years before bringing the rest of the family across the Atlantic. The family knew very little English in those early days, but they lived on a farm close to Italian immigrant friends, so the transition was gentle.[18] Salvatori later recalled, "In some indefinable way those early days on the farm served to shape my character, basic nature and even my philosophical outlook."[19] A one-room schoolhouse was the facility for Henry's first two years of schooling. Soon thereafter, the family moved to Florence, New Jersey, where he completed grammar school. After barely settling, the family packed its belongings and moved to Martins Ferry, Ohio, for one year, followed by another transition to Philadelphia. Salvatori attended and graduated from South Philadelphia High School in 1919 while working at his father's grocery business on the side.

Advanced education was a priority for Henry Salvatori. He was an aspiring scientist and put his knack for inquiry to work at the University of Pennsylvania, where he acquired his bachelor of science degree in electrical engineering in 1923. When a job with Bell Telephone Laboratories opened in New York, Henry jumped at the chance to earn a living and take part in its education programs for young engineers. As part of his work, he attended classes on scholarship at Columbia University three times a week until he received a master of science degree in physics.[20]

On his last day of class in 1926, Henry walked by a bulletin board hanging in the physics building. After passing it once, his curiosity conquered him, and he turned around to glance at it once more. This time, he considered the posting: "Wanted. Men with graduate work in physics to do research work in Oklahoma—if interested see Prof. Wells."[21] Henry Salvatori was satisfied at Bell Telephone. It was an impressive company and had the largest lab in the country with upward mobility opportunities. Yet the thought of the "Wild West" sparked the adventuresome graduate, and he made that visit to Professor Wells's office to get more information. After much prodding by the president of Geophysical Research Corp., Salvatori joined the small lab's Newark office.

Salvatori excelled at Geophysical because of his inventiveness. He produced a borehole differential thermometer that could read temperatures within 1/1000 of a degree, a steep improvement from the 1/100 of a degree accuracy the previous model held. Shortly after, Henry went to Tulsa in charge of a crew to determine exact depths for oil exploration. This "reflection method" had not been used by any other company at that time and still stands today as the industry standard-bearer. Salvatori continued to lead teams to develop this breakthrough technology, pinpoint oil reserves with great accuracy, and eventually purchased stock and worked for a new company, Geophysical Service Inc. (GSI). GSI prospered because of its revolutionary techniques, even through the country's difficult economic times. By the 1950s, the company had become the largest geophysical contractor.[22]

Salvatori resigned from GSI in 1933 while leading a crew in California. He was thirty-two years old and faced unemployment rates of nearly 25 percent, but he wanted to plant his own roots entrepreneurially. On August 15, 1933, Henry Salvatori started Western Geophysical. With an initial investment of $9,000, he acquired a small shop at 950 South Flower Street in Los Angeles to house the three-man, one-truck enterprise.[23] Salvatori built and equipped his only truck in six weeks at his home. Turning up his nose at the economic current around him, Salvatori worked fifteen hour days to build the company to ten crews in five states by the end of that first year.

By 1936, it was the second largest seismic contractor to GSI in locating oil and gas around the globe, and by 1955, the company became the world's largest offshore seismic contractor, present in twenty-six nations.[24]

As a bachelor, Henry's life couldn't have been more exciting—traveling the Wild West and experiencing a business breakthrough. His life changed one day when he visited Tulsa, Oklahoma, on a business trip. Salvatori met the talkative and outgoing Grace Ford at a dance. Grace, a beautiful ballet teacher, had been born and raised in the Tulsa area. While the two made an impression on each other, it wasn't until months later that they truly got to know one another better. MGM requested Grace Ford's ballet class to audition for a movie in Los Angeles. According to daughter Laurie, while Grace traveled only to chaperone her students, MGM actually tapped her for a part in Lionel Barrymore's first horror movie, *The Devil Doll*. While in LA, Grace phoned Salvatori to indicate she was in the area, but also conveyed she would be far too busy with rehearsals to see him. Early the next morning, a single red rose appeared at her hotel room. Fifteen minutes later, yet another arrived. And fifteen minutes after that, another, until her room was filled with roses.[25] Grace's aunt Eula escorted the couple to dinner at a Mexican restaurant the following night. Grace Ford and Henry Salvatori married in November 1937, the same year in which Western Geophysical branched out to include oil exploration of the Texas coast.

Their two children, Laurie Ann and Henry Ford, grew up in a beautiful, custom-built home on Bellagio Road in Bel Air, neighbors to Bill and Betty Wilson (Bill Wilson later became the first U.S. ambassador to the Vatican under Ronald Reagan). Grace spent her time raising the children and committing the family energy to various philanthropic causes. She was a strong woman, some would say a tad eccentric, but always wonderful and outgoing. Grace raised $400,000 in 1955 to support the construction of the Los Angeles County Music Center by raffling off a Cadillac Eldorado and continued to raise funds for the causes close to her heart until her death in 1990. Henry Salvatori also involved himself in causes near and dear to his heart.

Salvatori had grown up in a conservative household. His younger brother, William Howard, had in fact been named so by his Republican father during William Howard Taft's presidential term.[26] Salvatori had long repudiated the Rooseveltian welfare state and instead embraced the capitalistic free-market approach to solving societal ills. His entrepreneurial advances had helped California's postwar boom, and he realized that the opportunity to innovate free from big government's intervention was the key to American strength.

Henry Salvatori loved America. He also knew that America would be shaped by her prevailing ideas and wanted it to remain "the light of the world."[27] By the 1940s, Communism and the creation of the United Nations caused Henry much consternation but spurred him to action no less.[28] "It was only in the 1940s when I became concerned with the Communist threat to the free world that I began to take an interest in politics." He continued, "I was in San Francisco during the formation of the United Nations. I believed then that it was a mistake, and I thought that the Democratic Party was totally unaware of the future threat of Communist Russia."[29] His sweeping opposition to Communism pushed him to make several dramatic moves. He created the Anti-Communism Voters League in the 1950s to evaluate all candidates for office on their awareness of the Communist threat.[30] He gave $1 million to the University of Southern California to create the Research Institute of Communist Strategy and Propaganda in 1960. He then backed the original issues of William F. Buckley Jr.'s *National Review* and supported the American Security Council to fight the Soviet advance outside of the United States.

Most notably, however, by 1949 Henry was becoming more and more involved in political campaigns. He volunteered to be the Los Angeles County finance chairman for the Republican Party, California state finance committee chairman in 1951, and in 1952, Henry became fully engaged in Dwight Eisenhower's presidential campaign. President Eisenhower disappointed Salvatori on a philosophical level; Ike hadn't been as conserva-

tive as Salvatori had hoped, and Salvatori viewed the party leadership as a
large part of the problem.

He loved America and opposed Communism so much that by 1960,
while his company led the field on an international scale, he was ready to
take his earnings and become an advocate for the principles that brought
him success. Dr. Larry Arnn, professor at California's Claremont Institute
at the time, believed that Salvatori's "love of country was pure, selfless, and
intelligent."[31]

Year after year, Salvatori watched his party's eastern establishment shrug
at centralizing state power with little regard. When 1964 approached, he
became fully involved to change his party's leadership and volunteered to
be Barry Goldwater's California finance chairman for his presidential bid.
That campaign was a new style of conservatism, calling out the establishment leaders who consistently compromised with big government. He fervently supported Goldwater as opposed to the East-Coast candidate with
well-endowed coffers, Nelson Rockefeller. His ultimate goal was to find
replacements for what he saw as the sellout leaders of the Grand Old
Party.[32]

Henry's penchant for politics surpassed his desire to commit any more
time to Western Geophysical. He recognized the opportunities that had
been afforded to his immigrant family, and he was eager to give back to the
country he cherished. As such, he encouraged Litton Industries to take over
stock ownership of his company so he could focus more of his energy on
advocating for the ideas that he had come to admire. Salvatori retired as
CEO in 1967 to devote his full attention to conservative causes.

A. C. "Cy" Rubel

Born in Louisville, Kentucky, on March 30, 1895, Albert Chatfield
Rubel became known by his initials, A. C., or nickname, "Cy." Son of
Samuel and Nancy Rubel, Cy graduated from the University of Arizona
with a bachelor of science degree in 1917 and joined the U.S. Army. Fighting in France in World War I as a captain with the Corps of Engineers,

Rubel won the Distinguished Service Cross, the second highest award given to military heroes. In 1919, he was discharged and shortly thereafter went to work on an oil exploratory team through parts of Mexico.

Taking his oil experience with him, he later sought employment in Los Angeles at Union Oil in 1923 as an assistant geologist.[33] As years passed, Rubel worked his way up in the company, first by becoming chief geologist and then assistant manager of field operations. His superiors took note of his "unusual ability" and put him in charge of subsurface work at two oil fields south of Los Angeles. By 1931, company leaders promoted him to manager of field operations, one of the youngest employees in the history of the company to hold such a position, and he took on the responsibility for developing drilling and production methods used by the company. The *Los Angeles Times* reported that his rise in the company was "rapid," attributing his strength to his capabilities and ambition.[34] In 1938, Rubel was promoted to vice president and director of production, serving in this capacity until 1956 when he assumed the role of president.

Under his four-year tenure as president, Union Oil soared to record profits. When Reese H. Taylor, a subsequent president, died in the position in 1962, the company asked Rubel to return for a second stint. He served as president for another two years until his final retirement in 1964 at the age of seventy. The trade professionals and local leaders revered his success. The Los Angeles branch of the National Association of Accountants awarded him Southern California businessman of the year in 1963,[35] and he received the highest award given by the American Petroleum Institute: the gold medal for distinguished achievement.[36] When he retired his final gavel, six hundred shareholders stood on their feet clapping in admiration of his business savvy and success.

Entrepreneurial success wasn't his only accomplishment. Close friend Henry Salvatori described Cy as a "man of great integrity and a good family man."[37] Cy married Henrietta Rockfellow and the two had a son, John, and a daughter, Mary Ann. Cy and Henrietta actively pursued philanthropic opportunities with various causes including Occidental College where he was a trustee; Southern California Orthopedic Hospital; the California Cancer Research Institute; and the Boy Scouts of America where he held various committee chairmanships.

Writer Peter van Wyk believed Rubel had "a razor-sharp mind, a wry wit, and a propensity to ride fast."[38] He was outspoken, critical of government's capabilities, and didn't hesitate to speak his mind. In 1959, when Rubel became frustrated at the education America's young people absorbed at colleges and universities, he gave a speech to the Western College Placement Association and boldly lamented that the universities graduated too many "selfish, self-centered people."[39] Later, in 1966, he became so disgruntled with the Los Angeles county civil service system that he wrote a letter to say it was "so poor that only exceptional action will bring it out of its critical state."[40] Immediately the Board of Supervisors initiated reforms. Because of his clear opinions about how government should operate, he became the chairman of the County Citizens Efficiency and Economy Committee, which sought to reform government bureaucracy, succeeding in modernization and streamlining administrative practices.[41] He often criticized local officials, yet these same leaders still admired Rubel. Upon his sudden passing in 1967, county officials lowered flags to half-staff in tribute to his contributions to the community.

Similar to Tuttle and Salvatori, Rubel recognized free enterprise as a means to improving our country's national security. As such, he agreed to serve as finance chairman for the conservative gubernatorial candidate in 1962, Joseph Shell (he ran against Richard Nixon for the Republican nomination for governor); became a member of the Murphy for Senator finance committee in 1964; and fellow Californians elected him delegate to the 1964 national convention. He also took a leadership position as the western regional chairman for the Freedoms Foundation in Valley Forge and hosted two hundred of the two hundred and seventy-six Congressional Medal of Honor recipients at the Freedoms Foundation convention in 1966. For all of his work, close friend Holmes Tuttle described Cy Rubel as "a great patriot."[42] He held America on a pedestal and, as Henry Salva-

tori conveyed, "was greatly devoted to our American values and principles."[43]

The Speech

Tuttle, Salvatori, and Rubel held experiences of hardship and modest
beginnings in common. They all succeeded with hard work, an entrepreneurial spirit, and an American free-market system that afforded them the
opportunity to make their own, on their own. Authors Joel Kotkin and Paul
Grabowicz believe, "These men were ... corporate operatives who, in the
decades since the end of World War II, had helped transform California
into the nation's most populous and industrially advanced state."[44] They
were friends, but more than that, they were businessmen who felt charged
to strengthen the next generation's opportunity to enjoy the very same ben-
efits of American prosperity.

That late 1964 summer evening at the Cocoanut Grove altered the
course of America's future, but it wouldn't have occurred had it not been
for these three men who decided to get involved in a personal way. Upon
hearing Ronald Reagan's speech that night, Tuttle, Salvatori, and Rubel
knew the words struck a chord with listeners. They had heard dozens of
campaign speeches before, and rarely had they themselves been inspired
in such a way. The speech was so carefully constructed, charismatic,
thoughtful, and heartfelt. Clearly, Ronald Reagan was a talented orator, but
it was quite evident that Ronald Reagan personally believed every principled statement he made.

Ronald Reagan had a lot of practice giving speeches. In fact, the speech
he gave at the Cocoanut Grove was one he had been crafting for more than
ten years.[45] When he joined General Electric (G.E.) in 1954, Reagan
immediately began touring its plants, urban and rural, speaking to a wide
range of audiences from schoolchildren to prominent businessmen to factory workers.[46] Ronald Reagan, severely nearsighted, always removed one
contact lens prior to a speech so he could see the audience with one eye.[47]
With the other eye, he could see a basic outline for each of his speeches

sketched on four by six index cards. The cards contained simple phrases and mental triggers for his oratory and famous one-liners.[48] Instead of reading from a script as an actor might, Ronald Reagan talked *with* the audience, playing on historical allegory and allusions which he loved. He knew that reading text word for word from a script lost at least one-third of the audience along the way.[49] Over time, his speech entitled "Encroaching Government Controls" evolved from remarks against Communist infiltration of American life into an attack on big government.[50] To him, freedom and capitalism were "all or nothing" values; "You can't be a little bit Socialist and you can't be partly free."[51] Ronald Reagan was a natural salesman, learning to assemble his words to reach even the most difficult audiences.

In the fall of 1954, Reagan also began performing as the star host of *General Electric Theater*, a show which became the most popular Sunday evening program on television.[52] *General Electric Theater* ended in 1962 after Ronald Reagan refused to abide by the new regulations G.E. tried to impose on him. G.E., after a change in company leadership and facing threats of government anti-trust action, wanted Reagan only to promote its products and not discuss the evils of Communism and the income tax, which he had been doing for years. Ronald Reagan later wrote, "I traveled coast to coast speaking on behalf of conservative principles. Indeed, I chose to continue my speaking even when to continue meant the loss of my television show."[53] When he then became host of and occasional actor on *Death Valley Days*, he further honed his speaking style and skills in a studio furnished as a den with adorning bookcases and a crackling fire.

Tuttle, Salvatori, and Rubel knew Ronald Reagan's speech made an impact that night at the Cocoanut Grove because, not only were *they* inspired, but the speech electrified the crowd as well. Guest after guest approached the three organizers praising Ronald Reagan's performance, suggesting that he should be seen and heard more often.

While those eager to end their shifts noisily whisked away plates and glasses, Tuttle, Salvatori, and Rubel patiently waited for the keynote speaker to approach their table. As Ronald Reagan approached the threesome, they

knew something should be done, and they prepared to pitch an unprece-
dented idea. The men had decided that if Goldwater should win, it would
be because the ideas contained in Ronald Reagan's speech resonated with
the American people. The speech convinced them that a broad audience
needed to hear its message, and the sooner the better. Once Ronald Reagan took a seat at their table, the three pitched their off-the-wall idea; if they
could raise the funds necessary, would Ronald Reagan consider repeating
his speech for a national broadcast? "Sure," he responded, "if you think it
would do any good."[54]

Rather than giving the speech to a poised television camera, Ronald
Reagan suggested that he repeat the speech—one that he had given a version of hundreds of times—in front of a live audience to simulate the experience to which he was most accustomed through speaking engagements
to so many groups across the country, *General Electric Theater*, and campaign pep talks. The speech would be taped and prepared for broadcast at
a later date.

Los Angeles Republicans began arriving at NBC studios in Hollywood
to listen to the speech with anticipation. As they took their seats, movie star
Ronald Reagan prepared to deliver remarks that unknowingly would
change his life. After just a few lines, Ronald Reagan could tell that, oddly,
he wasn't the center of attention. Those sitting in the audience that day
buzzed with awe at the television cameras, studio lights, and film set. It was
the Hollywood experience that captivated them. In mere moments, with
much consternation and effort on Ronald Reagan's behalf, the audience
relaxed and tuned in to his near-perfect performance. Reagan used the
thirty minutes as a combination "family meeting and political rally, in turn
exhorting, shocking, sympathizing with, and inspiring his audience."[55] The
tape was ready to air with the consent of the Goldwater campaign.

Tuttle, Salvatori, and Rubel raised sufficient resources to put the speech
on air in California. But their project met scrutiny from the more senior
Goldwater officials. They aired it anyway, intending to demonstrate the
power of the remarks to the wary Goldwater leaders. That first broadcast of

the speech raised enough funds for the men to encourage the campaign, with their contributions in tow, to purchase thirty minutes of national airtime on NBC.

Days before the airing date, Ronald Reagan received a call from Goldwater who, he described in his memoir, was noticeably "uneasy" and "uncomfortable."[56] Goldwater politely conveyed that his advisors recommended against showing the Reagan speech in favor of a taping Goldwater did with General Eisenhower at Gettysburg. Goldwater himself admitted he hadn't seen the Reagan speech yet. Reagan assured Goldwater. "Barry," he said, "I've been making the speech all over the state for quite a while and I have to tell you, it's been very well received. . . ."[57] Goldwater decided to watch the tape for himself from his Cleveland hotel suite. When he was finished, Goldwater wondered, "What the hell's wrong with that?"[58]

Three hours before airing, and with prominent Goldwater staffers still insisting against its broadcast, the campaign received a call from the California team strongly urging its broadcast. After all, Salvatori, Tuttle, and Rubel had raised the funds necessary for the thirty minutes of airtime purchased by the campaign. And they were not willing to fill the time with anything other than Ronald Reagan's speech, they believed so strongly in its power. If the campaign chose to air a different program instead, it would have to come up with the money to run its own program just three hours before airtime. **

** In 2006, Thomas W. Evans authored a book, The Education of Ronald Reagan, in which he relies extensively on the collected papers of Lemuel Boulware, a man who hired Ronald Reagan for General Electric. Evans uses letters written by J. J. Wuerthner, another G.E. employee, to assert that Brothers for Goldwater, a group led by John Wayne, raised $60,000 which was subsequently given to the Goldwater campaign to be used for "Reagan's first nationwide TV political broadcast." While this claim is worthy of notation, the vast evidence suggests this theory is not altogether valid. Tuttle, Salvatori, and Rubel, the three men who organized the dinner where the idea was first generated and then continued to raise funds and plan for the NBC broadcast, clearly had a major role in its funding and production. It is plausible that subsequent airings of "The Speech" were funded by an allocation of a gift made by Brothers for Goldwater.

It was October 27, 1964, less than one week before Barry Goldwater faced President Johnson on Election Day. Ronald and Nancy Reagan joined some friends at their home to watch the twenty-seven minute broadcast. When it was all over, some of the most famous words entered American history:

> Those who would trade our freedom for the soup kitchen of the welfare state have told us that they have a utopian solution of peace without victory. They call their policy "accommodation." And they say if we only avoid any direct confrontation with the enemy, he will forget his evil ways and learn to love us. All who oppose them are indicted as warmongers. They say we offer simple answers to complex problems. Well, perhaps there is a simple answer—not an easy answer—but simple.
>
> If you and I have the courage to tell our elected officials that we want our national policy based upon what we know in our hearts is morally right. We cannot buy our security, our freedom from the threat of the bomb by committing an immorality so great as saying to a billion now in slavery behind the Iron Curtain, "Give up your dreams of freedom because to save our own skin, we are willing to make a deal with your slave masters." Alexander Hamilton said, "A nation which can prefer disgrace to danger is prepared for a master, and deserves one." Let's set the record straight. There is no argument over the choice between peace and war, but there is only one guaranteed way you can have peace—and you can have it in the next second—surrender.
>
> You and I have the courage to say to our enemies, "There is a price we will not pay." There is a point beyond which they must not advance. This is the meaning in the phrase of Barry Goldwater's "peace through strength." Winston Churchill said that "the destiny of man is not measured by material computation. When great forces are on the move in the world, we learn we are spirits—not animals."

And he said, "There is something going on in time and space, and
beyond time and space, which, whether we like it or not, spells duty."

You and I have a rendezvous with destiny. We will preserve for our
children this, the last best hope of man on Earth, or we will sentence
them to take the last step into a thousand years of darkness.[59]

The persuasive statement of conservatism also contained a plea for
financial support of Barry Goldwater via a small trailer at the bottom of the
screen suggesting where campaign contributions could be sent. This trailer
was a new mechanism to give ordinary Americans a call to action and was
the genius of finance chairman Henry Salvatori. According to the campaign management team of Herbert Baus and William Ross, Salvatori "first
hit upon the cornucopia of hitchhiking onto Goldwater television programs
a taped trailer asking for funds . . . [It] brought such brisk traffic in checks
and legal tender that the technique was continued by the national campaign to raise millions of dollars more."[60] Salvatori's techniques went on to
become widely utilized by campaigns. Baus and Ross believed Salvatori
"won permanent enshrinement in the finance chairmen's hall of fame by
the enormity of the challenge he coolly accepted and the Wagnerian
grandeur of his performance."[61] They go on to report, Salvatori "truly is the
genius of California financiers for conservative causes."[62]

Ronald and Nancy Reagan crawled into bed that night hoping the
speech had gone well, but a little uneasy with the public's response still
unknown. At midnight, a member of Barry Goldwater's campaign awoke
Ronald Reagan to convey the resounding success of the evening's broadcast. The campaign phones had been ringing constantly since the speech;
people wanted to pledge their support immediately, both in spirit and financially.

F. Clifton White, Goldwater's 1964 co-director of field operations,
remembered the deluge of activity following the speech. The campaign
office was "snowed under with telephone calls and personal visits," and
"checks showered in on the Goldwater campaign."[63] It's difficult to meas-

ure the campaign contributions acquired from that prerecorded speech, but estimates have ranged from $250,000 to $8 million, with the actual figure probably hovering around $1 million, a handsome sum for a 1964 event.[64] The speech raised more money than had any other political speech up until that time and provided an outpouring of both large and small donations from several hundred thousand contributors.[65]

The Republican National Committee aired the speech twice nationally, and in time the speech ran on more than three hundred local stations.[66] Demand for the speech was nearly incomprehensible. Henry Salvatori himself received calls from all over the country requesting copies of the tape, and taking his cues, he arranged for the small company which taped the original speech to have copies available for purchase by the various entities making requests. Fan mail poured into Ronald Reagan's mailbox. It was more than he and his one-day-a-week secretary could handle. They both worked around the clock to respond to messages from proponents, spending anywhere from two to five days a week thoughtfully replying to the thousands of letters and telegrams. Ronald Reagan later commented, "I never had a mail reaction like this in all my years in show business."[67] On average, more than one hundred speaking invitations arrived per week from all over the United States.[68]

Even while Goldwater followers tuned in and were inspired to action by the speech, mainstream press and political pundits missed the significance until sometime later. Nielsen estimated only 13 percent of those watching television, or 4.2 million homes, tuned in to Ronald Reagan's speech, an initially small audience.[69] None of the mainstream television or radio media commented on the speech. Only newscaster Fulton Lewis Jr.'s conservative radio show, *Top of the News*, touched on the speech's broadcast.

Goldwater lost to President Johnson in an historic lopsided election. His 38.5 percent paled in comparison to the Johnson-Humphrey duo that garnered 61.1 percent. But something special had occurred during this election. The loss, while dramatic, had coalesced conservatives in a way that suggested a future election may indeed have an opposite outcome. The ideas of anti-Communism, limited government, and opportunity resonated and provided a platform for this growing coalition, and one man emerged as the eloquent deliverer of its message: Ronald Wilson Reagan.

Astonishingly, more than $100,000 from Ronald Reagan's televised speech poured in even after the unfavorable 1964 election results were announced.[70] People weren't necessarily backing Goldwater, although many of them did. It was clear that voters were agreeing with a set of core principles articulated by Ronald Reagan. Shortened by some to simply "The Speech," "A Time for Choosing" became one of the most consequential speeches of all time for conservatives. The man who eloquently delivered it also won his place in their hearts. David Broder and Stephen Hess referred to it as "the most successful national political debut since William Jennings Bryan electrified the 1896 Democratic convention."[71] *Time* magazine said Ronald Reagan "provided just about the only dramatic moments in the whole, dreary Goldwater campaign."[72] And the three men who helped finance it overflowed with satisfaction. "That speech electrified the nation."[73]

That the speech did not lead to Goldwater's presidential victory is not the measure of its success. Instead, its far-reaching ramifications rest in the man whose career in public service was born. Political organizer F. Clifton White describes a conversation he had with Ronald Reagan over the telephone in December 1964 in his book, *Why Reagan Won*. When Mr. White inquired if Ronald Reagan had thought to run for governor, Reagan wondered aloud, "Clif, do you run for Governor on the basis of a single speech?'" White responded, "People have run on a whole lot less. . . . In politics, as in life, you have to take the opportunities as they come. You have a chance to catch the train now and ride it into Sacramento and the governor's mansion in 1966."[74]

His Moment Arrived

Less than two months following Goldwater's defeat, Tuttle, Salvatori, and Rubel gathered together at Tuttle's home. They continued to brainstorm how best to utilize Ronald Reagan and his talents for communicating and building a conservative coalition. They realized there would be a governor's race in California in 1966. Who better to be their candidate than Ronald Reagan? It would be a difficult road to be sure to win a bitter primary battle over San Francisco mayor George Christopher and ultimately take down the sitting two-term incumbent running for reelection, Governor Edmund G. "Pat" Brown. But they saw something in Ronald Reagan and the way he inspired fellow Americans to put their support behind him.

It was agreed that Tuttle, since he had known Ronald and Nancy Reagan the longest, and because of his natural abilities as a salesman, would visit the Reagans and pitch the idea. It wasn't the first time Ronald Reagan had been approached to run for office. In 1962, a group of men including Holmes Tuttle, Cy Rubel, and Tex Talbert asked Ronald Reagan to run for Senate. He declined because of the personal and financial sacrifice that he and his family would have to make. That spring when Tuttle asked Ronald Reagan to run for governor, Reagan replied, "You're out of your mind."[75]

Just as the three had not given up on airing "The Speech'" on national television, they did not give up on Ronald Reagan and continued to badger him to run. Time and time again Ronald Reagan turned down Tuttle, Salvatori, and Rubel. Yet they had gotten through. One day, Reagan relented: "If you fellows will arrange it for me to go on the road and accept some of the speaking invitations I'm getting from groups around the state, then I'll go out and speak to them and come back in six months, on the last day of 1965, and tell you whether you're right or whether you should be looking for somebody else to run for governor."[76] The three mailed a letter requesting funds, raising more than $100,000 to cover Ronald Reagan's travel expenses.[77] They also hired a well-respected political-management firm— Spencer-Roberts, a firm with thirty-four victories out of forty attempts under its belt—to help schedule speaking engagements.

The unofficial gubernatorial campaign tour started at the California Republican Assembly convention in San Diego. The crowd "went wild" over the movie actor, giving him standing ovations both prior to and following his remarks.[78] By the end of 1965, Ronald Reagan had traveled more than ten thousand miles up and down California to more than 150 speaking events to deliver "The Speech."[79] Even before officially announcing his intentions to run for governor of California, his speaking success put him ahead of Democratic governor Pat Brown in polls by 8.5 percent, and funds in excess of $140,000 from more than one thousand contributors arrived in the Friends of Ronald Reagan mailbox.[80]

The reaction he received from "The Speech" convinced him that a man of modest personal wealth could build support from common people. He gradually became prepared to ask Californians for their confidence and support.[81] From the comfort of his *Death Valley Days* studio on January 4, 1966, Ronald Reagan, smiling, made the official announcement that he would run for governor of California. Lee Edwards later wrote in a 1966 edition of *Human Events*, "At 54, Reagan is not running because he believes he is a political messiah or because he considers himself a great politician. He is running for the governorship of California because he was asked to by his Republican peers and because he was no longer satisfied merely to talk about his state of California."[82] In an interview with Lee Edwards, Henry Salvatori admitted that the trio would have never asked Ronald Reagan to run for governor if not for "A Time for Choosing."[83] Ronald Reagan beat then governor Pat Brown by a margin of 16 percent.

A Milestone

Looking back, Ronald Reagan said in his biography, "That speech was one of the most important milestones in my life—another one of those unexpected turns in the road that led me onto a path I never expected to take."[84] The *Washington Post* decades later admitted, "Reagan launched his political career in 1964, not by stuffing envelopes or running for the state Senate but with a nationally televised speech that immediately made him a top prospect for governor of California, the nation's biggest state."[85] When asked had he not been active during the 1964 Goldwater campaign, if he would have won in 1966, Ronald Reagan responded:

> I never would have been a candidate, because there was one thing I have to tell you. The farthest thing from my mind was running for political office. I liked my life. I thought it was an exciting life. I loved what I was doing, when in '65 — really as an outcome of that election and of the national speech that I made that went on the networks for Goldwater — people began coming to me.[86]

Ronald Reagan initiated dramatic reforms as governor of California. Beating Pat Brown by more than one million votes for the governorship, Ronald Reagan soared to popularity, balanced California's budget as required by law, made government's actions more efficient by cutting its rate of growth in proportion to California's population growth, achieved property tax relief, and reformed welfare. His efforts succeeded so well that the 1996 welfare reform put forward by the United States' Congress was modeled on the California initiative.

Because of his experience traveling California, listening to its citizens to determine whether or not to run for governor, Ronald Reagan came to believe, "A candidate doesn't make the decision whether to run for president; the people make it for him."[87] He acquired quite a following due to his successful gubernatorial terms, so the encouragement to run for even higher office was never lacking. Unsuccessful for the Republican convention nomination over President Gerald Ford in 1976, Ronald Reagan went on to capture the presidency away from Jimmy Carter in 1980, elected as the oldest president ever.

As president, Ronald Reagan's accomplishments catapulted the nation to a position of strength in the world. Soon after taking the oath of office, he signed the 1981 Economic Recovery Tax Act (ERTA) at his ranch in the Santa Ynez Mountains. His home, Rancho del Cielo, represented freedom to him. This ranch location formed the perfect backdrop for signing legislation that would get government off the backs of Americans and liberate them to make more of their own decisions. According to the Heritage Foundation, ERTA led to ninety-two straight months of economic growth starting in the fall of 1982—the largest period of peacetime expansion since 1854, the year our government started recording such trends.[88] The Dow Jones industrial average tripled. The Joint Economic Committee concluded in an April 2000 report,

> In 1981, newly elected President Ronald Reagan refocused fiscal policy on the long run. He proposed, and Congress passed, sharp cuts in marginal tax rates. The cuts increased incentives to work and stimulated growth. These were fundamental policy changes that provided the foundation for the Great Expansion that began in December 1982. . . . The economic record of the last 17 years is remarkable, particularly when viewed against the backdrop of the 1970s. The United States has experienced two of the longest and strongest expansions in our history back to back.[89]

When Ronald Reagan took office in 1981, federal expenditures increased an average of 17 percent each year. The government had no mechanism in place to reduce waste, fraud, or mismanagement of funds and employed nearly four hundred incompatible accounting systems. Early in his presidency, the president formed the President's Council on Integrity and Efficiency (PCIE) to "reduce waste, fraud, and mismanagement." Each year the group saved more than $20 billion by making sure funds were spent efficiently. With the implementation of new streamlined accounting procedures, the government began saving $1 billion annually just on interest alone.[90]

Ronald Reagan hoisted America on his back and carried her out of the malaise of gas lines, inflation, economic struggle, and military inferiority on the world stage. He halted gasoline price controls. The energy crisis ended abruptly. Gas prices tumbled. He battled the Soviet rhetoric and stood in front of the Brandenburg Gate in Berlin to declare, "Mr. Gorbachev, tear down this wall!" The wall fell, and the march of freedom continued its cadence, making Communism's unpopularity obvious to all. Ronald Reagan's accomplishments were far-reaching and life-altering both at home and abroad.

Not only did "The Speech" change Ronald Reagan's life, but it changed the lives of so many who listened with admiration when it was delivered. Martin Anderson, a Columbia University economics professor, watched "The Speech" and felt comforted that he was not alone in his New York City neighborhood. He later became a policy advisor to Ronald Reagan. David Stockman watched the broadcast from Michigan when he was eighteen years old and later served as President Reagan's director of the Office of Management and Budget. Housewife and mother Diana Evans viewed "The Speech" from her Oregon home and devoted the next sixteen years to helping Ronald Reagan's campaigns.[91] John Fund of the *Wall Street Journal* concluded, "Millions of people have been affected by 'The Speech,' both then and since. In 1992, I personally stood in an auditorium in Albania and watched as a group of English-speaking students cheered Mr. Reagan when a videotape of 'The Speech' was shown as their country held its first fully free elections."[92] Dick Armey, former House majority leader, conveyed, "Looking back at the Goldwater campaign in 1964, there's one thing that truly stands out in memory: Ronald Reagan's 'A Time for Choosing' speech. I dare say it was a speech unlike any we've heard before or since . . . Still today, that speech has never left my memory—nor the moment, the stirring in my heart. You see, Ronald Reagan actually revealed to us in 1964 something it took us years to understand: He knew the goodness of the American people and he had the decency to respect it. And we never really fully comprehended that about him until years later."[93]

In the summer of 2005, Discovery Channel/AOL conducted the largest, most comprehensive poll, asking citizens their choice for the "Greatest American." More than three million Americans voted Ronald Reagan as the person who had the biggest impact on the way we think, work, and live. He won this title over such figures as Abraham Lincoln, Martin Luther King Jr., George Washington, and Benjamin Franklin. Ronald Reagan had a meaningful and poignant impact on so many Americans who felt safer and prouder of their country following the successful implementation of his policies. It was no doubt because "'A Time for Choosing' became a pivotal event that changed the Republican Party from one of Rockefeller-era liberalism to Reagan conservatism. That in turn changed the course of the nation, which then led to victory in the Cold War and the virtual end of communism as a global threat."[94]

William French Smith, President Reagan's attorney, credited three men—Tuttle, Salvatori, and Rubel—with an enormous accomplishment. He said,

> I would say that if anybody could take credit for [Ronald Reagan] ultimately becoming the President of the United States, it would be those three. Because they promised to do for Reagan the one thing that he could not do without, namely to provide a political organization. They committed to provide a political organization and the necessary funding.[95]

Three self-made men built their fortunes from the ground and keenly recognized, and were grateful for, the factors contributing to their success. Tuttle later stated, "We believed in the free enterprise system.... We felt that if it was going to be preserved, instead of going around belly-aching about it we should go out and do something about it."[96] Holmes Tuttle, Henry Salvatori, and Cy Rubel hoped to give others the same chance they had to be successful starting from virtually nothing. As Joel Kotkin and Paul Grabowicz note: "These men lived in the future: they saw the solution to problems emerging from the application of rational business management principles that had made them rich, powerful, and self-assured; their eyes fixed on the creation of a stable new corporate order, dominated by the

technology and innovative genius that characterized the California entrepreneurial elite."[97]

Tuttle, Salvatori, and Rubel formed the nucleus of a tight circle that
changed the life of one individual who had felt compelled to participate in
the election of Barry Goldwater. Ronald Reagan wasn't the candidate back
then, nor had he seriously entertained the notion of running for office in
those days. Robert Bartley of the *Wall Street Journal* opined forty years later,
"What Henry Salvatori did with . . . Ronald Reagan is what we should be
encouraging millionaires to do with their money."[98]

According to Lou Cannon, "Reagan had arrived on the scene at precisely the right moment."[99] It was a moment in time. But the moment was
made possible by a group of men, friends, who saw an opportunity and
stood behind it. Ronald Reagan boldly declared in his "A Time for Choosing" speech, "If we fail, at least let our children and our children's children
say of us we justified our brief moment here. We did all that could be
done."[100] Ronald Reagan and the triumvirate that spurred his rise certainly
justified their brief moments on this earth. The Cocoanut Grove at the
Ambassador Hotel, the facility that hosted the event that changed our country, closed its doors in 1989, just as one of its most famous guests closed the
door on his presidency.[101]

Chapter Six

———————— ★ ————————

Antony Fisher

*"It is the battle of ideas which will decide
the future prospects of a free society."*[1]

—ANTONY FISHER

Antony Fisher was a chicken farmer who started breeding chickens with twenty-four eggs he smuggled from the United States. Yet this poultry farmer wasn't just any rearer and plucker of oven-ready birds. Rather, he was a knight, a pioneering engineer, an intellectual genius, and a committed free-market follower of Friedrich Hayek. He overcame death and war, business failure and financial setbacks, depression and exasperation, never losing sight of an objective he formed following his service during World War II and the Battle of Britain: the birth of a new organization devoted to the promotion of free-market economics and liberty.

Flying Officer A. G. A. Fisher was born Antony George Anson Fisher on June 28, 1915, to George and Janet Fisher, an upper-middle class couple. His father's family, the Thompsons, owned mines near the cultural center of Durham where his great-grandfather represented the city as a member of Parliament. Known as a generous, affable, and stylish guy, upon his death, Thomas Charles Thompson bequeathed a black suit to each of his employees to wear to his funeral.[2] In the years following his public service, he wanted to enjoy country living, so he purchased a home in the forest of East Sussex. It was in this forest that Antony and his younger brother, Basil, enjoyed their early years with their grandparents.[3] Antony's mother was the distant niece of Lord Anson, who had sailed around the world for the British navy, capturing a Spanish treasure ship along the way and depositing the loot at the Tower of London upon his heroic return. He also helped the New World colonists battle the French off the coast of the Carolinas; Anson County, North Carolina, remains his namesake today. Paying homage to family lineage, Antony's parents named him after family members on both sides; he took part of his name from his father, George, and part from his distant uncle, Lord Anson, thus becoming Antony George Anson Fisher.

As a two-year-old, Antony lost his father. George Fisher had been a captain in the Fourth Norfolk Regiment, but was shot by a Turkish bullet during a World War I battle in Gaza. As a result, Antony and his younger brother, Basil, depended on one another and became the best of friends to support one another during difficult times. The two went to school together at Eton, attended university together at Trinity College, drove fast sports cars together, and learned to fly airplanes together while jetting around Europe. In London, the pair topped the social atmosphere attending the most posh parties, dancing, and developing their close friendship. They maintained good values through their adventures—Fisher didn't drink, didn't smoke, and he made sure to do daily religious devotions.[4] Antony looked after Basil with the care of a father, especially after the loss of their mother to a painful and extended illness when they were in their early twenties.

In 1937, Antony, well dressed, handsome, and articulate, met Eve Naylor at a dance. The two loved to twirl around on the dance floor. Fisher married Naylor on July 29, 1939, at a church in Berkshire. Three weeks prior to his marriage to Eve, Antony volunteered for the Royal Air Force Reserve, and two days following his wedding, the Royal Air Force commissioned him and his brother as pilot officers for the Royal Air Force's One Hundred and Eleventh Hurricane Squadron.

The Battle of Britain, fought relentlessly in the sky for more than three months, stopped Germany from controlling the entirety of Northern Europe. It was a battle waged almost solely in the air between the British Royal Air Force and the German Luftwaffe, which had successfully attacked Belgium, Denmark, France, Holland, Norway, and Poland. Had Germany won that battle, it may have gone on to conquer the Soviet Union, gain control of its vast manufacturing plants and oil reserves, and dominate a large portion of our world, from Europe to North Africa into eastern Asia. The Battle of Britain, probably one of the most important battles of all time, halted Germany's advance, but it also had another, less well-known impact, too. It was in the death of a Royal Air Force pilot that a new organization sprouted, one that would inspire the emergence of free-market ideas worldwide.

The One Hundred and Eleventh Hurricane Squadron did most of the fighting during the Battle of Britain. On August 15, 1940, as one division attempted to push the German bombers back toward the English Channel, Flying Officer A. G. A. Fisher watched his brother, Flying Officer B. M. Fisher, veer from the fight over the village of Sidlesham in Sussex with smoke and flames spewing forth from his Hurricane plane. The Germans shot Basil Fisher's aircraft, which plummeted to the ground and crashed into a barn below, but not before Basil bailed. Unfortunately, his parachute caught fire on the way out, and it wasn't long before the cables burned through and Basil tumbled into a pond, his body recovered that evening. It was a loss A. G. A. Fisher felt deeply.

Basil's death was just one of so many during that war period. Antony's best friend, David Berry, died in a battle over France in 1940, too, along with two cousins who were killed in battles within the same summer. The loss of Basil, however, was a particularly devastating blow to Antony; his companion, the only close remaining family member, had just perished fighting a war Antony felt ill-equipped to wage.

Grounded by his commanding officer after the death of his brother, Antony instead became a Royal Air Force instructor to help with flight training. He soon realized, from his experiences and from viewing film footage of British air attacks, that a pilot's technical skills for shooting and the lack of training young pilots received in gunnery techniques were major factors contributing to Basil's death.[5] With expertise in engineering, Antony set to work on his Mecanno building set to create a deflection shooting device that could be used for training during the classes he now taught to young pilots. Recognition of a problem, analysis of it, and then an inventive solution to that problem came with ease to the bright engineer. The "Fisher Trainer" improved a pilot's shooting accuracy by simulating a realistic attack with a moving target.[6] The impact of his training tool has been described as a breakthrough invention:

> A significant but unknown number of [Royal Air Force] pilots survived the war because of Antony Fisher and his commitment to raising the standards of gunnery training. Some may have realised as much, but none would have known the high price that Antony paid for the insights that made him such a dedicated instructor, or the part played by the late Pilot Officer Basil Fisher in their survival.[7]

Because of his work, Antony Fisher earned the Air Force Cross for helping his comrades better prepare against an enemy in the sky, a remedy to the inadequacies Antony and his brother faced during the Battle of Britain.

Not only did Basil's tragic death lead to the invention of a pioneering device for training, but it also guided Antony's future life decisions. The gradual usurping of British liberties, and the conceit that this would alleviate social pressures following the war, caused Antony to reflect on freedom. His daughter, Linda Whetstone, suggests, "After the war, he realised that both his father and his brother had given their lives for the freedom of their fellow countrymen, yet he saw freedom diminishing, not increasing. Ration books, endless restrictions such as exchange control, and such petty regulations as to which colour you could paint your front door all seemed irrational and unnecessary.... He felt alone and depressed."[8] Those overwhelming feelings of discontent motivated Antony. When Fisher received a census form from the British government, rather than completing it, he trashed it. He assumed the census paperwork would be used by the state to usurp individual liberty. When the replacement questionnaire arrived, he filled in only the sections which he felt the government should know, causing census officials to fine him £8.[9] It was an introduction to Fisher's lifelong pursuit to defend principles of liberty.

While working at a bank in London following the war, Fisher became more and more involved with the Society of Individualists. This organization emerged during the war to engage in discourse on the rise of the state over classical liberalism. It was through his involvement that Fisher met many prominent leaders who believed as he did, including Ernest Benn, the group's founder and an economic individualist; S. W. Alexander, the free-market editor of *City Press*; and Oliver Smedley, the leader of the Cheap Foods League who opposed agricultural subsidies.[10] This small group of freedom-revering Brits encouraged Antony's fervent opposition to Communism and led him to read materials that endorsed his opinions. One of those publications was the anti-Communist *Reader's Digest*, which he began distributing to close family and friends as Christmas and birthday gifts.

In April 1945, Antony picked up the latest edition of *Reader's Digest* and read an abridged version of a piece that profoundly legitimized his thoughts regarding state power and Socialistic tendencies in Britain. *The Road to Serfdom* by Friedrich Hayek espoused his thinking in a clear and concise manner. In the book, Hayek wrote about Socialism in a way which explained its downfalls, not in terms of production and economics, but rather in terms of limiting freedom and personal liberty. When Fisher purchased the fully published version, he underlined, highlighted, and made notes over the passages that most affected him. Fisher later reported that the book "gave expression to many of his own fears and anxieties and how its combination of passion and rigour hardened his resolve to play an active role in reversing the political tide."[11] Fisher was so moved by *The Road to Serfdom* that he sought a meeting with its author less than two years later to obtain some guidance on how to become involved in fighting growing Socialism through public service.

Antony Fisher arrived at the London School of Economics one 1947 day to seek advice from author Friedrich Hayek. As the story unfolds, there were two explanations for the meeting's occurrence in the first place. Hayek, because of his work at the time to get the Mont Pelerin Society off the ground, probably felt compelled to accept the meeting if another ally would be found. Also, on Fisher's way down the corridor to Hayek's office, he purportedly passed Harold Laski in the hallway, the leading Socialist scholar of the day, thereby gaining a bit of further determination to act on his convictions before it was too late.[12] Instead of endorsing his desire to run for public office as Antony assumed he would, Hayek recommended against it. Fisher described the outcome of the meeting:

> My central question was what, if anything, could he advise me to do to help get discussion and policy on the right lines....Hayek first warned against wasting time—as I was then tempted—by taking up a political career. He explained his view that the decisive influence in the battle of ideas and policy was wielded by intellectuals whom he characterised as the "second-hand dealers in ideas." It was the dominant intellectuals from the Fabians onwards who had tilted the political debate in favour of growing government intervention with all that followed. If I shared the view that better ideas were not getting a fair hearing, his counsel was that I should join with others in forming a scholarly research organisation to supply intellectuals in universities, schools, and journalism and broadcasting with authori-

tative studies of the economic theory of markets and its application to practical affairs.[13]

Influenced by his mentor and teacher, Ludwig von Mises, who said, "What determines the course of a nation's economic policies is always the economic ideas held by public opinion," Hayek understood that the advance of Socialism could only be stopped by fueling the spread of the ideas that countered this trend among Britain's intellectual community.[14]

Recognizing his personal financial limitations in taking any action to the sort Hayek recommended, Fisher went to work to build his business and career as a way to grow his resources so he could act on his convictions as he desired. He was determined to pioneer the establishment of a free-market institute in Britain.

Fisher had always been a businessman at heart. When a friend introduced him to an engineer in 1934, Fisher collaborated with him by investing £1,000 to build the Deroy Car Company. The cars weren't designed with enough power, so the company folded just four short years later, and Antony lost his entire investment. At the same time, Antony joined the Close Brothers bank in London where he spent several months researching companies and putting together the vastly successful Lombard Trust, one of the first unit trusts in Britain. He also joined with a friend, Rex Fripp, to build a car rental company and gas station. The Hatfield Car Company was the first car rental company in Britain, and while the business succeeded before the war, it closed when its owners volunteered for military service. As with the Deroy Car Company, Antony took the burden of the finances for the car rental company upon himself, leaving the management to those around him—a trend he would emulate throughout his business endeavors.[15]

Fisher, after inheriting the family home upon his mother's passing, purchased a four-hundred-and-forty-acre farm called Thurston Hall, which he renamed Newplace, in Sussex in July 1945. The home included "four cottages, chauffeur's quarters, ornamental gardens, a three-acre lake, a waterfall, and grazing and arable grassland."[16] Along with the purchase came a herd of fifty-two shorthorn cattle. By 1950, Antony decided to quit his job in the city and move to his farm permanently. The farm had been losing about £2,000 each year, and he hoped to reverse that trend.[17] He purchased more shorthorn cattle, replaced the farm's workhorses with tractors, and bought two hundred day-old chicks. The chicks were meant to be an experiment, and he raised the young batch in a small, enclosed twelve by twelve foot unused cowshed. Once all two hundred chickens had been reared, Antony attempted to sell them. The local butcher laughed him out of the shop saying, "I lost [£1] on each of the 1,200 birds I sold last year, so why would I want your 200? Who is going to eat 200 chickens?"[18] Chickens had not found their way to English dinner tables yet as a sought-after meal. In 1951, Fisher confronted a disaster; foot-and-mouth disease wiped out his entire herd of cattle and much of the cattle across Britain.

As part of the state's subsidy program in agriculture, Fisher received compensation for his lost herd during the foot-and-mouth epidemic. With the proceeds, Fisher funded a trip to the United States. On this journey, Fisher spent time with prominent American scholars and thinkers of the day. He visited the newly established Foundation for Economic Education (FEE) in New York. There, staff introduced him to an economics professor, Dr. F. A. "Baldy" Harper, who helped Friedrich Hayek build the liberty-promoting Mont Pelerin Society. Harper invited Fisher to visit Cornell University's agriculture department, specifically, the university's broiler farm. There, Fisher witnessed fifteen thousand chickens being bred and raised in a single building. It was mass scale production of chickens such as he had attempted in Britain. According to journalist Gerald Frost, a broiler chicken, a mass produced one weighing between three and four pounds, was unknown in Britain. Britain had outlawed importing both birds and eggs, but Antony wanted to breed these particular chickens in Britain, so he smuggled twenty-four White Rock eggs by disguising them as Easter eggs in his carry-on luggage. Once the eggs hatched, those breeder chickens "were to be a key in the transformation of agriculture and of British eating habits."[19]

The result was the creation of the Buxted Chicken Company in 1954. The company started with Fisher's £1,000 and a £5,000 loan from a bank. Antony continued conducting research on the best techniques for breeding the chickens factory-style, started to process the birds for market himself, and partnered with a neighbor who would assist with the latter process. In later years, he was referred to as a "pioneer" in the production of broiler chickens because of his inventive methods.[20] After a year in the business, dozens of local farmers used Buxted Chicken to process their birds for market. Just four short years later, the company had 1.2 million chickens and did business across the country. Four years after that, in 1962, the company processed more than 25,000 birds per week, started raising turkeys, had a staff of more than two thousand (up from twelve), and acquired numerous other chicken companies along the way.[21] In 1964, Buxted Chickens produced more than 500,000 birds per week, making Antony Fisher Britain's largest poultry farmer (unsubsidized no less) and chicken the most widely consumed meat.[22]

With the 1947 Hayek visit on his mind while spending time now in the country, Antony continued to think about his philosophy and about the prevailing ideas of the time. He scribed opinion pieces for the *City Press*, often opining about Communism. He once wrote, "Communism is the poison offered to the people; socialism is the cup in which it is given; and the welfare state is the tempting label on the bottle."[23] Antony wrote his first book, *The Case for Freedom*, which was published in 1947 and laid out his philosophy as he saw it himself, with assistance from neither scholars nor academics. The eighty-six-page booklet touched on topics from inflation to privatization to housing shortages to Communist expansion and arms control. *The Case for Freedom* didn't garner a wide reading audience, but it became one more step in Fisher's philosophical development. He personally attested that he was not an intellectual, but he wanted to learn from intellectuals, the "second-hand dealers in ideas" as Hayek described them. As such, Fisher made arrangements to attend his first Mont Pelerin Society meeting in Beauvallon, France, in 1951. He was a rare businessman among the attendees, but made a lasting impression. Following the conference, the American contingency invited Fisher to visit the United States, and even asked him to provide remarks on British agriculture for the Venice Mont Pelerin Society meeting in 1954.

With his business enormously profitable, Fisher turned to Hayek's recommendation for the propagation of ideas he had been mulling over for years. He acknowledged the virtues of free enterprise witnessed personally in the entrepreneurial success he experienced, coupled with the obstacles he overcame in dealing with state restrictions. "[T]he only way...people prosper and improve themselves is when they are encouraged to develop their own talents and faculties, and are freed of the dead hand of welfarism," he once said.[24] The *Wall Street Journal* assumed that because Fisher was neither an academic nor an intellectual, he was not "spellbound by the inevitability of socialism" as so many of his countrymen were at the time.[25] The *Journal* went on to report, "What is surprising is that he rejected the common wisdom that promoting freedom, private enterprise and competition would be a futile attempt."[26]

Over the course of building his business, he had met people who would be good managers and intellectuals in building a new organization. He first looked to a former colleague in the Society of Individualists, Oliver Smedley, to help him build a think tank for Britain. With his newly acquired wealth and an abundance of conviction, Fisher pitched the idea of a free-market research institute to Smedley who agreed to join the project.

On November 9, 1955, the Institute of Economic Affairs (IEA) officially began as an educational and research trust registered as an educational charity. Three trustees each signed the Trust Deed and Rules of the Institute and contributed £100 to its initial capital: Antony Fisher; Oliver Smedley; and J. S. Harding, a colleague of Smedley's. IEA's mission is to "improve understanding of the fundamental institutions of a free society by analysing and expounding the role of markets in solving economic and social problems."[27] At the time when IEA was created, Britain faced the intrusion of more and more Socialistic policies including welfarism, high levels of taxation, increasingly coercive trade unions, nationalization, and state planning.

In a 1956 letter mirroring the advice given by Hayek in 1947, Fisher wrote to Oliver Smedley:

> Money spent on politics has very little effect on the actions of the average grown person. Most people are far too busy with their own affairs to get involved with the dreary subject of politics. It is of course necessary to have political machinery but if we are going to increase the number of people who are prepared to vote intelligently, we must start putting the right ideas in front of them at an early age.
>
> The Socialists got round this problem by getting a rich man to support the London School of Economics. . . . They teach young people at a time when they are actually exercising themselves in an effort to find out things. They are still at a formative age. Once young College and University students have got the right idea into economically [sic] they will never lose it and will spread these ideas as they grow up. In particular, those carrying on intellectual work must have a considerable impact through newspapers, television, radio and so on, on the thinking of the average individual. Socialism was spread in this way and it is time we started to reverse the process. It is probably impossible to do it in any other way but in any case with limited funds this method is the only way open to us.
>
> Therefore the Institute of Economic Affairs has been formed to propagate sound economic thought in the universities and all other educational establishments where we find it possible to do so.[28]

IEA's first project started strong. In July 1955, IEA commissioned George Winder to write a book that it would subsidize. *The Free Convertibility of Sterling* discussed floating exchange rates. Henry Hazlitt of *Newsweek* magazine reviewed the piece in a column. Professor Murray Rothbard also recommended the book be a part of suggested reading at the time. Because of Hazlitt's and Rothbard's promotion of the book, it sold out in three months.[29] This success only stimulated Fisher's need to hire staff to run IEA.

One person Fisher met during the years he spent building his business was Ralph Harris, who had given a speech in 1949 on economics, which Fisher found to be very interesting. Following Harris's remarks, Fisher approached him and outlined his early goals for IEA. He told Harris of his discussions with Hayek and of wanting to start "something which will do for the non-Labour Parties what the Fabian Society did for Labour."[30] Fisher relayed that his goal was one day to raise the funds to start such a project. Harris was so enthralled with Fisher's enthusiasm that he responded, "If you get any further I'd like to be considered as the man to run it."[31] Fisher never forgot that conversation. Six years later, with IEA off the ground but still needing qualified and motivated staff, Fisher knew just the man to run his new operation because, while he could finance the operation, his skills wouldn't be adequate to operate it successfully. Antony Fisher wrote to Ralph Harris in the summer of 1956 to gauge whether or not he was still interested in the project, and especially emphasized the success of IEA's first book. Harris agreed to join the IEA team and served as its director until his retirement in 1988. In later years, when Harris thanked Fisher for allowing him to run the organization without constant interference, Fisher responded that he didn't because he didn't know how.[32]

IEA's impact has been dramatic both in Britain and worldwide. Forty years after its inception, IEA has published more than five hundred papers and started its own monthly journal, *Economic Affairs*.[33] Its original published works included pamphlets of ten or fifteen thousand words called the Hobart Papers, which were highly marketable to the average student, academic, or journalist. The writers of these texts almost always came from the university setting, a way to keep the publications of academic quality. According to the *Washington Post*, the IEA "was the first . . . to operate on the boundary between university scholarship and public policy that have become so familiar and powerful today."[34] Over the years, IEA has featured writings from James Buchanan, Milton Friedman, Gottfried Haberler, Friedrich Hayek, John Jewkes, and Harry G. Johnson, among many other prominent economists and scholars. A Hobart Paper called *Resale Price Maintenance and Shoppers' Choice* by Basil Yamey in 1960 produced direct political consequences. It pointed out that Britain's Resale Price Maintenance (RPM), a law which required price fixing, should be abolished. Eliminating RPM would encourage big stores to cut their prices, thus saving the average Brit money every year. The pamphlet became widely discussed in the major media outlets and trade publications at the precise moment when the government began debating RPM's merits. In 1964, the conservative government abolished RPM, in no small measure because of IEA's efforts.[35] In the 1970s, IEA writers began advocating for reforming monetary policy, particularly abandoning the premise of full employment. Writers including Milton Friedman, David Laidler, and Alan Walters brought intellectual backing to those who pursued its abolition. Written in a letter from the chief economic advisor to the Department of Industry was the sentiment, "Not surprisingly, the Friedman/Laidler pamphlet excited considerable interest in Government circles and you will have received acknowledgement from some of our Ministers that it will receive attention."[36]

Still regarded by many as "eccentric," Fisher's IEA made free market ideas fashionable by selling more than 250,000 pamphlets worldwide by 1970.[37] Samuel Brittan of the *Financial Times* and Peter Jay of the *Times* (London) frequently found IEA's work worthy of being discussed in their publications, thus expanding the audience of those learning from IEA even further.[38] In addition, IEA's chief antagonist, the Fabian Society, had written a piece whereby it confirmed IEA's strength by labeling it part of the "New Right" and describing its philosophy as "coherently expressed."[39]

Hayek described how his first meeting with Fisher in 1947 impacted the direction IEA took in an interview with *Cato Policy Report*: "He [Fisher] thought you could sway mass opinion. What I insisted and what was strictly followed by the Institute was not to appeal to the large numbers, but to the intellectuals. My conviction is that, in the long run, political opinion is determined by the intellectuals, by which I mean, as I once defined it, the second-hand dealers in ideas—the journalists, school masters, and so on."[40] IEA published several of Hayek's works, including the 1961 *Agenda for a Free Society*, a 1960 symposium on *The Constitution of Liberty*, the 1972 *A Tiger by the Tail*, the 1975 *Full Employment at Any Price*, and the 1976 *Denationalization of Money*.[41] All in all, as author Richard Cockett describes, one of IEA's most notable accomplishments was that it created a "public platform in Britain for the two most powerful academic dissenters of all, Hayek and Friedman, who as we have seen, were not only instrumental in creating the Mont Pelerin Society and then the IEA, but who also remained the two most eloquent advocates of the free market into the 1980s."[42] By 1976, both of these men had been awarded the Nobel Prize for Economics.

The political climate of the 1970s gave IEA an opportunity to make a mark on Britain's future. Conservatives, under their leader Edward Heath, rose to power in 1970 after their 1964 defeat. In the years between 1970 and 1974, IEA hoped the free-market philosophy would be embraced by those who carried the conservative banner, including Margaret Thatcher, who served as secretary of state for education. Instead, the conservatives abandoned free-enterprise and the free-market approach. Heath's administration provided massive subsidies to firms in trouble, bolstered consumer demand due to unemployment, saw stampeding inflation, instituted price controls, and failed to fulfill its promise of privatization. Conservatives lost control of British government again in 1974. It was Margaret Thatcher, education secretary, who turned to IEA and those who had been inspired by it in the face of defeat for intellectual inspiration.

When Margaret Thatcher slammed Hayek's book *The Constitution of Liberty* on the table of the Conservative Party's research department and declared, "This is what we believe," it had been the work of IEA and its group of intellectuals that had given Thatcher her blueprint.[43] She had been attending events sponsored by IEA since 1975. In her memoir, she wrote, "I also regularly attended lunches at the Institute of Economic Affairs where Ralph Harris, Arthur Seldon, Alan Walters and others—in other words all those who had been right when we in Government had gone so badly wrong—were busy marking out a new non-socialist economic and social path for Britain."[44] Margaret Thatcher challenged conservative leader Edward Heath for control of the party in 1975 and became the first woman elected to this position.

Through the Centre for Policy Studies (CPS) in London, a group that owed its start to the intellectual inspiration of IEA and Hayek, IEA ideas and research were brought into the political arena. CPS took the pamphlets and books produced by IEA and sought to educate the conservatives under the leadership of Margaret Thatcher. CPS also served as the liaison between Margaret Thatcher and the IEA directors, Friedrich Hayek and Milton Friedman, by encouraging her to develop close relationships with these individuals. In one such meeting at a London hotel in 1978, Milton Friedman conducted a mini-session to IEA's Ralph Harris and Margaret Thatcher, suggesting that she arrange to end exchange controls in order to help the British economy transition to a market-based system.[45] The meeting had a profound impact on Thatcher; eliminating the controls became her first step toward free-market reforms once elected chancellor in 1979.

By 1979, IEA had become the "intellectual home of free markets, economic liberalism, and monetarism in Britain, and came into its own as the ideas of Keynes, Beveridge, and the Fabians were in retreat."[46] When Thatcher produced her "Stepping Stones" document for government reform, IEA had helped her draft it. The document outlined plans for reducing public debt, deregulating the public sector, and currency stabilization, among other reforms. Under the leadership of Margaret Thatcher, Britain privatized more than two-thirds of its state-owned enterprises with more than one million employees. Inflation was brought under control and trade unions were now subject to the law.

John Chamberlain called Thatcher's program for Britain "an IEA program."[47] Thatcher told an interviewer of her success: "It started with Sir

Keith and me, with the Centre for Policy Studies, and Lord Harris, at the Institute of Economic Affairs. Yes, it started with ideas and beliefs. That's it. You must start with beliefs. Yes, always with beliefs."[48] Milton Friedman also recognized Thatcher's reliance on IEA, specifically Antony Fisher: "the U-turn in British policy executed by Margaret Thatcher owes more to him than any single individual."[49] In a 1991 interview with author Richard Cockett, Milton Friedman said that Antony Fisher is the "single most important person in the development of Thatcherism."[50] Friedman later penned a piece for the *Times* (London) where he expanded on this sentiment: "Had the IEA never existed, Margaret Thatcher might still have become prime minister, but the reforms she presided over would not have been politically feasible, and most likely not even part of her platform. Seldom does a country, to plagiarise Winston Churchill, owe so much to so few and it is not irrelevant that Antony Fisher was also one of the Churchill 'few.'"[51] Ralph Harris described IEA's direct impact on Thatcher in *National Review*: "Margaret Thatcher's central reform of trade unions, state industries, monetary policy, and much else owed a great deal to the advisors and members of Parliament directly instructed in market analysis by IEA publications...."[52] British member of Parliament Oliver Letwin went on to contemplate Fisher's impact on the world even further when he said, "Without Fisher, no IEA; without the IEA and its clones, no Thatcher and quite possibly no Reagan; without Reagan, no Star Wars; without Star Wars, no economic collapse of the Soviet Union. Quite a chain of consequences for a chicken farmer!"[53]

Fisher's foresight and dedication to seeing the IEA succeed brought him numerous accolades from the intellectual community over and above his work with Thatcher. Sir Keith Joseph, once a proclaimed Socialist and later a conservative IEA convert, said of IEA, "If the IEA did not exist, how desperate would be the need to invent it.... All credit to that entrepreneur of entrepreneurs, Antony Fisher, who perceived the need to mobilise Ralph Harris on one of the most successful entrepreneurial ventures of this half century."[54] Friedrich Hayek, on the occasion of IEA's twentieth anniversary in 1977, said of Fisher: "If these ideas influenced the aims of the Institute he created a few years later [post the Hayek-Fisher meeting at the London School of Economics], I can now say honestly that it has achieved these aims far beyond what I then thought possible. . . . I now believe that the change of opinion which has been brought about in the last 20 years is in large measure due to the efforts of this Institute. . . ."[55]

IEA describes its core activities today as encompassing a quality publishing program; hosting conferences, seminars, and lectures; reaching young people; and getting its ideas across through the media. Rather than research and find new policy initiatives over the years, it sought to proselytize the ideas it knew worked already. If successful, the elected officials' support for IEA's ideas would follow in that order. IEA relies on the generous contributions of its core supporters, publishing sales, and conference fees for its programmatic resources. Fisher, in addition to funding the IEA's start-up costs, donated to the IEA each year from his Buxted Chicken profits.[56] He also provided a grant for the small office space in Hobart Place, Belgravia (thus the name of IEA's first pamphlet series, Hobart Papers).

The IEA has been called the "intellectual flagship of a growing fleet."[57] Milton Friedman characterized IEA's impact on the world: "The IEA's influence has not been confined to the United Kingdom. Its publications and the able group of scholars who became associated with it contributed greatly to the change in the intellectual climate of opinion around the world."[58] Even in the United States, IEA's impact has been felt: "Inside Washington's Capital Beltway, the American Enterprise Institute and the Heritage Foundation may seem the alpha and omega of the movement. But before there was George Mason University, there was the University of Chicago; and before there was the semi-scholarly quarterly the Public Interest, there was the Institute of Economic Affairs (IEA)."[59]

Not only did IEA itself impact the flow of ideas on an international scale, but Antony Fisher went on to use his successful IEA model to create similar organizations around the world. One of his first projects was to start the Fraser Institute in British Columbia in 1974, serving as its first president and helping it grow to become Canada's largest independent public policy institute. In the mid-1970s, Fisher persuaded a group of American businessmen to fund an American model of IEA. Under its first chairman, William Casey, who later became President Reagan's CIA director, New York's Manhattan Institute (then the Centre for Economic Policy Studies) emerged into a $6.3 million research group that puts quality books in the hands of publishers. Charles Murray's *Losing Ground* in 1984 is one such example. It also produces the conservative *City Journal* which is provided to ten thousand public servants, businessmen, and journalists each year.[60]

In 1979, Fisher, while sharing an apartment with Milton Friedman, helped start the Pacific Research Institute for Public Policy to meet the challenges faced in San Francisco. The group now addresses education reform under the theme, "Choice, Charters, Contracting Out, and Content."[61] Fisher also gave economist John Goodman a $25,000 grant to start the National Center for Policy Analysis in Dallas, Texas. The organization now operates in Washington, D.C., to build support for the privatization of Social Security. Fisher was also directly involved with starting Australia's Centre for Policy Studies, and the Adam Smith Institute (Great Britain) used his IEA as a prototype.

Fisher also assisted the development of new think tanks on an international scale through unconventional means. Frequently, subscribers to the free-market philosophy would receive invitations from Antony Fisher to attend various annual meetings from some of the groups he was involved with, and often a new organization would grow from this contact. Such was the case with Centro de Estudios en Educación y Economía in Mexico. Other times, it was simply an encouraging word from Fisher that inspired someone to start a group. The Hong Kong Centre for Economic Research, the Jon Thorlaksson Institute (Iceland), and the Institute of Economic Affairs (Ghana) are three such examples. Or perhaps one of Fisher's colleagues from an organization he started would one day find inspiration to do the same, such as David Theroux's Independent Institute or Chip Mellor's Institute for Justice. After a personal meeting with Fisher, several groups emerged, including the Centro de Divulgación del Conocimiento Economico in Venezuela in 1984, which began promoting freedom and the market economy by teaching economics courses and distributing books to students; the Centro de Investigaciones Económicas Nacionales in Guatemala, which reviews the economy and follows legislative action in Congress; and the Instituto de Libertad y Democracia in Peru, which helps citizens of ex-Communist countries acquire property rights.

In order to further collaboration among all the groups he helped build, Fisher established the Atlas Economic Research Foundation in 1981, which provides monetary grants and advice to more than eighty free-market-based think tanks worldwide, including Liberty Institute (Romania) and Unirule (China). All in all, by 2002, Fisher had a direct hand or indirect role through Atlas in forming ninety-nine policy think tanks around the world in places as diverse as Albania, Egypt, India, and Peru.

Instead of relying on university intellectual output, which seldom upheld the free market and liberty promoting positions, those ideas now had their own outlets. Think tanks generated their own research, publications, and platforms, no longer relying on the intellectual establishment for confirmation of their principles. The policy specialists employed by these groups formed the nucleus of many government agencies, both in the United States under Ronald Reagan, and in Britain under Margaret Thatcher.

The *Times* (London) acknowledged upon Fisher's passing, "The change in public opinion that has taken place in many countries in the last two decades is undoubtedly partly due to Fisher's vision."[62] As an obscure chicken farmer almost entirely unknown in the world for his accomplishments, the triumph of the free market owes Antony Fisher and a few others for its resurgence. For his efforts, Margaret Thatcher knighted Antony Fisher just five weeks before his death in 1988.

Fisher achieved many notable accomplishments during his time with the Royal Air Force, as a farmer, and as the creator of IEA. Following his passing, the *Times* (London) featured an editorial in which the writer described Fisher's life: "The qualities which Fisher displayed as a young officer—quiet analysis of a problem, readiness to reject current dogma in the search for an answer, originality and courage in devising an effective solution and practical ability of a high order in putting the solution into effect—again served our nation well in his post-war activities ... as a pioneer of new farming methods and his establishment of the Institute of Economic Affairs."[63] But it was this chicken farmer's gifts of time, energy, and a £100 investment that provided an alternative to the intruding Socialism of the day.[64]

──────────── ★ ────────────

Chapter Seven

Gerald "Spike" Hennessy

"Hillsdale deserves the appreciation of all who labor for freedom."[1]

—RONALD REAGAN

A two hundred acre "bastion of freedom" rests atop a rural Michigan hill, its red and light-orange brick walls a fortitude for independence, and its foundation deeply laid in academic standards and respected tradition.[2] Ranked for thirteen years as the top "Midwestern liberal arts school" by *U.S. News & World Report*, one of the "best college values" by *Barron's* and *Money Guide* magazines, and in the top ten of all private colleges by *Princeton Review*, Hillsdale College earned a strong reputation against all the odds.[3] The *Detroit Free Press* on January 25, 1981, explained what makes this school different from virtually every other public or private school in the country: "Hillsdale, after all, is famous as the little college that fights for rightness and independence. From the unlikely location of south central Michigan, it gained its national recognition by drawing its sword against the federal government. No trespassing, it told [the U.S. Department of Health, Education, and Welfare]; we'll hire, promote, subsidize, educate and influence with no interference from you."[4] Hillsdale College along with Grove City College in Pennsylvania stand proudly as the only two four-year institutions out of more than twenty-five hundred colleges and universities in the United States that do not accept public subsidies in the form of coerced tax dollars.

The Local Boy and a Farm Girl

Nestled in the small town of Hillsdale, Michigan, a local pharmacy served as a central hub for residents to catch up on the town's news, sip a chocolate soda at the twenty-four-foot marble counter, or pick up some advice or medication to solve a health ailment. The pharmacy's prestige came not from the medical assistance or social network it offered, but rather, from the prosperity it provided for its owners, the Hennessy family, over the years.

Gerald Hennessy, or "Spike" as he was affectionately known, was born in nearby Yale, Michigan, on July 30, 1906. His father, Herbert T. Hennessy, purchased the local Hillsdale pharmacy, Bull's Drug Store, located at 53 North Howell Street, from Samuel and Henry Bull in 1923. The family relocated to Hillsdale in 1926 when they bought the Sheffield Book Store just up the street at 30 North Howell Street and moved the pharmacy to its new location. Spike worked in his father's shop before deciding to attend Hillsdale College, the local school on top of the hill. He entered the sophomore class in the spring of 1926, set to graduate in 1928. In those days, Hillsdale was one of ten schools in Michigan approved by the North Central Association of Colleges and Secondary Schools, and nearly one-third of its students entered the teaching profession.[5]

Spike Hennessy worked to fit in as a new student at Hillsdale College by participating in school activities. Athletics, particularly football, had a prominent role in the college experience, spurred on with a new pep band and cheerleaders to boost school spirit. As a spunky sophomore member of the cheer squad, Spike led the rooting in the stands at football games, being

described by the 1926 yearbook as "full of pep and ginger."[6] He joined the
student council to act as a liaison between students and faculty and served
on the Inter-Fraternity Council as a member of Alpha Tau Omega, a fraternity founded in Richmond, Virginia, and the first fraternity recognized
following the Civil War. He also wrote for the student-published Hillsdale
College weekly newspaper, the *Collegian*. His college days in the era of rac-
coon coats and "rah rah" alongside academics gave him a solid social life
he relied on for the rest of his days.[7] He graduated from Hillsdale in 1928
in a class of seventy-three seniors.

After his college graduation, Spike Hennessy followed in his father's footsteps, graduating with his pharmacy degree in 1930 from Ferris Institute
(Ferris State University today) in Big Rapids, Michigan. Immediately, he
went to work with his father when the average price for a prescription was
25¢, officially becoming a partner in the business in 1935. As a hub in the
Hillsdale community, Spike continued to stay involved in Hillsdale College
happenings. He also attended numerous post-graduation social functions at
Hillsdale, one of which stood out from the others in 1936. Helen Mooty, a
new associate professor of economics at Hillsdale College, happened to be
at that particular event. She was a farm girl from a successful Iowan family,
a reserved, modest woman who went to Michigan to find work.

Helen was born on September 6, 1907, in the rich agricultural area of
Grundy Center, Iowa, home of the motto, "The good life." William and
May Mooty operated a thriving farm there and raised Helen and her
brother, William, with strong educations. Upon graduating from Reinbeck
High School in 1924, Helen attended the State University of Iowa (now the
University of Iowa), acquiring her BS in commerce in 1928 followed by her
MA in commerce in 1930. Helen Mooty joined the Hillsdale College eco-
nomics department's faculty in September 1935, following a brief sojourn
at Bradley Polytechnic Institute.

While Helen was quiet and unassuming, Spike Hennessy was outgoing
and had a quick sense of humor. Helen enjoyed listening to a good story,
while Spike loved to tell a good story. The two married within a few years,

but never had children. They instead embraced their extended families, especially their two nieces, became involved members of the community, and worked to expand the family business.

The Hennessy drugstore celebrated its golden anniversary with a reputation as the oldest retail business in Hillsdale operated by the same family. In the fifty years that the Hennessys owned the enterprise, it opened every day, including all holidays and Sundays. Under its motto, "Try Hennessy first," Hennessy's Drugs ran smoothly because of the contributions of many family members to its functions. Spike's mother, Grayce, and sister, Natalie, both worked in the shop, keeping it open for fifteen hours a day. The most important part of the business was, of course, its prescription sales, followed by its record-keeping services. Spike's father had even created his own medicine, an antacid known as Ogdendrox, only available at Hennessy's and by mail. By 1973, the medicine had been sent to every state in the union except Alaska and Hawaii.

Upon his father's death in 1950, Spike incorporated the business as Hennessy's Drugs, Inc. Gradually, the family acquired five other drugstores from Jonesville to Litchfield. Hennessy's Drugs flourished in the small town of Hillsdale, and because of their success and business expertise, Spike and Helen became more and more involved in the community.

Spike served as the president of the Hillsdale Chamber of Commerce for two years and as a director for eight. He led the Hillsdale Charter Commission in creating Hillsdale's new city charter in 1949 and achieved an appointment as the city's civil defense director in the 1950s. In addition to these leadership positions, Spike stayed involved with the Elks, Masons, Rotary, Hillsdale Golf and Country Club, and the Methodist Church. Helen kept up with the town's social network, playing bridge and maintaining the home.

Hillsdale College

Founded in 1844, Hillsdale College has a long tradition of commitment to Western heritage and liberal arts. The school's objective in teaching its students is in "educating for liberty." As part of its mission statement, Hillsdale College "considers itself a trustee of modern man's intellectual and spiritual inheritance from the Judeo-Christian faith and Greco-Roman culture, a heritage finding its clearest expression in the American experiment of self-government under law."[8] The college's founders proclaimed in the school's constitution, "The object of this institution is and shall be to furnish to all persons who wish, irrespective of nationality, color, or sex, a literary, scientific or theological education as comprehensive and thorough as is usually pursued in other colleges or theological schools in this country, and to combine with this, such moral, social and artistic instruction and culture as will best develop the minds and improve the hearts of the students."

United States Supreme Court Associate Justice Clarence Thomas summed up Hillsdale's founding:

> To a large degree, the principles of Hillsdale College are the principles of America. The founders of the college declared their gratitude "to God for the inestimable blessings resulting from the prevalence of civil and religious liberty" with which He has favored the people of this land, just as America's Founders called upon the protection of Divine Providence in their effort to secure for themselves and their countrymen the God-given, unalienable rights to life, liberty, and the pursuit of happiness. And the founders of this great College opened its doors to "all persons, irrespective of nation, color, or sex," just as America's Founders committed our nation to the idea that all human beings are created equal.
>
> Its traditional liberal arts curriculum introduces its students to the greatest books of both ancient and modern times. By studying these books, students become confident of the existence of permanent standards of right and wrong, and are led to discover through their own thinking the same truths that formed the basis of our nation, the "laws of nature and of nature's God" that underlie our unalienable rights and our tradition of limited government.[9]

Hillsdale College's distinguished alumni include Senator Albert Hopkins of Illinois; Congressmen Phil Crane of Illinois, Chris Chocola of Indiana, and Verner Main, Washington Gardner, and Spencer Fisher of
Michigan; Moses Luce, drafter of San Diego's city charter and Civil War
Medal of Honor winner; Dr. Elias Lyon, prominent scientist and former
dean of the St. Louis University Medical School; William Penfield, counsel for the United States during the 1903 Hague Tribunal; Dr. Mary Fulton, founder of Hackett Medical College and the Gregg Hospital for
women and children in China; Elizebeth Smith Friedman, code-breaker
during World War II; May Preston Slosson, the first woman to earn a PhD;
Bion J. Arnold, genius behind the electric trolley system in Chicago; La
Marcus Adna Thompson, inventor of the gravity-controlled roller coaster;
and poet Will Carleton, famed for the 1872 "Over the Hill to the Poor-
house," which brought him national literary prominence.[10]

Hillsdale College also has ties to many of the leading conservative
thinkers, authors, and scholars of all time. Edward Everett, America's first
PhD and the president of Harvard University, gifted his library to Hillsdale.
Conservative stalwart Russell Kirk (sometimes referred to as the "American
Cicero"), whose book *The Conservative Mind* led to a conservative insur-
gence in the 1950s, taught at Hillsdale College from 1971 to 1978, wrote
the school's mission statement, and eventually donated his entire library to
the college.[11] Austrian economist Ludwig von Mises entrusted his personal
library to the school, too, believing it "most clearly reflected the free market values for which I have given my life."[12] William F. Buckley Jr.'s complete collection of writings is being preserved by the college today.

Hillsdale's speakers program has hosted more than two thousand international and national scholars and leaders, from Margaret Thatcher to
Thomas Sowell to General Norman Schwarzkopf. [Even Frederick Dou-
glass, Booker T. Washington, and William Lloyd Garrison spoke to the
school in its 150-year history.] This small campus, ninety miles from a
major airport and home to only thirteen hundred students, has become the
epicenter of some of the most engaging and important discussions of all

time. In addition, it takes its lecture program on the road and conducts leadership seminars with these talented speakers.

The Hennessys and Hillsdale

Hillsdale may never have achieved its stature and high rankings without Spike and Helen Hennessy. They each served the college for more than fifty years in various capacities, from student to professor to trustee to committee chairman to donor. They saw Hillsdale through its darkest days with their commitment of time and gifts.

Because of their affinity for Hillsdale College, Spike and Helen paid close attention to the school's affairs, Helen through her role with the faculty, and Spike as a concerned alumnus. Hillsdale College faced trying times from the 1930s to the 1950s in particular, a period of time that nearly forced its doors to close for good. Hillsdale president Willfred Otto Mauck reflected on the 1933 situation: "It was a fearsome time of national and world Depression, with our endowment under a million dollars, our enrollment off some 75 percent, a bank holiday on, a very heavy debt, creditors moving in, the sheriff at the door, and the faculty unpaid even its meager salaries since the preceding February."[13] In 1934, a bank in Detroit won a $10,000 settlement from Hillsdale College because it had not paid on its loan with the bank—the field house and other real estate were in jeopardy. Slogans including "Hillsdale College Is for Sale for $11,000" headlined Michigan newspapers forewarning the college's demise.[14] Concerned and dedicated alumni and friends raised enough funds to pay the settlement and other outstanding loans at the time.

By 1942, little had changed. Efforts by members of the Hillsdale community sustained the college through these tough times. The chairman of the Hillsdale College Board of Trustees, Fred Freeman, spoke to the students, warning that the college topped a list of nearly six hundred colleges and universities in danger of shutting down.[15] To be sustainable, the college would need to decrease its budget by $170,000. President Harvey Turner turned to Hillsdale's faculty members in 1945 to put together a workforce to complete the construction on Herron Hall for the students. The faculty members served as plumbers and carpenters. When history professor Dr. Windsor Roberts moved into his new classroom, he had no chairs for the students, so he provided ten of his own and asked four hundred graduates for more furniture. The request brought in $1,513, so he was able to furnish more than just his own classroom. Considering that the faculty had not received a raise in 1944–45 and summer school had been cancelled, the faculty commitment was noteworthy.[16]

By this time, with no children and a successful pharmacy business, the Hennessys became annual contributors to Hillsdale College's sustaining fund to help alleviate its financial pressures. This fund, designed to assist the college through declining enrollments (due to World War II) and lower returns on the endowment, helped the college avoid relying on federal assistance during the war. It was only the beginning of their efforts to see this special place through difficult times.

Hillsdale College invited Spike Hennessy to join the board of trustees in 1951. In this same year, college president Dr. Harvey Turner once again addressed the college's bleak financial situation: "The picture at Hillsdale looks dark indeed as we reach mid-year of this mid-century. . . . Enrollment for the fall of 1951 looks even worse with the prospect of lowering the draft age to eighteen. . . . It is indeed a dark picture. . . . It looks now as if the going will be especially rough for the next three to five years. . . ."[17] Dr. Turner went on to predict an operating deficit of $27,000 for the 1950–51 fiscal year. It ended up being $65,000 at year-end. To make matters worse, the college borrowed $95,000 between 1949 and the summer of 1951 to meet payroll and other expenses. In January 1952, the Hillsdale State Savings Bank denied a loan of $50,000 to the college because of interest it forgave on a prior loan years earlier. Faced with mounting debt, Hillsdale College was unable to secure any more loans. Keeping the doors to the college open seemed more and more hopeless.

As a member of the board of trustees, Spike lamented the college's dire financial situation. Report after report confirmed that the college's long-term viability was threatened. Starting in January 1953 and a few times thereafter, Spike and Helen Hennessy personally financed the college's payroll and overdue bills.[18] Tony Fowler, a man who would serve Hillsdale College for thirty-seven years in various positions from bookstore manager to secretary of the board to vice president for administrative affairs, described the impact of the Hennessys' gifts: "I'm not sure the college would have continued without their support."[19] John Muller, in a 1982 memorandum to Hillsdale's faculty, wrote, "During the fifties, [Hennessy] was a central figure in keeping Hillsdale solvent."[20] Spike and Helen Hennessy kept Hillsdale College's doors open when it mattered most. But the Hennessys' commitment and work helped keep Hillsdale's doors closed to an intruder, too: federal usurpation of control.

Financial problems notwithstanding, the college faced critical policy issues starting in February 1959. The college began a series of debates over the sources of its funds and how federal taxpayer dollars would be used at the school, if at all. The first ruling involved the federal student loan program. The Prudential Committee of Hillsdale's board of trustees contemplated a measure that would allow students to accept subsidized loans from the federal government to assist with college tuition. This National Defense Student Loan Fund required a college to supply students with 10 percent of the loan, and federal taxpayers would supply the remaining 90 percent of the loan to the student. In a meeting of the full board of trustees on May 30, 1959, the board members broke a long tradition and created a formal policy allowing students to accept federal loans: "We agree that a private college ought not to receive government aid, but it is our opinion that this is not government aid to the college but to the student and that we will regret it if we do not participate in the program."[21] This policy came from a consensus among board members that financially deprived students would be hurt without the opportunity to take part in the loan program.

By 1962, federal education policy became consumed with recommending subsidy disbursements directly to schools, purportedly to improve their quality. These subsidies would likely be provided in conjunction with regulations that would inevitably shape the schools' policies. Hillsdale College had to make a decision about its activities and relationship with the government, keeping its difficult financial history in mind. Later Hillsdale College president Larry Arnn described the decision:

> Hillsdale College was forced to choose between two bad options. It could forgo the subsidies being offered and the regulations that would likely come with them, in which case it would suffer a disadvantage against its competitors who took the subsidies. Or it could accept what was offered and sacrifice its principles.[22]

The board of trustees decided in favor of principle against the federal subsidy and published a "Declaration of Independence." The most important paragraph stated,

> THEREFORE, BE IT RESOLVED, That it be the decision of the Board of Trustees of Hillsdale College to reaffirm its historic independence and to resist subsidization of its affairs by the Federal government. Acknowledging that the possibility of failure is a concomitant of independence, the Trustees place their trust in God and in the dedication and generosity of students, alumni and friends who share their views.[23]

Spike Hennessy, as a member of the board, helped lead the charge for the college to reaffirm its independence from the federal government's assistance, even though it was under heavy pressure to succumb to the subsidies. As a prominent Hillsdale businessman, his opinion was extremely valuable, because, as Tony Fowler later said, "A college in trouble needs to run like a business."[24] From his days as a student to his term on the board, Spike Hennessy had learned the value of independent education and more importantly, how precious private initiative can be.

So when in 1967 a special study task force led by the wealthiest man on the Hillsdale College Board of Trustees strongly recommended to "proceed at once with the program to obtain from federal sources all grants for which Hillsdale College may qualify to supplement our own fund-raising activities," Spike Hennessy was equipped to stand against this motion.[25] He had seen the college through some of its darkest days in the 1940s and 1950s—the personal investment and sacrifice of so many enabled the college to arrive at that 1967 day with virtually no obligations to the federal government. Even still, commentary in the *Wall Street Journal* considered Hillsdale College to be in a "state of supine poverty and neglect."[26] For the college not to take federal aid was daring and seemingly suicidal. Yet that is exactly what Spike Hennessy and the board decided to do. The motion to grab federal dollars failed in the board of trustees by a margin of sixteen to three.

The next battle Hillsdale faced was not by internal leadership; instead, it came when Congress amended the 1964 Civil Rights Act in 1972. Title IX, a series of changes to civil rights laws, specifically addressed discrimination in education and required all colleges and universities that accepted federal dollars to begin collecting race and sex data on its students and faculty and providing that information to the Department of Health, Education, and Welfare (HEW) as a condition of the federal government's financial assistance. In particular, the federal government insisted that Hillsdale College prepare a racial preferences program complete with a special plan to hire women for HEW's approval in order to be in compliance with the law.[27] These documents would serve to prove to the government that the college was not discriminating against women in particular.

Hillsdale College was the first college in America to prohibit discrimination based on race, sex, or religion in its written charter. It extended enrollment to blacks just after its 1844 founding and had one of the highest casualty rates among its graduates during the Civil War because so many of its alumni felt compelled to fight for equality.[28] It was the first college in

Michigan and the second nationwide to admit women alongside men in qualifications and provide four-year degrees. In fact, in 1972 when HEW first pushed its racial preferences paperwork on the school, Hillsdale employed 122 women to 103 men.[29] Its long record of equality aside, the federal government began asserting demands to Hillsdale College and all other educational institutions to install preferential treatment and adhere to political correctness, which was, in the words of John Chamberlain, "positively insulting when one considers the actual accomplishment of Hillsdale."[30]

By 1975, HEW declared Hillsdale College was a "recipient institution" of federal funds because its students accepted federal grants and loans. HEW believed Hillsdale College benefited from the federal dollars students received for their educations and, therefore, Hillsdale College was required to follow the Title IX provisions just like all the other schools that accepted federal subsidies outright had to do. In response, Hillsdale College trustees issued a resolution:

> [B]y consistent refusal of federal aid to education, federal grants in any and all forms of subsidy by the federal government . . . [the federal government] now seeks to impose its control . . . through the subterfuge that a few of the students of Hillsdale College receive federal aid through the medium of such programs as Veterans Benefits and the National Direct Student Loan Fund . . . [Hillsdale College will] hold to its traditional policy of equal opportunity without discrimination by reason of race, religion, or sex, but such nondiscrimination will be voluntary, thus preserving equality with dignity and encouraging friendship based on recognition of equal worth and mutual respect.[31]

This refusal to comply with Title IX by the board of trustees based on its upstanding record in dealing with matters of race and sex within its walls stood as a testament to the college's atmosphere of equality. Rather than relent and be forced to prove to the federal government year after year that its policies were in compliance with federal regulations, Hillsdale stood boldly on its own history.

Years of battling with HEW, and later the U.S. Department of Education, ensued when Hillsdale College refused to acquiesce to the government's requests. In 1979, HEW became the U.S. Department of Health and Human Services, and a new department, the U.S. Department of Education, was established. By 1982, the Sixth Circuit issued a ruling which was partially favorable and partially unfavorable to Hillsdale College. In short, it didn't find Hillsdale College guilty of violating Title IX by not filing the proper compliance forms, and it found that the U.S. Department of Education's insistence on cutting the federal financial aid Hillsdale students received was unjustified. However, the ruling also contained consent to the federal government to cut off any federal aid from students who attended a college like Hillsdale, even if the college is not found to have discriminated. The court also stipulated that Hillsdale could be subject to Title IX as a recipient institution if the U.S. Department of Education regulated them in a "program-specific" way.[32]

Together, Hillsdale and Grove City colleges appealed the decision to the U.S. Supreme Court (*Grove City v. Bell*). The Supreme Court ruled against the two colleges in 1984, saying that if one student receives financial aid from government sources, then the school he/she attends is a "recipient institution," and must conform to reporting guidelines and preferential treatment to uphold nondiscrimination clauses.

Now the trustees, undeterred and committed to Hillsdale College's core founding principles, set to face this Supreme Court ruling squarely. They had years of battle experiences (especially the initial 1967 vote of principle against forking over independence to the federal government), and these helped the trustees remain loyal to Hillsdale College's record of history, success, and principles, even in the face of the Supreme Court's unfavorable ruling. The trustees set upon a course to replace all federal student financial aid with private contributions. William E. Simon, in a foreword to John Chamberlain's *Freedom and Independence: The Hillsdale Story*, says, "Even at the expense of losing money, the principled independence of this college has led it to neither solicit nor accept government funding, and the chains attached, for its operations. Truly, how many other institutions of higher learning have demonstrated such noble standards at the expense of losing money? Virtually none."[33]

In that first year, the college needed to raise an additional $400,000 to make up for the lost student loans.[34] By 2000, that figure topped nearly $5 million dollars. Because of the direction set by Spike and Helen Hennessy, and with the help of so many other generous individuals, from 1986 to 1996, the decade following the cut student funds, the college raised $200 million from private sources, thus maintaining its complete independence. The college continues to build its network of financial supporters, many of whom have never visited the school but continue to support its principles and values from afar. Gifts to support its academic programs are testaments to its principles and to its core values.

Hillsdale College became an institution known for its commitment to freedom's virtues and rose to be one of the best private liberal arts schools in the country, and all of this occurred without handouts from the federal government. Not quite ten years following its decision to forego government subsidies, Hillsdale College continued to add to faculty and reduce the student-teacher ratio. It doubled the size of its library and expanded construction in its fine arts center, athletic complex, maintenance building, dormitories, and science building facilities, and 90 percent of the faculty members had doctorates in their areas of expertise.[35] In addition, 80 percent of Hillsdale's students received financial aid of one sort or another—but not a dime from federal sources. This, in no small measure, is partly due to the generosity of the Hennessys.

Today, Hillsdale College's curriculum is rooted in Western culture and avoids the multicultural and sexual identity courses that so many colleges and universities embrace. It neglects "Canine Cultural Studies" (University of North Carolina–Chapel Hill), "I Like Ike, But I Love Lucy" (Harvard), "The Unbearable Whiteness of Barbie" (Occidental College), and "Nip, Tuck, Perm, Pierce, and Tattoo: Adventures with Embodied Culture" (Alfred University) in favor of a curriculum that buttresses the sciences, teaching, and liberty. "The Founding of the American Republic," "The Western Heritage to 1600," "Austrian Economics," "American Religious Landscape," and "The U.S. Constitution" are just a few of the courses Hillsdale College offers its students.

A sampling of Americans demonstrated that only 25 percent could name more than one freedom guaranteed by the First Amendment, whereas more than half knew two or more members of *The Simpsons* family from the Fox television cartoon. A study by the McCormick Tribune Freedom Museum found that only one in one thousand people surveyed could list all five freedoms protected by the First Amendment: speech, religion, assembly, press, and freedom to petition the government on grievances.[36] Of the top one hundred universities listed by *U.S. News & World Report* in 2006, less than half offered a full course on the U.S. Constitution. Only two schools, the University of Georgia and SUNY Stonybrook, required their students to take a course on the Constitution. As an aside, the University of Georgia actually expects all of its students to pass an exam on the U.S. Constitution and the Georgia State Constitution before graduating. Hillsdale College also requires all of its students to take a course on the U.S. Constitution where "the goal is to understand the conditions requisite for the flourishing of human liberty."[37] It is Hillsdale College's freedom from the shackles of political correctness that enables it to teach its students more of the values that have led to America's success and greatness—and for that, our future is brighter.

Spike and Helen Hennessy not only kept the college solvent and free from federal meddling, but they also provided for the college in many other less public ways over the years. Spike Hennessy advised the Alpha Tau Omega fraternity boys as an alumnus and even financed an addition to the boys' house following World War II. In 1951, Mr. Hennessy, along with his mother and brother-in-law, furnished a faculty lounge in the Carr Memorial Library in memory of his sister, Natalie Hennessy Walworth, who died at a young age. The Hennessys also gave to the college on behalf of many of their family members and friends and designated funds to special projects such as the college's nationally distributed publication, *Imprimis*. Helen Hennessy was on the Board of Women Commissioners and even became treasurer for a time. This group helped raise resources for student scholarships, building projects, and other worthy causes.

Spike Hennessy served on the Hillsdale College Board of Trustees for thirty years and never missed a meeting.[38] Acting as chairman of the finance committee, Hennessy helped direct a $50,000 gift to Hillsdale College on October 15, 1966.[39] It is not clear whether or not he provided the gift himself or whether he helped attract the funds from an anonymous donor. In either case, during 1966, Hillsdale College's entire budget was $2.5 million, and this gift represented 2.5 percent of that amount. Freshmen students paid $1,415 in tuition while upper classman tuition was $1,340. The gift could provide full tuition scholarships for thirty-five students! Again in his capacity as chairman of the finance committee, Hennessy also helped attract good insurance for the college. He recognized the value of his efforts: "It is pretty nice to sit in a meeting and have something transpire and be able to say that we have the finest coverage that we can buy within our limit."[40] From the time of his early tenure until the end, the college went through drastic changes that have fortified its foundations for the long-term. When Spike's doctor recommended he step down from the board for health reasons, Spike wrote to the board of trustees to say, "During the past 30 years the stature of Hillsdale College has changed from a typical Liberal Arts College, one without an actual goal, to a nationally recognized institution, one with adequate motivation and established programs to become the best small Liberal Arts College in the United States.... [P]articipating with all of you has been a responsibility and an honor for me."[41]

When Spike lost his battle with emphysema and his heart gave way in 1982, he had made provisions in his estate plans to provide for Hillsdale College. Spike created the Helen Mooty Hennessy Scholarship for students to honor his wife when she passed away. From 1966 through the settling of their estate in 1994, the Hennessys gave Hillsdale College fifty-nine gifts totaling more than $2.5 million.[42] The college continued to receive benefits from his estate plans for more than ten years following his passing. Each year, when school officials received a generous portion of his bequest, they were reminded of how precious private initiative can be and of the sacrifice and commitment of so many who fought the important battles in Hillsdale's history.

Because of Spike and Helen Hennessy, the college got to where it is now, known around the country as the "bastion of freedom" and a "conservative showpiece." It stands as an institution of the best American ideals, and its principles have stood the test of time, remaining as they were when the college founders established its 1844 Articles of Incorporation. Twelve hundred students across America now have the opportunity to study those ideas so central to America's founding without adherence to political correctness or division by racial preferences and quotas. Instead, the college stands on its record, perched upon a hill in rural Michigan, attracting the world's best scholars, leaders, and policy makers to educate its students.[43]

But it is his family's success, starting from a humble, next-to-nothing Prussian beginning to operating the world's fifth and the country's third largest brewery, that supported the Heritage Foundation's growth.

The Family and Its Brewery

Adolph Coors, born in 1847 in a place now called Wuppertal, Germany, grew up as an apprentice working under local townspeople. His most important apprenticeship was with the Henry Wenker Brewery. During his tutelage there, both of Adolph's parents died, leaving him and his two younger siblings to fend for themselves. The brewery offered Adolph housing, food, and clothing in exchange for his work. To earn a little more on the side, Adolph kept the company's books, gaining a fundamental understanding of the finances and bottom line.

When upheaval descended on Germany in 1868, Adolph fled the country along with half a million of his countrymen. He came to the United States on board a ship as a stowaway. He arrived in Baltimore as a penniless Prussian, but with more than his share of ambition. Ashamed for not having paid his way, Adolph later took care of the bill. Adolph began his journey westward, working as a bricklayer, stonecutter, and finally as a brewery foreman for Stenger Brewery in Naperville, Illinois, in 1869. Two years later, Adolph intended to build his own brewery with the skills he had learned in Germany as an apprentice, but he needed to find the right location. He arrived in Denver and immediately bought a partnership in a bottling company. In the interim, while working at the bottling company, he continued to search for the appropriate site for his brewery. He recognized the importance of quality water, the key ingredient in making good beer, and aimed to find a place with impeccable water.

On the banks of Clear Creek in Golden, Colorado, Adolph Coors found the ideal location. The cold springs dusted with wintry snow trickled down from the Rocky Mountains; the water was fresh and crystal clear. At an abandoned tannery, Adolph Coors and his financial partner, Jacob

———————— ★ ————————

Chapter Eight

Joseph Coors Sr.

"A courageous, principled, far-sighted conservative who made a profound impact in many different worlds—in business, in national politics, in mass communications, in public policy...Joseph Coors, without whom there would be no Heritage Foundation."[1]

—EDWIN J. FEULNER

"Heritage is my legacy." Joseph Coors Sr. quietly spoke these words at an evening celebration shortly before his death. Heritage is a defining word in the long-standing tradition of historical families in the United States. Coors could have been reminiscing about his family's origins in Prussia and later Colorado. He could have been thinking of his ancestors' work to build the Adolph Coors Brewing Company. But neither of these descriptions were the intent of his personal acknowledgment. Instead, Joseph Coors Sr. conveyed his life's meaning and most valued accomplishment in the founding and subsequent success of an organization which without him might not exist. The Heritage Foundation is the legacy of Joseph Coors Sr.

Schueler, opened "The Golden Brewery" in 1873, long before Colorado had even become the thirty-eighth state.

By 1880, with the production of 3,500 barrels of beer annually, the company's profits soared, and Adolph Coors bought out his partner and became the brewery's sole owner. He also changed the name to Adolph Coors Company. Because of his rugged individualism and Golden's geographic disadvantage (both bottling and malt suppliers were great distances away), Coors began to develop his enterprise vertically. Living off very little income, Coors put every dollar back into the venture, making his own malt and building his own malt house, steam mill, bottling plant, and icehouse. The company eventually provided its own energy by burning the combustible waste products and tapping the natural gas fields located on its premises. All of these investments were made in cash—none on credit. The vertical alignment became a general philosophy of the company under the motto: "The more we do ourselves, the higher quality we have."[2] Ten years later, the brewery produced 17,600 barrels, and Adolph Coors had become an American citizen and a millionaire.[3]

The brewery faced battles from its earliest days. On Memorial Day in 1894, the Clear Creek's water rose over its banks and threatened the town of Golden and the Coors brewery. The flood swept a new addition to the brewery completely away, and the Coors family members retreated from their home for higher ground when waters threatened to sweep it downriver, too. Adolph Coors, in an effort to save the mainstay of his brewery, sent an assistant across the raging waters with a specific purpose. Coors decided to offer cash to four families living on the opposite bank. Hours later, workmen tore down their homes and carved a new trench for the river—the Clear Creek still has a bend in its path near the brewery today.

When Colorado's statewide prohibition made most of his business dealings illegal on January 1, 1916, the brewery struggled, but Adolph and his three grown sons kept the company in business. Predicting the tide against breweries, the family diversified its business and started a porcelain com-

pany, creating cooking utensils and scientific items. Later this porcelain
was used by the U.S. government for insulators at the Y-12 uranium enrich-
ing plant in Tennessee which provided the fuel for the Hiroshima atom
bomb.[4] The Coors Company also entered the real estate market, started
producing cement products, and the idle brewing equipment began making malted milk (which was mostly sold to the candy maker, Mars, Inc.)
and a near beer called "Mannah."

The Coors brewery paid its employees well, but Prohibition forced
Adolph to ask them to take pay cuts to get the company through the difficult time. The employee union refused to cooperate in the new environment and went on strike. It was the Coors Company's first taste of union
demands on employers. Adolph's son, Adolph Jr., told his father,
"[N]obody...should ever tell this family how to run its own business."[5]
Adolph fired the striking employees, and the union placed Coors on its
"unfair" list.[6] Before Prohibition, 1,568 breweries existed. Following the seventeen year ban, only 750 reopened. The Adolph Coors Brewing Company
survived.

Adolph Sr., the sole proprietor and holder of 100 percent of the shares
of the Coors Company, transferred the shares to family members in 1923.
With these transfers, Adolph Sr. advised each recipient to put the stock in
trusts without dividends so the profits could be reinvested and the company
grown.[7] It was a strategy that helped build the Coors Brewing Company
over the years.

The Grandson

By the time Prohibition ended, Adolph Coors had died, and he had
passed the company's management to his son Adolph Coors Jr. Adolph Jr.
had been educated at Cornell University in chemical engineering and
shared his father's commitment to quality and financial discipline. After
joining the company full-time, Adolph Jr.'s first accomplishment was to
invent the strong chemical porcelain that no one else supplied; the invention established the very porcelain company that helped Coors get through
Prohibition.

Adolph Jr. married Alice May, and the couple had three boys: Adolph III, William, and Joseph. The two raised their children in the white, Queen Anne home that was nearly swept away by the Clear Creek decades earlier. Joseph Coors, a quiet boy, had inherited his disposition from his grandfather Adolph Sr. He graduated from a Colorado public school and followed his father's footsteps to Cornell University where he acquired his degree in chemistry in 1939, followed by his master's in chemical engineering in 1940. Coors took his degree directly to DuPont where he worked on plastics. He then accepted a position with the National Dairy Association. These business experiences gave him important learning opportunities, which he applied in his future career. Joseph Coors joined the Coors Company's Porcelain Company (now Coorstek) in 1946.

No member of the Coors family would get a place at the helm of the company without first earning it. Joseph Coors did what so many of the Coors family members did; he worked hard from the bottom up under expectations of discipline and perfection. Joseph Coors worked in the clay pits mining the materials needed for porcelain just west of Golden. Even his brother Adolph III had been seen from time to time pulling weeds in their southern Colorado barley fields.[8] When he was rearing his own sons, they began in the company in much the same way—sweeping floors and working for the waste treatment part of the company.

His hard work paid off. Joseph Coors served Coors Brewing Company as a board member from 1942 until his retirement from the board in 2000. He also worked as a technical director (1946–1975), executive vice president (1975–77), company president (1977–1980), chief operating officer (1980–1987), and vice chairman of the board of directors (1985–2000).

Coors and his brother William propelled the company from a provincial Western brewery into a modern, highly successful corporation. Together, the two brothers, with their chemical engineering backgrounds, pioneered a new brewing technique whereby beer would be filtered and packaged cold. Therefore, it would be unpasteurized, fresher, and of higher quality once it arrived at distribution outlets. Most other American beers are sold pasteurized after passing through a heating unit which kills the yeast before being cooled. If left in a warm temperature, this beer will spoil; it also goes through a change of flavor when pasteurized.

The Coors brothers also propelled the development of the first two-piece aluminum can. Joseph and William Coors followed the philosophy of their grandfather and his fiscal conservatism. The Coors Company held the rights to the production of this new liquid container, but rather than produce cans for the entire market's demand, Coors Container Co. sold the patent to other packaging production companies including Continental Can Co. and American Can Co. In order to produce cans for the entire industry, they would have had to borrow funds from banks to get the large-scale operation running—and the Coors Company had never operated on credit.[9] Sticking to their grandfather's commitment to self-sufficiency, the company produced only its own cans—billions of them. The two brothers also initiated the first far-reaching recycling program by offering a 1¢ return on Coors aluminum cans in 1959. By 1970, the company itself purchased cans from consumers for recycling for 10¢ a pound.[10]

The Rocky Mountain brew could be found in only eleven states in the West (where it led its competitors in each state except for Texas where it couldn't be found in all areas) for much of the 1900s. President Eisenhower requested his supply of Coors beer be brought to the White House on board an Air Force plane. President Ford packed Coors in his luggage on return trips to Washington from ski vacations in Colorado.[11] Henry Kissinger carried cases back from his trips to California. And actor Paul Newman required Coors beer on ice at all his movie sets and refused to be seen in a picture drinking anything but Coors beer, believing it is "the best American beer, bar none."[12]

Starting in the mid-1970s, the company opened markets into two or three new states each year.[13] Joseph Coors served the Coors Brewing Company for forty-one years, and during that time its production grew from roughly three hundred thousand barrels annually to more than twenty million when he retired. It had become the nation's third and the world's fifth largest brewer.

While the Coors Company grew in strength, both Joseph and William lived modestly, sharing an office with desks a foot apart at the company headquarters. Since their grandfather's first steps on American soil, the family "shunned ostentation."[14] Their children went to public school, they occupied humble homes, drove regular old cars, and took small allowances from the company so they could reinvest in its future. Joseph's children even had to go to their friends' homes to see color television as late as the 1960s. Coors biographer Dan Baum wrote, "None of the brothers minded their humble lifestyle. They had all they needed. Coorses didn't work for money. They worked to make the best product possible. Their products were beer and ceramics, so that's where the money went."[15]

The Coors Company had always treated its employees well. Their salaries were higher than average for the Denver area, workers received free beer in the cafeteria, and the working conditions were in upscale, spacious, computerized areas.[16] Even still, the Coors brothers faced trouble through the years, especially when dealing with organized labor—a nuisance their father and grandfather had also confronted over the years. In 1957, they successfully battled the local chapter of the International Brewery, Flour, Cereal and Softdrink Workers Union for 118 days at Coors. They were angered upon learning the union fined workers who crossed a picket line, but got through the strike by hiring college students and asking the supervisors to pick up the extra work.

In 1968, thirteen construction crews went on strike. When the company refused to negotiate their contracts, many of the men resigned their union membership and came back to work.[17] On April 5, 1977, workers went on strike at the Colorado brewery under Joseph Coors's tenure as president. The AFL-CIO launched a nationwide ten-year boycott of the beer, and its sales suffered dramatically. In California alone, the state that provided more than 45 percent of its total volume, sales plummeted by 15 percent.[18] Two months later, a radical group bombed a Coors warehouse in California and threatened Joseph Coors's life. Coors took this threat with extreme seriousness. Fifteen years before, in February 1960, his older brother, Adolph

III, had been killed in a botched kidnapping attempt. The strike ended after twenty months, and the next year the employees voted down the Teamsters' attempt to organize the workforce. Joseph Coors in particular saw unions as a heavy hand trying to tell him how to run his business.

Joseph had learned through the generations of Coors family entrepreneurship the respect for hard work and self-sufficiency. Anytime government or unions intruded into the affairs of a proprietor's business, it hurt. He knew how Prohibition had damaged the firm. When the government first introduced zip codes in 1963, Joseph Coors refused to implement the new mail system on his Coors Brewery stationery for years in protest of the added government regulation.[19] He saw for himself how the battles over time with the unions affected sales and growth. Above all, he despised encroaching powers restricting his freedom to run his enterprise as he saw fit.

As president of Coors, he was a public figure, and he began to become more involved in public affairs, both in Colorado and on a national scale. Encouraged by his favorite authors David Hume, Adam Smith, and Mark Twain, Joseph Coors became more deeply involved in popularizing his conservative principles. In particular, he read Russell Kirk's *The Conservative Mind*. As the grandson of a successful entrepreneur, he found comfort with Kirk's thesis on the importance of tradition and "wisdom of our ancestors." Dan Baum, a Coors biographer, wrote, "For Joe, it was all right there in Kirk's book: If family tradition had taught Joseph anything, it was that progress grew out of the freedom to manage one's own property, that the division between owner and employee was honorable, that nobody was 'entitled' to anything he didn't earn himself, and that government efforts to 'perfect society'—whether through alcohol prohibition or taxation for social programs—only bred misery."[20]

Joseph Coors was incensed at the prominence of "entitlements" that seemed to permeate American culture. Whereas his grandfather had arrived without a penny in his pocket and became a millionaire in seventeen years through his own hard work and skill, Joseph was skeptical if this was possible now—not because of people themselves, but rather because of confiscatory taxation and other restrictions on freedom. In a rare *Wall Street Journal* interview in 1981, Joseph Coors said, "Freedom of action— the freedom to start or carry on a business and act in a responsible fashion, to be successful—is basic to the capitalist system.... If a person has these freedoms, as my grandfather and father had, then he is able to build up an operation."[21] Such a philosophy, a philosophy threatened, propelled Joseph Coors to become more involved in promoting these values for the future.

Joseph Coors volunteered for the Goldwater campaign in 1964, attended several campaign strategy sessions, and he liked what Goldwater had to say. When actor Ronald Reagan gave a televised speech on behalf of Goldwater, Joseph Coors was mesmerized. So much so that he bolted straight to his father following the 1964 campaign and asked what he would think if his son considered running for the Jefferson County School Board. Because of Adolph III's kidnapping and murder, their hopes to remain relatively obscure, and the family's general stay-out-of-the-press approach to life, Adolph Jr. was skeptical of his son's new aspirations, but he relented and supported the move.[22]

Before he started his race for the school board, Coors received a visitor at the Coors Company headquarters from a University of Colorado political science professor. An opening had just emerged on the school's board of regents. According to this professor, Coors's conservative philosophy, which opposed the rampant march of Socialism on campuses and in the corridors of faculty lecture halls, would be a welcome addition to the board. After refusing to consent to run immediately, Coors did agree to meet again with the professor and a conservative member of the board of regents. Together, the two school representatives convinced him to run a statewide campaign for the slot. His campaign literature touted his message to the voters: "I believe that the University of Colorado should be dedicated to preserving and strengthening the cause of freedom in America.... There is nothing that I want more than for your children and mine to be able to look forward to a bright tomorrow in a free America...unfettered by excessive government control."²³ Colorado voters elected Joseph Coors to a six-year term on the University of Colorado Board of Regents in 1966, the same day that a man he came to admire deeply, Ronald Reagan, was elected governor of California.

Joseph Coors spent his time on the Board of Regents supporting policies to calm the rebellious campus atmosphere. He fought tirelessly against the radical student group Students for a Democratic Society (SDS), a leftist organization that supported draft resistance during Vietnam, blocked students from meeting with CIA and military recruiters on campus, and threatened all who stood in its way. In November 1968, Joseph led the charge to ban SDS from campus, which succeeded for three weeks until the board held a new vote, and the university president broke the tie in favor of SDS.²⁴

Through his work in the university system in Colorado, Coors became personally acquainted with Ronald Reagan. When Governor Reagan slashed the University of California budget by nearly 30 percent, radicals pounced and protested. Coors flew to the Republican Governors' Association meeting in Palm Springs, met Ronald Reagan and shook his hand for the first time, and pledged his support to the embattled governor.²⁵ Joseph Coors also booked Ronald Reagan to speak on his Colorado campus. Following the speech and accompanied by Lyn Nofziger, Reagan's press secretary, Ronald Reagan and Joseph Coors headed back to the airport. It was then that Coors leaned over to then-governor Reagan and asked with a twinkle in his eye, "If you become president, can I be secretary of the treasury?"²⁶ Reagan responded with a smile, "Sure, Joe."

Joseph Coors became a national delegate from Colorado for the 1968 Republican convention in Miami and was proud to cast one of the seventy-eight votes Ronald Reagan received. Reagan was defeated at that convention but still remained governor of California. Even through the defeat, he wanted to look for ways to advance his national platform. He called on Joseph Coors, a man he fondly remembered and liked, to sponsor some radio programs he intended to record to continue building his conservative base. Joseph Coors arranged for the Adolph Coors Company to sponsor the weekly broadcasts which became an important venue for Ronald Reagan to refine his conservative views. It was through these broadcasts that Reagan coined the term "welfare queen" and used the phrase to propel his welfare reform package as governor.[27]

The Heritage Foundation

Joseph Coors particularly liked being on the University of Colorado Board of Regents. He wasn't a natural politician, disliked facing the cameras and the publicity, and wasn't a skilled communicator on issues. Above all, he regretted the eventuality of having to compromise to accomplish goals and move forward. Yet he still wanted to have an impact, so he carefully considered how he could contribute to advancing his ideas. He determined he had one possession to give: money. Joseph Coors didn't live a luxurious lifestyle and had plenty to spare. He asked his assistant, a young Jack Wilson, to conduct a "nationwide search for the right 'investment.'"[28]

During his hunt, Wilson wrote a letter to Colorado senator Gordon Allott to inquire about investing in conservative causes. Senator Allott's longtime mail sorter, Barbara Hughes, happened to be out of the office the day the letter arrived, and her fill-in saw the opening text of the letter: "Dear Senator Allott. You remember me. I was news Director at KBTR in Denver. . . ."[29] Because of the media call-letter reference in the body, the substitute routed the letter to Allott's press secretary, a young grassroots organizer from Wisconsin, Paul Weyrich. Ordinarily, the letter would have found itself upon the senator's stack of incoming correspondence, or perhaps with his administrative assistant.

The letter's contents requested the senator's advice: "I have been hired by Joe Coors to help him determine where he should put his money so it can further the conservative cause."[30] When Weyrich came across that letter from Jack Wilson, he was thrilled. Paul Weyrich, aide to Senator Strom Thurmond Jim Lucier, and a Library of Congress researcher, Victor Fediay, had been strategizing about how to help conservatives advance their ideas in the country.[31] They had come to the conclusion that starting a group to provide *timely* policy-related information to members of Congress from a "principled perspective" could help immensely. The Brookings Institution had been providing the powerful liberal coalition with the ammunition it needed to secure its policy objectives for more than forty years, and conservatives had no alternative on Capitol Hill. Lucier, Fediay, and Weyrich had spent a couple years pitching the idea for a new organization to businessmen across the country, but no one stepped forward.

The letter indicated that Weyrich's call for action would finally be answered, assuming he could convince the benefactor of the project's importance. Weyrich called Jack Wilson and asked him to come to Washington a few weeks later. While in D.C., Weyrich carefully described the proposal to start a conservative organization to inform Congress. Wilson flew back to Colorado to report what he'd learned to his boss, and Weyrich began gathering endorsements from Senator Thurmond, Senator Cliff Hansen, Representative Ed Foreman, and Representative Henry Schadeberg to use as supporting materials to convince Coors that this was the right project.

When Wilson told Joseph Coors of the Weyrich proposal, he was immediately interested in the project. Coors agreed to fly to Washington himself to investigate the proposition. The program Weyrich organized to brief Coors personally on the proposal included comments from each of those who formally endorsed the project and a visit to the Nixon White House where Coors met with Lyn Nofziger, a man he had known since his days on the University of Colorado Board of Regents. It was during this visit's stop at the White House that Joseph Coors decided the project had merit.

Being a methodical and cautious businessman, Coors requested a budget and an organizational plan before agreeing to help fund the venture. Weyrich's political mentor, Fritz Rench, happened to be in Washington, D.C., that day, and Rench cancelled his existing plans and immediately put together a budget and a prospectus for the new group. He worked for three days from Senator Thurmond's office to compile the business plan.[32] Coors approved of the detailed documents, and the new group designed to counter the Left began as a subsidiary of the Coors Company. The Analysis and Research Association operated for only a short time before Coors, unhappy with its early staffing and failure to acquire further corporate sponsors, decided he wanted an alternate vehicle to the subsidiary. Weyrich, in a conversation with a fellow conservative, learned of a tax-exempt organization, the Robert M. Schuchman Memorial Foundation (named after the first president of Young Americans for Freedom who died from a brain embolism at the young age of twenty-seven) that could be easily taken over for their purposes. Joseph Coors agreed to the transition, and a new entity formally began operating in northeast Washington, D.C., just blocks from the Capitol.

Paul Weyrich, along with a young Edwin Feulner, then chief of staff to Representative Phil Crane, began the new organization, together with an investment from Joseph Coors of $250,000, a $300,000 building commitment, and a pledge for millions more down the road.[33] It wasn't long before a philosophical split within the Schuchman Foundation's board of directors caused another change.[34] Some members wanted to rely on publications and conferences as the major project initiatives, while others wanted to affect the policy process directly. Feulner and Weyrich believed strongly in the latter course. They wasted no time and set the stage for a new nonprofit organization, one that they could direct to work on issues that Congress grappled with daily.

The new venture did not yet have a name. And Joseph Coors was becoming impatient. He called Weyrich and demanded, "You will have a name by tomorrow morning."[35] While walking with his wife near his home in Annandale, Virginia, Weyrich saw a sign that said, *Coming Soon: Heritage Town Houses.*[36] The Heritage Foundation, an agreeable name to Joseph Coors, was officially incorporated in the District of Columbia in February 1973 and went on to become one of the country's largest and most effective advocacy organizations.

The Heritage Foundation planted its roots in a Washington, D.C., office suite housed in a building once occupied by a Korean grocery store and a

halfway house for drug addicts, just blocks away from its present location.[37]
The Heritage Foundation produces policy papers, books, newsletters, and
reviews of various policy-related issues that it delivers—often by hand—to
one thousand members of Congress and the administration and six thousand journalists, editors, academics, and supporters. Scores of its policy recommendations and corroborative evidence have appeared in the pages of
the most read newspapers' op-ed sections. It aims to present the information to these decision makers *prior* to key votes in order to influence legislative action. Some of the key issues it addressed from its
inception—indexing tax rates against inflation, tax cuts, welfare reform, privatization, and school choice—have become law. It has come so far from
its humble, early roots to become a powerhouse for creating, promoting,
and inspiring conservative policy changes that are crucial to America's
future success.

For an institution whose workers were once dubbed "little nobodies,"
the Heritage Foundation's policy victories and other accomplishments have
been far-reaching, but primarily came to bear during the Reagan administration.[38] The organization's work is perhaps best documented by its *Mandate for Leadership* publication, which it produced prior to Ronald
Reagan's 1980 election on a gamble that he would win. It took less than
one year to complete the project—nearly three thousand manuscript pages
in the first draft. More than 250 people worked for months on the final one
thousand page book to present government-wide policy reform recommendations to Ronald Reagan, not one of them receiving any compensation for his efforts.[39]

The *Mandate for Leadership: Policy Management in a Conservative
Administration* was a government-wide study into the thirteen government
agencies, and it recommended more than two thousand policy changes.
President Reagan distributed copies of *Mandate for Leadership* at his first
cabinet meeting. The new director of the Office of Management and
Budget, David Stockman, said, "Leaders in both the new administration
and the Congress will find in this work all of the tools they need to 'hit the

ground running.'"[40] The United Press International called the heavy book "a blueprint for grabbing the government by its frayed New Deal lapels and shaking out 48 years of liberal policies."[41] The paperback version earned a place on the *Washington Post's* best-seller list. Some fifteen thousand copies sold—a huge number considering that policy discussions dominated its contents.[42] By the end of Ronald Reagan's first term, authors of the *Mandate* suspect nearly 60 percent of the two thousand recommendations had been implemented or initiated—some 1,270 reforms, including the 1981 tax cut, a sub-minimum wage for youth, and the "Star Wars" defense system.[43] In addition, several dozen of the *Mandate's* authors acquired appointments in the administration because of their work. The *Mandate* cost the Heritage Foundation more than $250,000 to produce, but it was a meager sum considering its broad impact.

Then came Ronald Reagan's reelection. The day after he won, presidential counselor Edwin Meese placed a 580-page *Mandate for Leadership II* in his hands. This time, the volume contained 1,300 policy provisions for the new administration, and within a week all the relevant chapters had been distributed to members of the cabinet. It was, according to the *New York Times*, "the hottest ticket in town . . . a major media production."[44] It primarily called for a reduction in spending through privatization measures in Social Security, public housing, and air-traffic control. Following his reelection in 1985, the Heritage Foundation presented Ronald Reagan with a fifty-four-page briefing book on how to deal with Soviet Premier Gorbachev before his Geneva summit.

The Heritage Foundation continued to publish similar books for subsequent leaders and administrations. It produced *Mandate for Leadership III: Policy Strategies for the 1990s*; *Mandate for Leadership IV: Turning Ideas Into Action*; and 2001's *Priorities for the President*. Each of the well-researched volumes gave conservatives a platform and a how-to guide to make government smaller and more efficient.

Ten years after the Heritage Foundation got its start, its impact on the country could be seen by all. In 1984, after the Heritage Foundation delivered its *Mandate* to Ronald Reagan, it purchased an eight-story facility just blocks from the Capitol. It had become the largest think tank in Washington with a $10 million budget and more than one hundred employees.[45] Even the liberal *New Republic* claimed it to be "the most important think tank in the nation's capital."[46] Lee Edwards, conservative author and scholar, reported, "Just a decade after its birth, Heritage became a physical as well as an intellectual landmark in the nation's capital."[47] At that time, even the *New York Times* admitted that the Heritage Foundation surpassed the Brookings Institution in impact, saying it had become "the most influential of these organizations."[48]

Twenty years after the Heritage Foundation's start, Newt Gingrich put together his "Contract with America" legislative agenda and included proposals that the Heritage Foundation researchers recommended. Among those, an adoption tax credit for families which eventually became law. The president of the U.S.A. Committee for International Association of Voluntary Adoption Agencies and NGOs, William Pierce, said that without Joseph Coors's funding "there would be no Heritage Foundation and without Heritage, there would have been no expert to pick up on an idea promoted by the National Council For Adoption adoption tax credits." "So," added Mr. Pierce, "it would not be surprising if those adoptive parents who consume a malt beverage were to pick one with the name 'Coors' on it to toast the man whose vision indirectly led to their getting financial help to build their family through adoption."[49]

In 1995, the Heritage Foundation launched a Website, Townhall.com, that combined daily writings from conservatives in one place, along with job bank information, upcoming events, and book recommendations. Townhall.com features writings from more than one hundred authors and news and information from more than 120 different organizations. The Website started operating as its own entity separate from the Heritage Foundation in 2005 in order to expand its role further.

The Heritage Foundation, according to Conservative Movement historian George Nash, "deliberately assumed the role of facilitator, liaison, and clearinghouse for the entire conservative public policy network."[50] Today, it connects more than two thousand scholars and activists around the country through its Resource Bank; produces an annual three-inch thick *Guide to Public Policy Experts*, which contains contact information for the nation's conservative leaders; and publishes a pamphlet called *The Insider*, which compiles news from around the globe as it relates to conservatism and the spread of freedom.

Joseph Coors didn't only help the Heritage Foundation by providing critical funds, although at one time, he gave more than half of its budget.[51] He also served on its board of directors, offering keen insight into efficient operations and management and advice from his own entrepreneurial experience. He convinced its top leaders of the need to run it like a business by paying careful attention to the bottom line, and he sought to ensure it had a sufficient operating reserve set aside for the tight times.[52] *Policy Review*, a journal put forward by the Heritage Foundation, gave conservative scholars an opportunity to get their messages heard on cutting edge research or studies that affect policy. Heritage president Edwin Feulner sold the journal to the Hoover Institution, because he thought the money to produce it could be used better elsewhere, probably in no small measure due to Coors's input.[53]

Coors also had a special appreciation for marketing as a result of his entrepreneurial experience with the Coors Company. He acknowledged that the Coors Company's slow pace of growth was due largely to spending less than $1 per barrel of beer on marketing. Adolph Coors Sr. opposed allocating resources to marketing, but Joseph and William Coors began to appreciate its importance over the years. While the Coors Company sold its merchandise, the Heritage Foundation sold its ideas. Authors John Micklethwait and Adrian Wooldridge suggest, "Heritage is as passionate about selling conservative ideas as Coca-Cola is about selling fizzy drinks."[54] As part of its marketing strategy, the Heritage Foundation utilized a short two-page brief that could be hand-delivered to busy members of Congress on the fly, and it maintained a stack of colored note cards with brief sound

bites pre-scrawled for conservatives to use on upcoming television interviews. "Marketing is a big component of our program here. It's something
we stress,'" President Edwin Feulner told the *Wall Street Journal*.[55] Historian James Smith agrees. "What Heritage has shown is that ideas are products that can be marketed, bought, and sold just like anything else," he
said.[56]

In 1999, the Heritage Foundation celebrated its twenty-fifth anniversary.
President Edwin Feulner tucked a small business card into the breast
pocket of his suit. On it was the figure $100,957,372, the tally of the Her-
itage Foundation's most recent fund-raising drive, the largest for a public
affairs organization in the country.[57] The organization at that time
employed more than 180 workers and operated on an annual budget of $30
million. This budget had grown to be one-third larger than that of its coun-
terpart, the Brookings Institution, and the Heritage Foundation had
become the most quoted think tank in the country.[58]

The still-growing Heritage Foundation's impact is profound; as of 2007,
its near $40 million budget and more than $150 million in net assets indicate its staying power. Conservatives at all levels of government and the pri-
vate sector now rely on the Heritage Foundation to make their decisions.
Senator Tom Coburn in 2005 even kept a copy of *The Heritage Guide to
the Constitution* at his side during the Senate Judiciary Hearing of Supreme
Court Justice Samuel Alito. With hard work, precision, and ambition, the
Heritage Foundation's story of surging growth paralleled that of the Adolph
Coors Company. On the evening of its twenty-fifth anniversary, Joseph
Coors announced, "Nothing has ever happened in my life that has made
me prouder."[59]

The Television News Inc.

In 1973, conservatives had no evenhanded source to turn to for their
news reporting. They relied on ABC, NBC, and CBS in addition to major
newspapers of the day such as the *New York Times* and the *Washington Post*.
Paul Weyrich, along with an investment banker, Robert Pauley, suggested

that Joseph Coors start a television news network to provide twenty-four hour accurate and objective coverage of the day's leading stories. This was seven years before CNN, long before any of the other cable news stations that cover the news today, and before satellite television. The only alternative to the network news at the time was syndicated newsfilm services that provided sports and feature service to their clients via air-express post. Using the mail, the newsfilm services couldn't provide news because by the time the film reached the local outlet, it was no longer new. Transmitting news electronically through network audio-video hookups into telephone company lines, like the big three networks did, was cost prohibitive. Weyrich's convincing encouraged Joseph Coors to recognize the unmet need that he could fulfill. Coors had the resources to make it work, and if they were lucky, it could become an alternative to the liberally biased news departments at the big three networks.[60]

With the backing of the Adolph Coors Company, Television News Inc. (TVN) started broadcasting out of New York City in May 1973. With a budget of $2.5 million and a crew of fifty reporters, cameramen, and secretaries, TVN provided twenty-five film packages of hard news, sports, and features through line-fed video that stations could add into their newscasts as they wanted. It was, at the time, the "only non-network source of national and international newsfilm for the nation's commercial TV stations."[61] Coors hoped this strategy would allow local newsrooms to have more autonomy from their mother networks. The news coverage went to more than eighty stations in sixteen U.S. states (from California to Missouri to Massachusetts) and Canada.

In early 1975, TVN began preparations to set up its own television transmission through a domestic satellite. This new technology would have made it the first television network to make such a bold initiative.[62] It budgeted between $10 and $12 million to build satellite ground stations. Joseph Coors believed that satellite programming and its freedom would attract dozens of new stations to the Television News feeds. But the timing just wasn't right. The network lost nearly $500,000 each month in operation, a handsome sum even for Joseph Coors. In the first year alone, the Coors Company lost more than $2 million on the venture, but the next year eclipsed the first with losses of $3 million.[63] By the venture's end, it had cost Joseph Coors more than $8 million, a figure which totals more than $30 million today.[64]

TVN's demise is attributable to a source other than timing, as well: the mainstream media which had everything to lose with its success. Coors had been nominated by Nixon and resubmitted by Ford for a position on the board of directors for the Corporation for Public Broadcasting. Months of hearings on his nomination in the Senate Communications Subcommittee followed and included accusations and charges of character incongruity. Senator Lowell P. Weicker Jr. alleged, "A pattern of insensitivity and bad judgment...threads through everything the man [Coors] does."[65] Committee chairman Senator John Pastore told Coors publicly during one of the hearings, "No nomination which has come before this subcommittee has bothered me more than yours."[66] Charles Baker, executive director of the Institute for American Democracy, testified against the Coors nomination and criticized him for "directing more personal and corporate resources into the battle for his beliefs than any other living super-patriot."[67] It was an odd attack, considering Joseph Coors was a man who used to "[think] you can write to your congressman and get something done."[68] Coors was not deterred by the criticism; rather, he believed it reinforced the need for conservatives to step forward on behalf of their principles.

Both Senator Weicker and Senator Robert P. Griffin used the hearings to pressure Coors to resign his chairmanship of the TVN board. Coors made his intentions clear: "More than anything else, I am seeking this job because the President of the United States asked me to. I consider it a dictum."[69] Joseph Coors didn't back down, and the subcommittee rejected his nomination. All of the major news networks carried stories for months on Coors's Senate hearings as did the major newspapers, including the *New York Times*, the *Wall Street Journal*, and the *Washington Post*. He became labeled the "ultraconservative zealot."[70] The stations which were considering carrying TVN's feeds at the time had no positive reinforcement to do so. Rather, they faced scrutiny from being connected to this "zealot."

While TVN ultimately shut down in October 1975, less than two years after its start, its activities were not without positive consequence. Charles Gibson, immediately prior to joining ABC's *World News* as a correspondent, spent a year covering the Nixon resignation and Watergate trials for TVN. A more compelling individual, however, also acquired experience at TVN. Hired to be Joseph Coors's news director was a young and inexperienced conservative publicist: Roger Ailes. He had never been a journalist before, but he had coordinated television spots for Richard Nixon. Twenty-five years before he would turn Fox News into the most-watched news network, Roger Ailes got his first newsroom experience working for a project funded by Joseph Coors.

Ailes took the lead in changing two key components of TVN's methods. He first suggested making the news segments shorter than they were at one and a half minutes. He hoped this would attract news outlets that used "currently fashionable 'action news' formats."[71] He also was one of the forces behind building the satellite ground stations to challenge the three networks. TVN didn't make it to see Ailes's plans to fruition, but CNN used the technology just five years later.

Rupert Murdoch asked Roger Ailes, who led CNBC in 1996, to lead his new venture, Fox News. Murdoch suspected a gap in the news media market. All those who were fed up with network news and the likes of CNN wanted an alternative source and would perhaps turn to a new outfit for their news if it could get off the ground. Ailes's formula included emphasizing talking heads and controversy, minimizing foreign reporting, and using intellectual debates to stimulate interest, all under the rubrics of responsible journalism. Ailes noted at the time, "We are committed to providing viewers with more news in less time that is fair and balanced."[72] He used a tactic with Fox News that he had tried with TVN: short news segments. Only this time, it worked. Fox News surpassed CNN in 2002 as the most watched news channel and has never looked back.

Fox's successes are immeasurable. Trent Lott said during the 2000 Florida recount, "If it hadn't been for Fox, I don't know what I would have done for the news."[73] Newt Gingrich declared, "If there is one channel on in a Washington office that I visit, it's usually Fox."[74] Most impressive, though, has been Fox News's impact on the news market in general. Capturing interviews with key conservatives and covering stories that relate to conservatives have tended to encourage the other networks to cover similar perspectives, especially following Fox's surge in ratings.

The Strategic Defense Initiative

The Soviet threat burdened President Reagan in the early 1980s. Thousands of Soviet warheads pointed in America's direction, and the uncertainty surrounding the relationship between the two countries only put the entire administration on edge about what would come of it all. Joseph Coors was, at the time, a committed anti-Communist. He told a *Wall Street Journal* reporter, "I am a strong believer that communism is wrong and a strong believer that socialism is not the best way for people of the world to be controlled or governed."[75] Coors had also refused to open his beer market to the millions of Chinese beer drinkers all because they were Communists, and the Coors Company repudiated doing business with the Communists, no matter how much it restricted the bottom line.[76]

Joseph Coors maintained his contacts with Ronald Reagan, especially leading up to the 1976 presidential campaign and into his 1980 victory. Even though he had been nominated to a prominent post by President Ford, Coors remained loyal to Ronald Reagan. They were "ideological soul mates."[77] Coors once told a reporter that Ronald Reagan "would be better able than Ford to do the things I think are important for this nation. For example, we need to balance the budget.... We should try to reduce the amount of bureaucratic involvement in the business world.... What says it all is that adage, 'The government that governs best governs least.'"[78] Author Dan Baum describes the congruity of the two men: "They were of a piece—simple men of uncomplicated vision, conservative in their gut, rooted in the West and instinctively mistrustful of the East."[79] Coors contributed the maximum legal amount to Ronald Reagan's campaign long before he even announced his 1976 candidacy.[80] He also personally funded more than $18,000 in newspapers ads in Florida before the Republican primary and continued to help Ronald Reagan whenever he could—whether financially or otherwise.[81] One of the more poignant ways Coors helped President Reagan came from a joint acquaintance with whom Coors reconnected in the administration once Reagan was elected president.

Edward Teller was the father of the hydrogen bomb. He and Joseph Coors had participated in some of the same anti-Communist gatherings in the 1960s, and Teller had invited Coors to visit the Lawrence Livermore Laboratory to see the new technology he was developing when Coors worked with the University of Colorado Board of Regents. The technology was a sort of "Star Wars" vision of defense that could shield America from incoming ballistic missiles through a system of weapons and high-tech sensors that would destroy the impending threat midair. Concurrently, after Reagan was elected governor of California, he went to see Teller at the Lawrence Livermore Laboratory to learn more about "Star Wars" and the new technology that could help the United States defend itself against a rogue Soviet warhead.

Years later, Teller recruited a group of prominent businessmen close to Ronald Reagan to form the High Frontier group. Those individuals included Joseph Coors, Jaquelin Hume, and William Wilson among others. The Heritage Foundation financed the High Frontier group's first study, which concluded that a global ballistic missile-defense system could be created and implemented.[82] In January 1982, the group, escorted to the White House by Joseph Coors, held a meeting with President Reagan. Originally scheduled for fifteen minutes, Reagan allowed the meeting to last for more than an hour. Teller informed the president of the anti-missile defense possibilities.

Ronald Reagan, a former spokesman for General Electric, worked under the motto "Progress is our most important product," and was receptive to the anti-missile system. In a February 7, 1983, speech, just six weeks before he announced his Strategic Defense Initiative (SDI), Reagan said, "God gave angels wings. He gave mankind dreams. And with his help, there's no limit to what can be accomplished."[83]

The Soviets, and Gorbachev in particular, learned of the new technology and feared that the shield would negate their lead in offensive weapons and their prospective "First Strike" advantage. The USSR's economy couldn't handle additional military expenditures to speed up work on its own missile defense project. This reality forced General Secretary Gorbachev to place SDI on the negotiating table. If the USSR would give up some if its offensive weapons, would the U.S. abandon SDI? The implications and Soviet fears of U.S.-acquired SDI brought Gorbachev to the Geneva and Reykjavik arms reduction talks. Gorbachev aimed to negotiate reductions in his nuclear arsenal, contingent on Ronald Reagan scrapping SDI. Ronald Reagan forcefully said time and time again, *"The SDI is not a bargaining chip."*[84] But during the Reykjavik meeting, it became quite clear this was the only way Gorbachev would make a deal. At the last minute, after agreements had been reached without a discussion of SDI, Gorbachev tested Ronald Reagan and declared with a smile, "This all depends, of course, on you giving up SDI."[85] Ronald Reagan stood up, announced that the meeting had ended, and left abruptly. It was the beginning of the end of the Soviet Union. Ronald Reagan wrote in his autobiography, "Some people may take a different view, but if I had to choose the single most important reason, on the United States' side, for the historic breakthroughs that were to occur during the next five years in the quest for peace and a better relationship with the Soviet Union, I would say it was the Strategic Defense Initiative."[86]

All the Rest

For his work promoting his values, Joseph Coors became known as the "godfather" of the Colorado mafia—a supposed reference to his close relationship with President Reagan and his uncanny ability to accomplish his goals.[87] Bertram Wolfe, former Soviet Communist turned author and scholar, once wrote to Coors lamenting, "I have been very much disturbed by the poor and unjust press reports you were getting in Washington."[88] Coors didn't seem to care much about the media critiques and responded, "It is not my normal nature to want publicity but I seem to be getting a good deal of it anyway."[89]

Perhaps congruent with the media's treatment of his efforts, Coors paid particular attention to the mainstream press and funded several efforts to curb its influence. He served on the board and contributed to Morality in Media, which seeks to reduce obscenity in the media. He funded and joined the board for the Christian Broadcasting Network in the 1980s, the first Christian station in the country and the largest ministry on television. He helped Reed Irvine's Accuracy in Media, an outfit that seeks to correct biased and erroneous news reporting. Coors also helped strengthen the National Journalism Center first led by M. Stanton Evans, an institution which over its history has graduated more than 1,200 aspiring journalists and placed them in positions of prominence in the media from the *Wall Street Journal* to *Forbes* to MSNBC.

Coors also continued building new groups and new initiatives—a hallmark of his philanthropy. He helped Paul Weyrich establish the Committee for the Survival of a Free Congress. While Heritage contributed to the intellectual and policy debate on the Hill, Free Congress was set up as a political action committee and could, therefore, engage in activities to promote the election of those members it found to subscribe to its core values. Coors subsidized House Speaker Newt Gingrich's travel and other promotional activities for his book *Window of Opportunity*, which proposed reforms to the U.S. government.[90] He assisted Phyllis Schlafly's efforts to kill the proposed Equal Rights Amendment to the Constitution. He provided a $250,000 loan (which he forgave) to Ward Connerly's American Civil Rights Coalition to promote Proposition 54, an attempt to block state and local authorities from collecting race-based data in California.[91] He gave $100,000 toward the purchase and preservation efforts of Rancho del Cielo,

President Reagan's California ranch, which now stands dedicated to young people as a dynamic facility to teach Reagan's convictions and accomplishments. He contributed generously to causes including Young Americans for Freedom, Young America's Foundation, and the Leadership Institute. He also served on the board of overseers for the Hoover Institution on War, Revolution, and Peace—a center at Stanford University devoted to the study of international affairs.

When Joseph Coors said, "Heritage is my legacy," he meant it. His family's commitment to building the Adolph Coors Company and his experiences in developing the Conservative Movement from the ground up have created a triumphant heritage which will remain his legacy forever. So many groups and policy measures often led by the Heritage Foundation's innovative approach wouldn't exist today without his philanthropy. Just as Adolph Coors gouged a new path for the Clear Creek when his company's future was threatened by rising water, so, too, Joseph Coors helped carve a new path for America's future.[92]

Chapter Nine

———————— ★ ————————

John Engalitcheff

*"I will do my best to use my American training and education
for the benefit of this country and for the community."*[1]

—JOHN ENGALITCHEFF

He was a Russian prince by birth and an American inventor when he died. He is unknown to most, yet his story reads like the fairy tale children yearn to hear night after night at bedtime. This prince led a regal young life being born into a monarchical dynasty complete with riches and wealth, titles and jewels. When the Bolshevik Revolution threatened his family, Prince Jean Engalitcheff relinquished it all and risked his life to fight Russian Communists, ended up in a German prison, and eventually found his way to the United States. He worked tirelessly from the depths of desperation to amass a $100 million personal fortune that he would eventually turn over once again. This time, a significant portion of the accomplished entrepreneur's wealth went purposefully to negate the spread of Communism and preserve American freedom.

The uprising of workers against Czar Nicholas Romanov culminated in January 1905 with the massacre referred to as Bloody Sunday. This democratic revolution of sorts eventually molded into a totalitarian regime commandeered by Vladimir Lenin. Prince Ivan and Princess Barbara Engalitcheff gave birth to Prince Jean in July 1907, just two years after the first Russian revolution. They lived in a Moscow palace during the winter and at a country estate for the warm summer months. Prince Ivan Engalitcheff, a graduate of the Russian Imperial Academy of Art, was a chamberlain in the imperial Russian court, famous for its art and couture fashion. During the first two years of young Prince Jean's life, more than two thousand Russians were executed as a result of the czar's defense of his imperial powers.

Rasputin, the Russian peasant with alleged abilities to heal the czar's son's hemophilia, came to save the monarch's heir in 1908. After snatching the ear of the czarina herself, Rasputin wielded his influence until his murder in 1916. His death signaled the ultimate rise of radicals in Russia, and the Bolshevik revolution would begin just months later in 1917. Communism, the ultimate repression of freedom, took hold and overwhelmed the nation for more than seven decades.

Upon the Romanov family's abdication of authority, the Russian Provisional Government kept the family safe in various locations. The family was later imprisoned by the Soviets and then destroyed when Lenin ordered the gruesome execution of the czar, czarina, and their royal heirs.[2] The Engalitcheff royal family—Prince Jean's parents, Prince Ivan and Princess Barbara, and sister, Eugenie—fled their inherited positions and wealth. A peasant who had received word that they were in grave danger knocked on the door of the family estate and saved their lives with his warning, just two hours prior to the arrival of Soviet Cheka who had orders to arrest them. Prince Ivan, Princess Barbara, Jean, and Eugenie left an hour later on a train bound for southern White Army–controlled Russia, having swallowed a few selected jewels with which to start a new life. At the time, Jean's two brothers, Cyril and Nicholas, served in the White Army. In 1919, upon the

White Army's defeat, Prince Ivan and Princess Barbara escaped to Serbia, leaving the boys behind. Separated and fleeing for their lives, the family didn't reunite until each had finally set foot on American soil twelve years later in Maryland.

Prior to Prince Jean's arrival in New York and then Baltimore, he served as a navy apprentice seaman for General Wrangel's navy. Members of the White Army, as it was called, objected to the atheism promoted by the Bolsheviks and wanted to give the people the ability to choose their form of government freely. Wrangel's troops, with the support of the Brits and the French, fought War Commissar Leon Trotsky's Red Army advance near Crimea (Ukraine) in 1920. Jean eventually landed in a German prison because of his efforts. He had risked his life to reverse the spread of Communism early in his youth and never lost sight of that objective.

Upon his release from prison, Prince Jean traveled all over Europe in search of his family. His journey must have been difficult. Years later, after watching the movie *Dr. Zhivago* at a Laurel, Maryland, drive-in, he commented that the overflowing trains shown in the film were nothing compared to his personal experience. Close friends heard him say once, "You don't know what it means to be hungry," but months of doubting his next meal gave him this keen perception.[3]

Jean finally tracked down his parents and sister in Belgrade, Yugoslavia. He remained at his family's side and graduated from a Russian high school within the Yugoslav capital. It is unclear exactly when he graduated, or if he pursued further education while there. Biographer Susan Monshaw reported that he attended one year of postsecondary schooling at a Belgrade university before he achieved a scholarship to attend Johns Hopkins University in 1925.

While four of the family members had found each other in Yugoslavia, Prince Jean's two brothers wouldn't be reunited until some years later. Brother Cyril, a graduate of the Imperial Cavalry School at Saint Petersburg, served as a captain with the White Russian forces in the World War before fleeing the Bolsheviks. He arrived ahead of the other family members in New York on November 2, 1923, from Bremen, Germany, on board the ship, *George Washington*. Jean's other brother, Nicholas, appears to have arrived in the United States under the name "Anghelcovitch" in January 1924. He married the daughter of Czar Nicholas's aide, Miss Natalie Platoff, and sculpted for a living in Baltimore.

The two brothers worked tirelessly to raise the necessary funds to enable their parents, sister, and brother Jean to get to the United States. Cyril in particular suffered from a long illness in Baltimore, his family attributing his early death on August 27, 1933, to self-deprivation (he was just thirty-six years old).[4] He conserved all financial resources and neglected his own personal nourishment in order not only to get his family to the United States, but also to support them once they arrived. Though he paid dearly with his life, Cyril succeeded. Prince Ivan received a letter in 1924 from his son, who had saved enough for their transportation. Once immigration quotas permitted, Prince Ivan and Princess Barbara departed Europe for the land of freedom and opportunity.

Ivan and Barbara Engalitcheff arrived in New York City as refugees from Bremen, Germany, on June 19, 1924. They disembarked from the ship named *President Harding* and registered to enter the country under the names "Ivan and Varvara Engalitscheff." Their misspelled names were likely due to the communication confusion during the entry process. Ivan used his artistic abilities to set up a studio in Baltimore where he painted portraits until his death in 1937. Barbara made a living as a seamstress. According to a friend of the family, Georganna Long, "If you had your trousseau sewn by Mrs. E, you were top-notch."[5] Her skill in sewing this bridal wear earned her a high reputation in Baltimore. Barbara Engalitcheff continued to live in Baltimore with her daughter, Eugenie, who also specialized in needlework, until her passing in 1953. Eugenie married the White Russian Georges Rodzevitch (son of Czar Nicholas's sister Olga) and arrived in Baltimore via Paris, France, in 1929. Georges worked as an architect and interior decorator, often receiving prestigious commissions in Baltimore. Perhaps appropriately, he designed the Russian Orthodox Church of St. Nicholas in Baltimore in 1955, which still stands today.

Prince Jean, upon his American entry under section 4(c) of the Immigration Act of 1924 as a "nonquota immigrant student," arrived with nothing except a dream to make a new life for himself and his family in the country of opportunity and freedom. Upon entry, he relinquished his aristocratic title of "prince," as did the rest of his family, and thus he was called John Engalitcheff Jr. The family finances in the early days of getting settled in America were described by the Naturalization Service of the Department of Labor as "desperate" because of the passing of the family financier, brother Cyril, in 1933.[6] Their poverty in Baltimore contrasted starkly with the riches and palaces they once enjoyed in Moscow.

John Engalitcheff enrolled at Johns Hopkins University and became a well-liked student at the Baltimore establishment. Limited in English language skills (he could speak no English when he arrived), though proficient in four other languages, including Russian, French, German, and Serbian, Engalitcheff pursued an educational track requiring limited linguistic abilities: engineering. He struggled through courses in English, while mastering his mathematics and physics classes. Assignments took hours to decipher—he often reread paragraphs multiple times to understand their meanings. He later commented, "In college I took Mechanical Engineering on the firm conviction of my family that I was mechanically inclined. On looking back, that conviction apparently came from my inability to conquer Latin and my complete dislike of it."[7] Friend and colleague Fred Long reported that he "spoke to the dean of the Engineering College in French, to his advisor in German, and to his chemistry teacher in Russian."[8] He passed all his courses the first year, except English.

John Engalitcheff's time at Johns Hopkins meant a great deal to him. He kept a letter from the admissions office framed behind his desk through his working years which said, "Please admit [Mr.] Engalitcheff to your classes. The question of credits will be determined later."[9] His gratitude became evident years later when his wife helped establish a mechanical engineering laboratory at Johns Hopkins University to honor his accomplishments there following his passing.

Just prior to his graduation on June 10, 1930, with a BE degree in mechanical engineering from Johns Hopkins, Mr. Engalitcheff's time in America was running short. Under the Immigration Act of 1924, once his studies were completed, he would be forced to leave the country he had come to love and respect. He applied to enter Canada but was formally rejected by its commissioner of immigration. He pleaded by letter to Harry Hull, commissioner general of the U.S. Department of Labor, to allow him to work in the United States. Another rejection letter arrived in his mailbox.

In June 1930, John Engalitcheff wrote the Honorable Harry Hull once again and said, "There is no country to which I can go as I am not a citizen of any country. I am not a subject of Soviet Russia, and actually am a political exile of that government. It is absolutely impossible for me to go there.... I am not intending to break the law, but it is actually the only thing that I can do at present."[10] John Engalitcheff respected America and rule of law, but felt he had no alternative but to stay in the United States without an appropriate visa. He went on to describe his affinity for the country that had provided him the opportunity to advance personally through his studies at Johns Hopkins. "Although not a citizen of the United States, which I greatly regret, nevertheless, I will conform with all the laws, rules, regulations, and customs of this country, just as if I were a citizen."[11] Words which rang true throughout his life thus closed the body of the letter to Mr. Hull: "I will also do my best to use my American training and education for the benefit of this country and for the community."[12] It was a commitment that he lived and exemplified time and time again. John Engalitcheff secured his American visa and shortly after became a U.S. citizen.

John Engalitcheff graduated from Johns Hopkins at an inopportune time. In the midst of the Great Depression, job prospects were few; unemployment peaked at 46 percent on the eastern shore of Maryland, and the region's worst drought in history wreaked havoc on local agriculture.[13] It was a time when young graduates, the "lost generation" as it was eventually known, had few worthwhile professional opportunities. He was lucky, however, and the Johns Hopkins graduate, sporting a mustache and small spectacles, accepted a position with a refrigeration company in Dayton, Maryland, moving away from his family and Baltimore home to earn $26 a week. The company built, sold, and installed air-conditioning systems for small theaters.

Not long after joining the firm, the refrigeration company "abruptly and unexplainably" dismissed him.[14] He moved to Detroit, Maryland, and worked for the Maryland Air Conditioning Corporation for a few short years to practice and perfect his engineering skills. It was at this time that John married Caroline Rogow-Pennington, a "socially prominent divorcee" and a 1935 graduate of the Johns Hopkins nursing program.[15] Their marriage lasted thirteen years before they were divorced in Orange County, Florida, in 1948.

Engalitcheff married Virginia Porter Watson on September 25, 1948. Affectionately referred to as "Bunny," Virginia was the love of his life. Her prestigious family background fit comfortably with the lifestyle they eventually achieved. A graduate of an all-girls school, Smith College in Northampton, Massachusetts, Virginia had two children from a prior marriage. Page Reid Watson and Kenneth Clayton Watson grew up in the often demanding Engalitcheff family with their mother and stepfather. The family made their home in Gibson Island, Maryland, in a house John Engalitcheff's brother-in-law designed. Virginia belonged to the Gibson Island Club and the prestigious Baltimore Country Club, signing most of the bills through their lifetime until John was accepted for membership decades later. She enjoyed gardening, spending time tending to the flowers and outdoor façade. John Engalitcheff tenderly cared for her later on, devoting much of his spare time to improving her quality of life, while Virginia Engalitcheff grew to respect and accept her husband's values, following his wishes even after his passing.

Following a short stint with Chrysler Airtemp, Engalitcheff moved back
to Baltimore from Detroit in 1938. At that time, with the help of a few local
laborers, he built an air conditioner coil by hand and sold it for $2,450 to
York Refrigeration of York, Pennsylvania. Upon its successful sale, the
young and talented engineer sought to use his skills and leadership to build
his own enterprise. After pawning his wife's wedding ring for $1,000 and
scrounging up $250 in cash, Engalitcheff started a new company in an
aging garage on West Redwood Street.

Engalitcheff named his business Baltimore Aircoil Company (BAC).
Engalitcheff tenderly explained, "This is a good and wonderful nation and
to show my appreciation for what people in Baltimore have done for me I
named my company the Baltimore Aircoil Co."[16] His patriotism and indebt-
edness to the country he admired couldn't have been more apparent. BAC
manufactured air-conditioning products and evaporative condensers and
experienced moderate success in these early years. It was a growing field
and his firm, young and fresh, was revolutionizing the way people lived
with the advent of air-cooling mechanisms.

Eventually, Engalitcheff moved his facilities into a Waverly, Maryland,
manufacturing building. Just three short years after the birth of BAC, Engalitcheff accepted a commissioning with the United States Navy and enlisted
as a lieutenant in 1942. He shut down the business, left his wife behind,
and served the country he loved to preserve the freedom he enjoyed. The
United States of America had given him opportunity when he had few possessions or wealth, and he was proud to serve when his country now needed
him the most. His fluency in German took him to the Brazilian jungle
where he helped manage a helium plant that the Americans had seized
from the Germans. In those days, helium served a variety of purposes. It
fueled dirigibles that protected against enemy submarines and warships.[17]
Researchers of the Manhattan Project who built the first atomic bomb used
helium as a key ingredient. Doctors provided helium as a form of anesthetic
as well as a treatment for soldiers suffering from respiratory disorders. While

Engalitcheff's naval assignment may not have been as dangerous as others, helium was an important component of America's military success.

In 1945, Engalitcheff returned and restarted Baltimore Aircoil, hiring back many of those who had lost their jobs when he closed down the shop. From the beginning, Engalitcheff surrounded himself with employees who exemplified his most valued attribute: motivational character. Upon meeting a potential hire for the first time, he asked three questions: "What does your daddy do?" "Where did you go to school?" "How did you go to school?" The response to this final question gave him the information he sought to determine if the individual had expended personal initiative and effort. He had worked hard to get where he was and wanted those around him to value that.

A "Groundhog Day disaster" struck his manufacturing plant in 1956 when the Waverly facility burned to the ground in the wee hours of the morning, destroying the entire enterprise.[18] Firemen fought the ten-alarm blaze in freezing rain through three explosions. Initial damage was estimated to be $500,000 at the time, though Engalitcheff reported, "not even a letterhead was left."[19] In today's dollars, the fire caused $3.7 million worth of damage. Less than two days later, Engalitcheff had set up temporary offices in a rented house. Baltimore Aircoil rebuilt in the countryside of Dorsey, Maryland, along the railroad tracks and white picket fences of nearby farms. The personal sacrifice, struggle, and accomplishment that came with rebuilding the plant clearly affected Engalitcheff. He later commented, "The proudest day of my life came when we raised the American flag at our plant in Dorsey."[20] The red-bricked facility doubled its sales to $3 million in that year following the fire. He maintained the employment of all those who worked in the Waverly plant. It was one of those moments that employees would never forget, an example of his commitment to those whose lives depended on him and the company's success.

Personal testimonies of Engalitcheff's generosity abound. Once, when a BAC employee tragically died young due to an aneurysm, Mr. Engalitcheff asked his controller to sit down with the employee's wife to determine her monthly out-of-pocket expenses. Engalitcheff supported the widowed family over many years, sending the children to private school, but never giving more than necessary. He wanted them to contribute to their own futures, too, being careful to not overrun his generosity by becoming a welfare bank for the family.

After a fire destroyed an employee's home and belongings, Engalitcheff called a staff meeting of all employees on the shop floor. He implored each employee to give at least $1 to him to get back on his feet. He also requested any furniture donations be brought to the plant, and he would take care of transporting the goods to the family.

In most infant companies, there are slow times when work seems hard to come by. Even in those early days, Mr. Engalitcheff valued his employees and did all he could to take care of them. When Joe Pope started with Engalitcheff earning a salary of 25¢ an hour in 1939, his employment was intermittent at best, sometimes working for two weeks and being laid off for the next two. Recognizing Joe's need for a steady job, Mr. Engalitcheff told Joe he'd pay him if he'd paint his house during an "off" period. This care for the human condition radiated from Mr. Engalitcheff throughout his days. During another such slow period, rather than lay off his employees, Engalitcheff commissioned them to build him a sailboat. Sailing was a hobby the Engalitcheffs enjoyed immensely. John Engalitcheff was known to hop on his sailboat alone and stay at sea for hours at a time. Instead of furloughing his workers, the BAC employees drafted and built his new steel sailboat on the shop floor. Employees trusted Engalitcheff, and more specifically, the company, to take care of them above all. Perhaps because of this, employees rejected nine attempts to unionize the enterprise.

While his brilliant mind and leadership skills led to BAC's vast success, he still maintained paternal relationships with those employees who worked for him, remembering each by name and holding award ceremonies for their accomplishments. Ed Schinner, a young engineer who joined BAC in 1965, believed his fairness, understanding, and "extreme" generosity were demonstrated best by his profit-sharing company philosophy. In the days when profit-sharing was rare, Engalitcheff believed that the company's success was due to the hard work of all the BAC employees, and as a result, they were entitled to a portion of the revenue. Salaries were boosted by 15 to 25 percent based on the company's performance. Accordingly, Schinner reported that the employees believed they were "ordinary people doing extraordinary things."[21]

Engalitcheff's concern about the world and community around him became evident through his management of BAC. When neighbors complained about excessive speeds and traffic near the plant, Engalitcheff gathered the couple hundred employees to suggest sternly that they respect the children and families who lived nearby. Following the disappearance of an employee's wallet, Engalitcheff advised workers that stealing from him or the company would be better than taking from a colleague.

Engalitcheff arrived each morning promptly at nine a.m., adorned with a tan brimmed hat and attired in a crisp, white dress shirt with cuffs. He was a demanding employer with a commanding presence. Ed Schinner described him as a man with an endearing personality but a short fuse. When faced with frustration, diatribes flowed out of Engalitcheff's mouth at warp speed, Russian and English garbled together. Many who witnessed these episodes would chuckle at the sound and sight of his exasperation. And yet, he was quick to apologize and recognize his weaknesses.

Mr. Engalitcheff exemplified a style aptly described by Ed Schinner as "managing with your feet".[22] Rather than sit behind his desk, he spent time getting dirty in the shop with those who made his ideas reality. In fact, he required all of his new engineers to spend time in the shop working through exhaustion to earn respect from and appreciation for the everyday laborers. A recent bout in the plant's shop attempting to make actual the ideas he created and studied over and over in his mind with the assembly-line workers was reflected by an occasional disheveled appearance.

According to colleagues who worked side by side with him, Engalitcheff had a brilliant mind, able to originate new techniques and products,

while he struggled with materializing the components of analytical engineering. Norva Pope, an administrative employee in the BAC main office,
believed "he was a person that didn't know what the word 'impossible'
meant. His mind never stopped thinking."[23] Whether on a work trip to Belgium or on holiday in Jamaica, his mind never rested. While on annual
vacations in Jamaica, Engalitcheff checked in on the engineering team
daily to receive the latest test results from the lab, and he'd lounge on the
beach reworking ways to improve BAC's products. A wave once splashed
over him and swept his new design plans out to sea, much to his frustration.

Engalitcheff's pioneering creations led to forty-seven lifetime patents,
twenty-three in the field of evaporative cooling devices. The Vatican's diplo-
matic headquarters, Seattle's Space Needle, St. Louis's Gateway Arch, and
New York's Madison Square Garden and Guggenheim Museum all incorporated BAC cooling towers into their structures' circulation systems. Several countries house BAC plants, including Australia, Belgium, China,
Italy, Japan, Malaysia, Mexico, South Africa, and Spain. Today, what once
was revolutionary (reusing water rather than expelling it as waste) now is
standard in the air-cooling industry.

Engalitcheff earned the American Society of Heating and Air-Conditioning Engineers' Distinguished Service Award in 1963, the F. Paul Anderson Award in 1981 (the society's highest award), and was inducted into the
ASHRAE Hall of Fame in 1996. Engalitcheff became only the eighth man
in Maryland's history to earn the presidential "Export E" award for his work
to advance free markets and trade abroad. Maryland governor Spiro T.
Agnew described the award: "If our national economy is to be stabilized, our
international security preserved, our foreign commitments honored, America's industries must expand foreign trade. . . . Baltimore Aircoil Company
has done just that—and through its highly successful design and manufacture of refrigeration, air conditioning and process cooling equipment, has
developed international demand for its specialized products."[24] Agnew concluded, "The Company's good citizenship, I understand, not only reflects
but is inspired by its founder and present chairman, Mr. Engalitcheff."[25]

Engalitcheff's ability to see a need and then fill it led to Baltimore Air-coil's vast success and continues to inspire its growth today. It was the first refrigeration company, according to the *Baltimore Sun*, to have an assembly line process and is known today as the world's largest manufacturer of evaporative cooling devices, thermal storage, and heat transfer equipment, with more than two thousand employees.[26] New York Stock Exchange outfit Merck & Company, Inc. purchased Baltimore Aircoil in 1970 for $44 million in stocks, and Mr. Engalitcheff stayed on for two more years through the transition before retiring. In 1985, AMSTED Industries purchased the Baltimore Aircoil unit of Merck & Company for $92 million.[27] In 2005, a brand-new, 95,000 square-feet global headquarters opened across the country road from its previous location.

Upon his retirement from BAC in 1972, Mr. Engalitcheff turned his energy and attention to his wife's painful arthritic hands. He agonized over how to help alleviate her discomfort. Following the surgery on Virginia's hands in 1980, Dr. Raymond Curtis confided in Mr. Engalitcheff that a lack of proper equipment slowed the rehabilitation process. He believed a device that enabled an individual to practice performing actual tasks required in daily life would vastly improve recovery for arthritic patients. Mr. Engalitcheff, led by the desire to help his ailing wife, his experience at BAC, and with the assistance of close friend Jack Doub, invented a medical instrument to simulate "real world" activities. It incorporated a barber-chair base to account for various heights of patients, too. The patented "Work Simulator" formed the basis of Mr. Engalitcheff's hobby enterprise, Baltimore Therapeutic Equipment Co., and led to twenty-four additional patents on medical equipment. His desire to make life better for people could not have been more clearly demonstrated.

Even still, Engalitcheff remembered the commitment he made when he first became a U.S. citizen; improving his community was part of that objective. Engalitcheff believed that Americans didn't always fully appreciate the freedom and free enterprise economy they were so accustomed to. He sought to give back to the country that afforded him the opportunity to achieve the American Dream. In the 1950s, Engalitcheff's enthusiasm grew in support of ideas he felt could transform the world, namely capitalism, anti-Communism, and free expression.

One of Engalitcheff's first projects became a film called *Only the Strong*. The title originated from a passage of a Blue Ribbon Defense Panel report: "The road to peace has never been through appeasement, unilateral disarmament, or negotiation from weakness. The entire recorded history of mankind is to the contrary. Among the great nations, 'Only the Strong' survive."[28] The anti-Communist film creation demonstrated Engalitcheff's commitment to freedom and "peace through strength", which emanated from his personal experiences and desire to build on American prosperity and freedom. Proud and patriotic, Engalitcheff staged a showing of his film to the entire BAC workforce on the plant floor with rented television sets.

Engalitcheff's involvement steadily deepened over the years. He was honored when asked by the secretary of the Navy to participate in the Naval War College's 1969 Global Strategy Discussions in Newport, Rhode Island. He distributed books to employees depicting the horrors of the Soviet gulags. A certificate recognizing his personal "contribution to national security" hung on his office wall, along with the numerous heating and refrigerating engineering awards, society membership placards, and a portrait of Barry Goldwater. One time, he invited two of his younger employees who held similar values to a dinner honoring a man he admired: Barry Goldwater. After a speech by Richard Nixon, Engalitcheff returned to work the next day offering all employees access to the fax machine if they should choose to send him a supportive letter. During an election season, he provided literature about the candidates and sternly reminded employees, "It is your God-gift to vote... That's what this country is about."[29]

More dramatically, John Engalitcheff used his wealth to support causes that upheld his values. A skeptic businessman at heart, Mr. Engalitcheff took time to become fully committed to various associations. He sauntered in unannounced to the offices of those organizations he financed, peppering the staff with question after question. He never left his decisions to chance. In fact, his engineering mind led him to demand thoughtful and thorough responses from organizations before his support would be provided. Once he received a sponsorship card in the mail requesting financial resources for Young Americans for Freedom. He sent a stern response back to the group's chairman at the time, wondering how he could have received such a mailing when Engalitcheff had been an annual contributor to the organization for years. He had confused Young America's Foundation, an organization he had supported for quite some time, with Young Americans for Freedom. This perceived oversight did not go unnoticed by Mr. Engalitcheff and was indicative of the way he dealt with those beneficiaries of his contributions.

According to John Fisher, the past president of the American Security Council Foundation (ASCF), Engalitcheff started giving $10 to the group by mail. After some time, he "just appeared one day" at the ASCF offices to inspect the organization for himself.[30] Mr. Fisher showed him a slide presentation, and shortly thereafter, Engalitcheff transferred $4,000 in stock. The relationship grew from there. He gave $100,000 in 1972 to promote a television documentary encouraging "Peace Through Strength," and served on ASCF's governing board.

Membership of ASCF tripled from 1978 to 1981, a period at the height of John Engalitcheff's activity with its work. ASCF built a Coalition for Peace Through Strength, comprised of 252 members of Congress who supported a strong United States foreign policy. In 1983, 249 sponsors passed a "Peace Through Strength" resolution in Congress. In 1984, the American Security Council aired its "Peace Through Strength" program on 174 stations in one week. It went on to show more than nine hundred times on television to educate Americans on the danger of appeasement.[31] Former Soviet KGB operative Oleg Kalugin admitted, "When President Reagan started this program . . . [the Soviets] were scared. . . . They were convinced they would never be able to match the U.S. program for purely financial reasons."[32]

In a true twist of irony, a man who perhaps more than any other was committed to witnessing the defeat of Communism, collapsed at the feet of the American leader who brought Communism to its knees. On November 15, 1984, just days after Ronald Reagan's reelection of historic proportions, the president invited forty figures to the White House Blue Room for a reception to honor their commitment to "Peace Through Strength." Mr. Engalitcheff was one of those dedicated men set to receive the Presidential Eagle pin that day. As the line progressed and the hand of Ronald Reagan approached Engalitcheff's lapel, he collapsed. Cradled on the White House floor in the arms of the man who had vowed to destroy Communism since his days as a Hollywood actor, Engalitcheff quietly apologized for the disruption. President Reagan was heard responding, "Don't worry. We just want you to get better."[33] Days later, a massive stroke took John Engalitcheff's life. His colleague Ed Schinner recalled the timeline of the events: "The White House boxed up his Colombo-style coat and brimmed hat. By the time they arrived at the offices of Baltimore Aircoil, he had passed away."[34]

Some said that the excitement of the day probably instigated the stroke. And they were probably right. After all, Ronald Reagan was the one man who had had the courage to stand up to Communist oppressors, and Engalitcheff was overjoyed and humbled in his presence. After attending a Conservative Political Action Conference dinner shortly after Reagan's 1981 inauguration, Engalitcheff remarked, "It meant an awful lot to me to hear President Reagan in person."[35] He fervently admired Ronald Reagan.

Engalitcheff's wife, Virginia, lived six years longer, suffering from the effects of arthritis until April 19, 1990. She honored her husband's values and ideas by keeping their will intact following his passing. Their estate, built from initial capital of $1,250, was primarily divided among nine organizations. Each preserved and formed the foundation of the Engalitcheff legacy with the bequest received, each given a minimum of $4 million and some receiving as much as $13 million. It is ironic that a man who came from a country where tradition required wealth to follow families through inheritance ignored these roots and largely bypassed family to give his wealth back to the country for which he was most grateful.

This Russian-born entrepreneur dreamed of seeing the defeat of the USSR's Communist government by the United States. Accordingly, American Security Council Foundation (ASCF) received more than $9 million for its programs upon Mrs. Engalitcheff's passing. In addition to establishing the first and only advanced degree for the study of national security, ASCF was also credited by Ronald Reagan as having helped establish the theme of his foreign policy approach based on its 1978 "National Strategy for Peace Through Strength." President Reagan conveyed, "One thing is certain. If we're to continue to advance world peace and human freedom, America must remain strong. If we have learned anything these last eight years, it's that peace through strength works."[36] The fall of the Berlin Wall and the collapse of the Communist bloc rendered ASCF's mission complete at that time, a feat that would have surely inspired Mr. Engalitcheff's pride. His dream had come true.

The Fund for American Studies, after the receipt of Engalitcheff's funds, renamed its Georgetown internship program the Engalitcheff Institute on Comparative Political and Economic Systems in 1994 as a testament to his upbringing and later exile to the United States. More than one hundred students participate in this summer program each year, gaining real-world experience through valuable internships and academic competence at Georgetown's premier course training. Former BAC president and member of the Fund for American Studies' Board of Regents Fred Long knows, "He'd be delighted to know that there's an institute at the Fund for American Studies named after him."[37] These young people will become America's leaders down the road—a legacy of Engalitcheff's staunch support of freedom.

Ronald Reagan comforted Mr. Engalitcheff while incapacitated on the floor of the White House during his final hours. It is perhaps a testament of will then, that Mr. Engalitcheff's generous bequest to Young America's Foundation helped comfort Ronald Reagan and his family during the president's last years. Ronald and Nancy Reagan lived at their hilltop ranch, Rancho del Cielo, or Ranch in the Sky, for more than a quarter century. It was the place where Ronald Reagan felt most at ease, a place where he was capable of doing his best thinking about how to expand the free world. Lou Cannon once said, "There is more of Reagan in this ranch than in all the speeches he ever gave."[38]

When Ronald Reagan could no longer care for the Ranch and his medical costs continued to rise, in order to keep him comfortable in his Bel Air home, Nancy Reagan decided to sell the Ranch. An agreement with a developer threatened to destroy the historic property, a place where Ronald Reagan signed the largest tax cut in American history and hosted important world leaders including Mikhail Gorbachev, Queen Elizabeth II, and Margaret Thatcher. Instead, Young America's Foundation, equipped to undertake such an endeavor because of John Engalitcheff's legacy gift, stepped forward to save the precious piece of history, and in so doing, partially alleviated the medical cost burden on the Reagans.

Young America's Foundation had a long history with Ronald Reagan. In 1974, the Foundation financed a nationally syndicated radio program featuring then California governor Ronald Reagan. Governor Reagan's addresses, focusing on a variety of issues including taxes, crime, and foreign policy, helped strengthen the future president's national reputation. During each year of his presidency, Reagan hosted briefings at the White House for Young America's Foundation student leaders who attended the National Conservative Student Conference in Washington, D.C. In 1993, President Reagan addressed the conference saying, "Together we worked to accomplish much of what has come to be known as the 'Reagan Revolution'. . . . Young America's Foundation has been a refuge for students seeking an alternative to the politically correct environment enforced on many campuses. I know the conference will send you back to your campuses better informed, motivated, and trained. Your work is vital to the future of the nation."[39]

It was a logical next step in Young America's Foundation's relationship with President Reagan to come forward during his time of need to protect the place he loved so much. Ronald Reagan had been there for countless young Americans over the years, those who found inspiration in the character of the man who took time to speak directly to them. During his presidency, he spoke to student audiences at Moscow State University, Fudan University in Shanghai, University College in Ireland, Notre Dame University, and the University of South Carolina, among many others. Even as he was leaving office, Ronald Reagan looked to the future of America and its young people: "And are we doing a good enough job teaching our children what America is and what she represents in the long history of the world?...We've got to do a better job of getting across that America is freedom—freedom of speech, freedom of religion, freedom of enterprise. And freedom is special...It's fragile; it needs [protection]."[40] For Young America's Foundation, whose own history and ethos is tied directly to President Reagan, saving the Ranch, "a true national treasure" according to the *Washington Post*, offered an unmatchable opportunity to protect his ideas and advance conservative principles. John Engalitcheff's gift gave Young America's Foundation confidence to take on such an important task.

Saving and preserving Ronald Reagan's Western White House—Rancho del Cielo—was a crucial step in ensuring future generations know of and are inspired by Ronald Reagan's vision and lasting accomplishments. Young America's Foundation hosts thousands of students, scholars, members of the media, and leaders at the Reagan Ranch, including the crew of the U.S.S. *Ronald Reagan*, Robert Novak, Pat Sajak, General P. X. Kelly, Marvin Olasky, Mrs. Louis L'Amour, Governor George Allen, Dinesh D'Souza, and John O'Sullivan. They join a list of other well-known individuals who have visited Rancho del Cielo over the years, including Attorney General Ed Meese, Heritage Foundation President Edwin Feulner, Focus on the Family's James Dobson, Lieutenant Colonel Oliver North, and Charlton Heston, as well as authors Peggy Noonan and Nelson DeMille.

The Reagan Ranch has been featured on every major broadcast and cable news network: ABC, CBS, NBC, Fox, MSNBC, CNN, and Fox News. In addition to news shows such as *Good Morning America* and the

Today show, the Ranch has been featured in historical specials produced by the History Channel, the Travel Channel, CNN, and even Entertainment Tonight. In print, the Ranch has been highlighted in such well-read publications as *Time, Newsweek,* the *Washington Post,* the *Washington Times,* the *New York Times,* the *Los Angeles Times,* and *Human Events.* Stories featuring the Ranch have appeared in publications with a combined circulation of more than thirty million.

Conferences and seminars bring scholars, authors, media personalities, and the country's most accomplished conservative thinkers in front of young audiences. The full impact of this opportunity for young people to study and be inspired at the Ranch will never truly be known. But Fred Long, former president of BAC, reported on the importance of the gift, "That could well be the thing that he values most out of his contributions—that he helped buy the Reagan Ranch. Reagan was his hero."[41]

Young America's Foundation's preservation of Rancho del Cielo plays a vital role in preserving Ronald Reagan's lasting accomplishments and adding to his overall popularity. In the late 1990s—and now into the twenty-first century—Ronald Reagan was *the* most popular individual to represent conservative success as a public policy leader. President Reagan left office in 1988 with an average approval rating of 53 percent, a number that actually declined to as low as 50 percent in 1992, and held at 52 percent in 1993. All the while the Left and revisionist historians worked hard to tear down President Reagan's lasting accomplishments, attempting to discredit his involvement in the fall of Communism and the economic prosperity the nation enjoyed in the post-Reagan years. In the years since Young America's Foundation has been at work saving the Western White House, conducting its student programs, and strengthening its media outreach initiatives, President Reagan's national approval ratings have climbed from the middle of the road to the top.

John Engalitcheff helped the world learn about Ronald Reagan and his accomplishments because of the gift he gave. Many who now know of

Ronald Reagan's deep commitment to freedom hadn't yet been born when he was president of the United States. A February 18, 2005, Gallup Poll found that more Americans named Ronald Reagan "the Greatest United States President" than any other candidate.[42] The poll, conducted just before Presidents' Day, a holiday celebrating the birthdays of George Washington and Abraham Lincoln, found that Reagan was named more often than any other president in history. Twenty percent of the sampling responded with that answer. The 2005 poll marked the first time *any* single president has received more than 18 percent of the total vote.

Close associate Ed Schinner commented, "I couldn't imagine the pride that [Engalitcheff] would have to think that his money, his work ethic, and the thing that he created ... went to fund the purchase of the Ranch."[43] The Reagan Ranch today is used to inspire young people with the value both Ronald Reagan and John Engalitcheff most cherished: freedom. It is the centerpiece of Young America's Foundation's student outreach programs. This bold undertaking fosters the virtues of individual freedom, limited government, patriotism, and traditional values in America's future leaders. In teaching young people about Ronald Reagan's accomplishments, the group instills the ideas that have been the core of its mission for more than forty years.

Engalitcheff's gift did more than save the Reagan Ranch. His confidence in Young America's Foundation inevitably encouraged other individuals to invest in the future of America with subsequent and formative gifts to the Reagan Ranch project. Those individuals who recognized the project's potential at critical moments and took lead roles in ensuring that the property and student programs were utilized to their maximum potential include Virginia Knott Bender, Robert and Joan Cummins, Richard and Helen DeVos, Fred Kirby, Thomas L. Phillips, and Norma Zimdahl. Together, these generous benefactors gave legitimacy to the Reagan Ranch project, ensuring Rancho del Cielo's longevity will endure generations past Ronald Reagan's death, much like George Washington's Mount Vernon or Thomas Jefferson's Monticello.

Today, Mr. Engalitcheff's legacy is also carried forward by the men and women who worked side by side with him at Baltimore Aircoil Company and Baltimore Therapeutic Equipment Company. His generous spirit encouraged those around him to make similar gifts to causes they believe in, and for that, Mr. Engalitcheff continues to give back to the country he so fondly admired.

Mr. Engalitcheff had been so profoundly impacted in his childhood by the horrors of Communism; he felt the immeasurable responsibility to ensure that American freedom not only survived, but could counter future threats to liberty. This Russian turned fervent American patriot, with $250 and a $1,000 wedding ring, started a company that would eventually enable him to alter the course of the American Conservative Movement, our country, and our world in a way few other Americans have. All totaled, John and Virginia Engalitcheff gave $102 million to causes from their estate. Not many people think to leave their fortunes to causes committed to advancing mutually held ideas and protecting their country's future, but John Engalitcheff did. Joe Pope, one of the original BAC employees, tearfully said it best, "He was a prince in his country, and he was a prince in this country."[44]

---------- ★ ----------

Acknowledgments

O ur deep appreciation goes to all those men and women whose gifts have yet to be fully recognized by conservatives for their immeasurable impacts. Though the space limitations required us to focus on only a few, we know stories remain. We thank you, profusely, for the encouragement and inspiration you provide when you choose to endow your ideas with a gift to the Conservative Movement.

On practical matters, we thank two research colleagues for their outstanding work in preparing original materials and finding stories that should be included. Sara Linert, a student at Crown College (St. Bonifacius, Minnesota), and Luke Hellier from Saint John's University (St. Joseph, Minnesota) provided invaluable time and effort to this project, and we are grateful for their commitment. We also thank Daniel Wanke, a student at Purdue University (West Lafayette, Indiana) and a Young America's Foundation Sarah T. Hermann Intern Scholar, for his study of the courses offered on the United States Constitution at American colleges and universities.

The loving encouragement from our spouses, Michelle Easton and Eric Hoplin, kept our spirits lifted and minds focused. We are indebted for their editing and counsel which made this piece the best it could be.

In addition, there are numerous individuals who assisted our research efforts at various institutions across the country. In particular we gratefully acknowledge:

Clare Batty	Institute of Economic Affairs
Carol Bowers	American Heritage Center, University of Wyoming
John Cervini	Hillsdale College Development
Mary Curry	National Security Archive, George Washington University
Michelle Easton	Clare Boothe Luce Policy Institute
Burt Folsom	Hillsdale College
Jim Fowler	*National Review*
Arlan Gilbert	Hillsdale College
John Gizzi	*Human Events*
Carol Leadenham	Hoover Institution Archives
Bobbi Levien	Western Historical Manuscript Collection, University of Missouri–Kansas City
Pat Loper	Hillsdale College
William Massa	Sterling Memorial Library, Yale University
Linda Moore	Mossey Library, Hillsdale College
Benjamin Pezzillo	Ronald Reagan Presidential Library
Delores Proubasta	Society of Exploration Geophysicists
Sandy Ruskowski	Baltimore Aircoil Company

John Pollack	Rare Book and Manuscript Library, University of Pennsylvania
Steve Slattery	Fund for American Studies
Sherri Smith	Kansas City Public Library
Jennifer Sternaman	Ronald Reagan Presidential Library
James Stimpert	Milton S. Eisenhower Library, Johns Hopkins University
Barbara Truesdell	Center for the Study of History and Memory, Indiana University
Rebecca Wendt	California State Archives
Linda Whitaker	Arizona Historical Foundation
Anna Wilhelm	Jackson County Historical Society
Ray Wilson	Ronald Reagan Presidential Library
Hans Zeiger	Hillsdale College

Finally, this book could not have come together without the important advice and assistance from the following individuals:

Darla Anzalone	Meghan Espinoza
Larry Arnn	John Fisher
Jason Barbour	Mark Fisher
Kimberly Martin Begg	Mike Fisher
Sara Banks	Dan Flynn
Jessica Bleess	Molly Flynn
William F. Buckley Jr.	Tony Fowler
Lisa M. Buestrin	Brett Glawe
Patrick Coyle	Darla Glawe
T. Kenneth Cribb	Jon Glawe
Harry Crocker	Kraig Glawe
Midge Dean	Merrilu Gordon
Frank Donatelli	Lesley Hoplin
Manny Espinoza	Mark Hoplin

Richard Kimble
Jessica Koebensky
Nikki Kosinski
Elli Leutheuser
Frederick Long
Georganna Long
Rich Lowry
Dan Manion
Chris Manion
Don Mossey
Mitchell Muncy
Kate Obenshain
Ronald Pearson
Thomas L. Phillips
Joe Pope
Norva Pope
Tina Quick
Alfred Regnery
Ricardo Reyes
Thomas Robinson
Marji Ross
Ben Sacher
Fred Sacher
Ken Sacher
Krissy Sacher
Ruth Sacher
Ed Schinner
Peter Schweizer
Marc Short
Vernon Smith
Candace Smith
Thomas Spence

Herb Stupp
David Sturrock
Christian Tappe
James B. Taylor
Wayne Thorburn
Clark Vandeventer
Linda Whetstone
Kirby Wilbur
Flagg Youngblood
Hans Zeiger

Index

Notes

Introduction

1 Margaret Thatcher, "Speech to General Assembly of the Church of Scotland," May 21, 1988, *BBC Sound Archive*, OUP transcript, http://www.margaretthatcher.org/speeches/displaydocument.asp?docid=107246.

2 Rick Bragg, "All She Has, $150,000, Is Going to a University," *New York Times*, August 13, 1995, sec. 1.

3 *Tampa Tribune*, "The Most Unlikely Philanthropist," October 4, 1999, 8; Rick Bragg, "Oseola McCarty, A Washerwoman Who Gave All She Had to Help Others, Dies at 91," *New York Times*, September 28, 1999, sec. B.

4 Rick Bragg, "She Opened the World to Others; Her World Has Opened, Too," *New York Times*, November 12, 1996, sec. A.

5 Phil Kloer, "Preview," *Atlanta Journal and Constitution*, December 5, 1995, sec. D.

6 Harvey Blume, "Q & A With George Soros," *Boston Globe*, August 20, 2006, sec. D.

7 Chris Blackhurst, "Man of Contradiction: Billionaire, Financier, Mover of Markets, Guru, Philanthropist, Philosopher," *Evening Standard*, January 11, 2006, 29.

8 *Pittsburgh Post-Gazette*, "Money Talks: George Soros, A Very Concerned Citizen, Is Using Wealth to Oppose Bush's Re-Election," October 13, 2004, sec. A.

9 Orville Schell, "Sounding the Alarm on America's Direction," *Los Angeles Times*, May 23, 2004, sec. R.

10 Carlo Wolff, "Author Illuminates the Essential George Soros," *Boston Globe*, March 31, 2002, sec. C.

11 David Bank, "Boss Talk: The Man Who Would Mend the World—For Social Gains, George Soros Insists Government Funding Must Augment Philanthropy," *Wall Street Journal*, March 14, 2002, sec. A.

12 Garry Wills, "Scaife Has Good Reason to Hide," *Times Union*, October 27, 1998, sec. A.

13 John G. Craig, "Mission: Implausible Dick Scaife Couldn't Keep His Probe of Kangas a Secret," *Pittsburgh Post-Gazette*, March 28, 1999, sec. B.

14 Mark Jurkowitz, "Scaife Sleuthing," *Boston Globe*, July 8, 1998, sec. F.

15 Mark Jurkowitz, "The Right's Daddy Morebucks, Billionaire's Cash Fuels Conservative Journalism's Fires," *Boston Globe*, February 26, 1998, sec. E.

16 Rob Trenkle, "Extremists Target Unions," *Las Vegas Review-Journal*, April 17, 1998, sec. B.

17 Joe Conason, "The Right Connections; The Starr in Richard Scaife's Eyes," *Washington Post*, March 16, 1997, sec. C.

18 Phil Kuntz, "Citizen Scaife: Heir Turned Publisher Uses Financial Largess to Fuel Conservatism," *Wall Street Journal*, October 12, 1995, sec. A.

19 Debra Saunders, "Richard Scaife a Victim of '90s McCarthyism," *Milwaukee Journal Sentinel*, April 23, 1998, 18.

20 Arthur C. Brooks, *Who Really Cares* (New York: Basic Books, 2006), 18.

21 Ibid., 21.

22 Ibid., 21–22.

23 Henry Regnery to William F. Buckley Jr., May 17, 1951, box 10, folder 14, Henry Regnery Papers, 1909–1996, Hoover Institution Archives [HIA from here forward].

24 Brooks, *Who Really Cares*, 20.

25 Ibid., 18.

26 Charles Dunn, "On the Generosity Index, Conservatives Top Liberals," *Virginian-Pilot* (Norfolk), November 22, 2004, sec. B.

27 James Piereson, "Investing in Conservative Ideas," *Commentary*, http://www.commentary.org/article.asp?aid=11905048_1.

28 Martin Morse Wooster, "Chairs of Entrepreneurship Are Bad Business," *Wall Street Journal*, May 25, 1990, sec. A.

29 Ibid.

30 Milton Friedman to Ron Robinson, October 9, 1992, Young America's Foundation files.

31 Milton Friedman, personal letter to undisclosed individual, September 15, 1976, Young America's Foundation files.

32 Penelope Overton, "Kramer and Yale Settle Dispute," *Hartford Courant*, April 3, 2001, sec. A.

33 John Hechinger and Daniel Golden, "Poisoned Ivy: Fight at Princeton Escalates Over Use of Family's Gift," *Wall Street Journal*, February 7, 2006, sec. A.

34 Ibid.

35 Ibid.

36 Ibid.

37 James Piereson, "Only Encouraging Them," *Wall Street Journal*, November 18, 2005, sec. W.

38 Wooster, "Chairs of Entrepreneurship."

39 Ibid.

40 Laura Vanderkam, "Donors: Wise Up About Giving," *USA Today*, November 6, 2003, sec. A.

41 Stephen Moore, "Vision and Philanthropy," The Bradley Center for Philanthropy and Civic Renewal, February 16, 2005, 2.

42 Jason DeParle, "Goals Reached, Donor on Right Closes up Shop," *New York Times*, May 29, 2005, sec. 1.

43 Thomas Edsall, "Rich Liberals Vow to Fund Think Tanks; Aim Is to Compete with Conservatives," *Washington Post*, August 7, 2005, sec. A.

44 Ian Wilhelm, "Conservative Grant Makers Must Change to Be Effective, Leaders Say," *Chronicle of Philanthropy*, March 3, 2005, 25.

45 Kay Sprinkel Grace and Alan Wendroff, *High Impact Philanthropy* (New York: John Wiley and Sons, Inc., 2001), 45.

46 *Chicago Sun-Times*, "The Motley Fool," December 25, 2005, sec. A.

47 Bragg, "Oseola McCarty," sec. B.

48 Aleksandr Solzhenitsyn, *November 1916: The Red Wheel II* (New York: Farrar, Straus and Giroux, 1999), 42.

49 Ibid.

Chapter 1

1 Herbert C. Cornuelle, *Mr. Anonymous* (Burlingame, California: William Volker and Company, 1951), 134.

2 American Bible, Matthew 6:2–4 (Revised Standard Version).

3 Cornuelle, *Mr. Anonymous*, 175.

4 Photograph of Roselawn, folder 22; William Volker & Co. Records (KC59); Western Historical Manuscript Collection-Kansas City [WHMC-KC from here forward].

5 *Kansas City Star*, "The Price of Success," June 27, 1915.

6 Ibid.

7 Ibid.

8 Harold Luhnow, *Unpublished Biography of William Volker*, 1948; folder 3; William Volker Company Records (KC59); WHMC-KC, 15.

9 Cornuelle, *Mr. Anonymous*, 33.

Notes

10 Henry Van Brunt, "William Volker's Hard Head Made Millions: His Soft Heart Gave Millions Away," *Kansas City Star*, January 11, 1948, sec. C.
11 Ibid., 68.
12 Ibid., 37, 66.
13 Cornuelle, *Mr. Anonymous*, 53.
14 Ibid., 93.
15 Luhnow, *Unpublished Biography*, 13.
16 Cornuelle, *Mr. Anonymous*, 132.
17 Ibid., 79.
18 Ibid., 89.
19 Ibid., 81.
20 *Kansas City Star*, "The Price of Success."
21 Ibid., 16.
22 Shirl Kasper, "Saving Place: William Volker's Legacy and His Beloved Roselawn," *Jackson County Historical Society Journal* 44, no. 1 (Spring 2003), 7.
23 Luhnow, *Unpublished Biography*, 15.
24 Luhnow, *Unpublished Biography*, 36.
25 *The National Cyclopaedia of American Biography* XXXV (New York: James T. White & Company 1949), 205.
26 Luhnow, *Unpublished Biography*, 29.
27 Cornuelle, *Mr. Anonymous*, 94.
28 Jay Shafritz, *International Encyclopedia of Public Policy and Administration* (Boulder, Colorado: Westview Press, 1998), vol. 3, 1712.
29 Andrew Dunar, "Truman and Pendergast," *Journal of Southern History* 67, (2001), 1.
30 Cornuelle, *Mr. Anonymous*, 153.
31 Ibid., 153.
32 William Volker Fund, *A Brief Statement of Policy*, 1955, (Burlingame, California), box 2, Felix Morley Papers, Herbert Hoover Presidential Library, HHPL, 6.
33 Luhnow, *Unpublished Biography*, 22.
34 Shirl Kasper, "Welcome to Roselawn," *Kansas City Star Magazine*, January 12, 2003, 11.
35 *New York Times*, "Education Notes," May 19, 1946, sec. E.
36 Cornuelle, *Mr. Anonymous*, 99.
37 William Volker Fund, 7.
38 John Blundell, *Waging the War of Ideas* (London: Institute of Economic Affairs, 2001), 34.
39 Here, classical liberalism is used in its traditional nineteenth century European use, with regard to minimizing the role of government interference, rather than the current American meaning.
40 Handwritten note to Friedrich Hayek, May 7, 1945; folder 41; William Volker Company Records (KC59); WHMC-KC.
41 Ronald Reagan, "Remarks at the Conservative Political Action Conference Dinner," March 20, 1981, *The Public Papers of President Ronald W. Reagan*, Ronald Reagan Presidential Library, http://www.reagan.utexas.edu/archives/speeches/1981/32081b.htm.
42 John Jewkes to Dr. Albert Hunold, personal letter (December 20, 1947), quoted in Richard Cockett, *Thinking the Unthinkable, Think-Tanks and the Economic Counter-Revolution 1931–1983* (London: Fontana Press, 1995), 115.
43 R. M. Hartwell, *A History of the Mont Pelerin Society* (Indianapolis: The Liberty Fund, 1995), 95.
44 Ibid., 160.
45 Vernon Smith, personal interview with author Nicole Hoplin, August 5, 2005.
46 Ibid.
47 Milton Friedman and Rose Friedman, *Two Lucky People* (Chicago: University of Chicago Press, 1998), 333.
48 Ibid., 202.
49 Hartwell, *History of the Mont Pelerin Society*, xv.
50 Scott Thompson and Nancy Spannaus, "George Pratt Shultz: Profile of a Hit Man," *Executive Intelligence Review* 31, no. 48 (December 10, 2004), 1.
51 Blundell, *Waging the War of Ideas*, 96.
52 Henry A. Turner, *Politics in the United States: Readings in Political Parties and Pressure Groups* (New York: McGraw-Hill, 1955), 198; Nash, *Conservative Intellectual Movement*, 25.
53 Henry William Spiegel, *The Growth of Economic Thought* (Durham, North Carolina: Duke University Press, 1991), 746.
54 Nash, *Conservative Intellectual Movement*, 18–19.
55 Richard Weaver, *Visions of Order* (Wilmington, Delaware: Intercollegiate Studies Institute, 1995), xii.
56 Luhnow, *Unpublished Biography*, 23.
57 Herb Cornuelle to Felix Morley, January 8, 1952, box 2, Felix Morley Papers, HHPL; Henry Regnery to Harold Luhnow, September 15, 1952, box 46, folder 11, Henry Regnery Papers, 1909–1996, HIA; Harold Luhnow to Henry Regnery, March 25, 1949, box 46, folder 11,

Henry Regnery Papers, 1909–1996, HIA.
58 Jim Powell, "Why Liberty Flourished in the West," *Policy* 17, no. 3 (Spring 2001): 51.
59 George H. Nash, *The Conservative Intellectual Movement in America* (Wilmington, Delaware: Intercollegiate Studies Institute, 1998), 348; William Volker Charities Fund, "Minutes of Meeting of Directors," Sept. 20, 1952, William Volker Company Records (KC59), WHMC-KC, 3.
60 Mehr Freiheit, "Ludwig von Mises," http://www.mehr-freiheit.de/idee/mises.html.
61 Harold Luhnow to Felix Morley, October 25, 1953, box 2, Felix Morley Papers, Herbert Hoover Presidential Library [HHPL from here forward].
62 Robert Allan Williams, "The Phenomenon of Privatization," December 6, 2003, http://www.authorsden.com/visit/viewshortstory.asp?AuthorID=17785.
63 Harold Luhnow to Henry Regnery, April 26, 1950, box 46, folder 11, Henry Regnery Papers, 1909–1996, Hoover Institution Archives [HIA from here forward].
64 Henry Regnery to Pierre F. Goodrich, April 6, 1962, box 44, folder 27, Henry Regnery Papers, 1909–1996, HIA.
65 William Volker Fund, 4.
66 William Volker Fund, 3.
67 Luhnow, *Unpublished Biography*, 19.
68 William Volker Fund , 3.
69 Milton Friedman and Rose Friedman, *Capitalism and Freedom* (Chicago: University of Chicago Press, 1982), x.
70 Cornuelle, *Mr. Anonymous*, 134.

Chapter 2

1 John B. Crane, "Henry Regnery," *Richmond News Leader*, April 16, 1956.
2 Henry Regnery, *Memoirs of a Dissident Publisher* (Chicago: Regnery Books, 1985), 5.
3 Wayne S. Cole, *America First: The Battle Against Intervention, 1940–1941* (Madison, Wisconsin: University of Wisconsin Press, 1953), 15–16.
4 Felix Morley to Henry Regnery, January 27, 1963, box 22, Felix Morley Papers, Herbert Hoover Presidential Library [HHPL from here forward].
5 Regnery, *Memoirs*, 7.
6 Ibid., 8.
7 Ibid., 10.
8 Ibid., 18.
9 Henry Regnery to Felix Morley, July 11, 1958, box 22, Felix Morley Papers, HHPL; Henry Regnery to Felix Morley, February 6, 1974, box 22, Felix Morley Papers, HHPL; Henry Regnery to Felix Morley, July 31, 1974, box 22, Felix Morley Papers, HHPL; Henry Regnery to Felix Morley, May 26, 1976, box 22, Felix Morley Papers, HHPL; and Henry Regnery to Felix Morley, December 8, 1977, box 22, Felix Morley Papers, HHPL.
10 Henry Regnery to Felix Morley, August 17, 1961, box 22, Felix Morley Papers, HHPL.
11 Regnery, *Memoirs*, 21–22.
12 Ibid., 29.
13 Ibid., 34.
14 Crane, "Henry Regnery;" *Book Industry*, "Regnery Charges Censorship of Ideas," March 1964, 70.
15 Henry Regnery to Pierre F. Goodrich, May 4, 1972, box 44, folder 27, Henry Regnery Papers, 1909–1996, Hoover Institution Archives [HIA from here forward].
16 Henry Regnery to William F. Buckley Jr., November 30, 1951, box 10, folder 14, Henry Regnery Papers, 1909–1996, HIA.
17 Regnery, *Memoirs*, 32.
18 Henry Regnery to Felix Morley, January 30, 1964, box 22, Felix Morley Papers, HHPL.
19 Regnery, *Memoirs*, 39.
20 Ibid., 33.
21 Ibid., 45.
22 Ibid., 33.
23 Henry Regnery to Felix Morley, October 30, 1974, box 22, Felix Morley Papers, HHPL.
24 *Time*, "The Drowning Children," March 1, 1948, 92.
25 Regnery, *Memoirs*, 41.
26 Henry Regnery to William F. Buckley Jr., May 14, 1951, box 10, folder 14, Henry Regnery Papers, 1909–1996, HIA.
27 Henry Regnery to William F. Buckley Jr., May 28, 1953, box 10, folder 14, Henry Regnery Papers, 1909–1996, HIA.
28 Henry Regnery, "A Memorandum on the Henry Regnery Company," May 1961, box 81, folder 16, Henry Regnery Papers, 1909–1996, HIA.
29 Henry Regnery to J. Howard Pew, November 29, 1960, box 22, Felix

YOUNG AMERICA'S
F O U N D A T I O N

Dear Friend,

Thank you for all you do to advance freedom. Enclosed you will find an inscribed copy *Funding Fathers: The Unsung Heroes of the Conservative Movement*, by my colleague, Nicole Hoplin, and me.

This book tells the untold, behind-the-scenes stories of some of the men and women who made the Conservative Movement the force it is today. We researched and wrote these stories to inspire you, our friends and supporters, and thank all "unsung heroes" for the generous and personal sacrifices that have been made to advance freedom.

We hope you enjoy *Funding Fathers* and the inspirational stories about our fellow conservatives who also gave so much to our shared cause. We encourage you to share these stories and help us inspire future support for our Movement. Thank you, again, for all you do!

Sincerely,

Ron Robinson
President

F.M. Kirby Freedom Center
110 Elden Street
Herndon, Virginia 20170
800-USA-1776
www.yaf.org

The Reagan Ranch
217 State Street
Santa Barbara, California 93101
888-USA-1776
www.reaganranch.org

Morley Papers, HHPL.

30 William J. Casey to Henry Regnery, January 29, 1953, box 13, folder 13, Henry Regnery Papers, 1909–1996, HIA.

31 Henry Regnery to William F. Buckley Jr., May 17, 1951, box 10, folder 14, Henry Regnery Papers, 1909–1996, HIA.

32 Henry Regnery to William F. Buckley Jr., December 5, 1951, box 10, folder 14, Henry Regnery Papers, 1909–1996, HIA.

33 Henry Regnery to William F. Buckley Jr., January 31, 1952, box 10, folder 14, Henry Regnery Papers, 1909–1996, HIA.

34 Henry Regnery, "Henry Regnery: A Conservative Publisher," *The Alternative*, October 1971, 15.

35 Henry Regnery to William F. Buckley Jr., May 28, 1953, box 10, folder 14, Henry Regnery Papers, 1909–1996, HIA.

36 Henry Regnery to Felix Morley, December 18, 1975, box 22, Felix Morley Papers, HHPL.

37 Ronald Reagan to Henry Regnery, personal letter, June 19, 1985, quoted in Henry Regnery, *Memoirs of a Dissident Publisher* (Chicago: Regnery Books, 1985), unnumbered page 1.

38 Henry Regnery to Pierre F. Goodrich, June 25, 1962, box 25, folder 13, Henry Regnery Papers, 1909–1996, HIA.

39 *Human Events*, "Fifteen Years of Publishing: Henry Regnery Company," February 23, 1963, 151.

40 Ibid., 151.

41 Regnery, "Henry Regnery: A Conservative Publisher," 15.

42 Harry Crocker, interview with author Nicole Hoplin, August 4, 2005.

43 William J. Casey to Henry Regnery, January 29, 1953, box 13, folder 13, Henry Regnery Papers, 1909–1996, HIA.

44 Henry Regnery to J. Howard Pew, November 29, 1960, box 22, Felix Morley Papers, HHPL.

45 Ibid.

46 Henry Regnery to Felix Morley, October 14, 1960, box 22, Felix Morley Papers, HHPL.

47 Henry Regnery to J. Howard Pew, November 29, 1960, box 22, Felix Morley Papers, HHPL.

48 Henry Regnery to Pierre F. Goodrich, June 25, 1962, box 25, folder 13, Henry Regnery Papers, 1909–1996, HIA.

49 Henry Regnery to Felix Morley, October 20, 1967, box 22, Felix Morley Papers, HHPL.

50 Henry Regnery to Mrs. Esther Chambers, October 27, 1967, box 14, folder 12, Henry Regnery Papers, 1909–1996, HIA.

51 Stephen J. Tonsor, "Tribute to Mr. Henry Regnery," *The Philadelphia Society*, April 27, 1996, http://www.conservativeclassics.com/hrlp2.html.

52 Walter R. Collins, "Two Vigorous New Book Publishing Houses Based in South Bend," *South Bend Tribune*, March 5, 1978, 6.

53 Henry Regnery to Henry Salvatori, January 6, 1977, box 67, folder 4, Henry Regnery Papers, 1909–1996, HIA.

54 Felix Morley to Henry Regnery, December 17, 1976, box 22, Felix Morley Papers, HHPL.

55 Henry Regnery to Russell Kirk, May 10, 1979, box 40, folder 1, Henry Regnery Papers, 1909–1996, HIA.

56 Michelle Easton, personal e-mail communication with author Nicole Hoplin, July 11, 2005.

57 William Regnery to Foundation for Foreign Affairs, November 7, 1945, box 23, folder 3, Henry Regnery Papers, 1909–1996, HIA.

58 The Philadelphia Society, *Our Mission*, http://www.phillysoc.org.

59 Henry Regnery to Felix Morley, May 2, 1974, box 22, Felix Morley Papers, HHPL.

60 Regnery, *Memoirs*, 248.

61 Ibid.

Chapter 3

1   George Will, "For Senator Barry Goldwater," *National Review*, December 31, 1980, 1645.

2   John B. Judis, *William F. Buckley Jr. Patron Saint of the Conservatives* (New York: Simon and Schuster, 1988), 18.

3   Mark Royden Winchell, *William F. Buckley Jr.* (Boston: Twayne Publishers, 1984), 2.

4   Scott Kraft, "Being Bill Buckley; He's No Longer a Lone Voice in the Conservative Wilderness. But the Letters, Columns, and Books Keep Coming," *Los Angeles Times Magazine*, August 26, 2001, 16.

5   William F. Buckley Jr., "The Ivory Tower," *National Review*, October 25, 1958, 277.

6   Aloise Buckley Heath, "Supper at Great Elm," in *W.F.B. – An Appreciation by His Family and Friends*, eds. Priscilla Buckley and William F. Buckley Jr. (New York: Private Printing, 1979), 214.

7   Judis, *William F. Buckley*, 20–21.

8   Ibid., 21.

9   William F. Buckley Jr., *The Jeweler's Eye* (New York: G.P. Putnam & Sons, 1968), 349.

10 Judis, *William F. Buckley*, 21.

11 Nemesio Garcia Naranjo, "A Friend of Mexico," in *W.F.B. – An Appreciation by His Family and Friends*, eds. Priscilla Buckley and William F. Buckley Jr. (New York: Private Printing, 1979), 50.

12 Ibid., 26.

13 William F. Buckley Jr., *The Right Reason* (Garden City, New York: Doubleday & Company, Inc., 1985), 442.

14 Naranjo, "A Friend of Mexico," 50.

15 Ibid., 31–32.

16 Judis, *William F. Buckley*, 32.

17 Buckley, *The Right Reason*, 443.

18 Judis, *William F. Buckley*, 30.

19 Aloise Buckley Heath, "Supper at Great Elm," 200.

20 Priscilla Buckley, "Foreword," in *W.F.B. – An Appreciation by His Family and Friends*, eds. Priscilla Buckley and William F. Buckley Jr. (New York: Private Printing, 1979), ix.

21 Judis, *William F. Buckley*, 36.

22 Priscilla Buckley and William F. Buckley Jr., "Memorandum to: Aloise, John, Priscilla, Jimmy, Jane, Billie, Patricia, Reid, Maureen, Carol," in *W.F.B. – An Appreciation by His Family and Friends*, eds. Priscilla Buckley and William F. Buckley Jr. (New York: Private Printing, 1979), 218.

23 Judis, *William F. Buckley*, 48–50.

24 Ibid., 48.

25 Ibid.

26 Chris Manion, personal interview with author Ron Robinson, June 20, 2006.

27 Winchell, *William F. Buckley, Jr.*, 4.

28 Ibid., 4.

29 Judis, *William F. Buckley*, 55.

30 Ibid., 69.

31 Ibid., 70.

32 Evan Galbraith, "Pat Buckley, R.I.P.," *National Review Online*, April 16, 2007.

33 Galbraith, "Pat Buckley."

34 William F. Buckley Jr., *God and Man at Yale* (Washington, D.C.: Regnery Publishing, Inc., 1986), lxv.

35 Ibid., lxv.

36 William A. Rusher, *The Rise of the Right* (New York: William Morrow and Company, Inc, 1984), 41.

37 Ibid., 40.

38 McGeorge Bundy, "The Attack on Yale," *Atlantic Monthly*, November, 1951, 50–51.

39 Judis, *William F. Buckley*, 95.

40 Henry Regnery, *Memoirs of a Dissident Publisher* (Chicago: Regnery Books, 1985), 170.

41 Judis, *William F. Buckley*, 105.

42 Ibid.

43 Ibid., 109.

44 Rusher, *The Rise of the Right*, 43–44.

45 William F. Buckley Jr., "Publisher's Statement," *National Review*, November 19, 1955, 5.

46 Lee Edwards, *The Conservative Revolution* (New York: The Free Press, 1999), 79.

47 George Will, "Thankful Praise for Birthday Boy Buckley," *Times Union*, November 24, 2005, sec. A.

48 George Will, "Grim Conservatism Cracks a Smile with Bill Buckley," *Newsday*, December 5, 1985, 99.

49 Victor Lasky to Henry Regnery, October 26, 1955, Henry Regnery Papers, box 10, Hoover Institution Archives.

50 Buckley, "Publisher's Statement," 5.

51 Judis, *William F. Buckley*, 133.

52 William F. Buckley Jr., "Regular Features," *National Review*, November 19, 1955, 6.

53 Henry Regnery to Pierre Goodrich, June 21, 1957, Henry Regnery Papers, box 25, Hoover Institution Archives.

54 William F. Buckley Jr., "Notes and Asides," *National Review*, December 31, 2005, 17.

55 Judis, *William F. Buckley*, 140.

56 Buckley, "Notes and Asides," 17.

57 L. Clayton Dubois, "The Sniper," *Time*, November 3, 1967, 70.

58 Rich Lowry, "We Need Your Help," *National Review Online*, June 12, 2006.

59 Ibid., 368.

60 Buckley, *The Jeweler's Eye*, 17.

61 Dwight Macdonald, "Scrambled Eggheads on the Right," *Commentary*, April 1956, 367, 371–372.

62 William F. Buckley Jr., "The Week," *National Review*, November 28, 1980, 1434.

63 John Micklethwait and Adrian Wooldridge, *The Right Nation* (New York: The Penguin Press, 2004), 50.

64 Jeffrey Hart, *The Making of the American Conservative Mind*

Notes

National Review and Its Times (Wilmington, Delaware: ISI Books, 2005), 269.

65 Ronald Reagan, "The Defense of Freedom and Metaphysics of Fun," reprinted in *National Review Online*, June 10, 2004, http://www.nationalreview.com/document/reagan200406100924.asp.

66 Rusher, *The Rise of the Right*, 80.

67 Joseph Sobran, "Morituri," *Wanderer*, June 8, 2006, http://www.sobran.com/wanderer/w2006/w060608.shtml.

68 Rusher, *The Rise of the Right*, 228.

69 Judis, *William F. Buckley*, 140.

70 John Saloma 3d, "Old Right? New Right? One Right," *Nation*, January 14, 1984, 14.

71 *National Review*, "The Sharon Statement," September 24, 1960, 173.

72 Judis, *William F. Buckley*, 189.

73 Herb Stupp, interview with author Nicole Hoplin, June 19, 2006.

74 Ibid.

75 Judis, *William F. Buckley*, 231.

76 George H. Nash, *The Conservative Intellectual Movement in America* (Wilmington, Delaware: Intercollegiate Studies Institute, 1998), 109.

77 Ibid., 287.

78 *Time*, "Who's Who Among Campus Celebrities," October 27, 1967, 61.

79 Judis, *William F. Buckley*, 265.

80 Regnery, *Memoirs*, 167.

81 Judis, *William F. Buckley*, 241.

82 Ibid., 257.

83 Buckley, *The Jeweler's Eye*, 39.

84 L. Clayton Dubois, "The Sniper," 70.

85 Ibid.

86 Hart, *American Conservative Mind*, 3.

87 L. Clayton Dubois, "The First Family of Conservatism," *New York Times*, August 9, 1970, 28.

88 L. Clayton Dubois, "The Sniper," 71.

89 Ibid.

90 Judis, *William F. Buckley*, 267.

91 Rich Lowry, personal interview with author Nicole Hoplin, July 12, 2006.

92 Judis, *William F. Buckley*, 288.

93 Ibid.

94 Ibid., 290.

95 Ibid., 288.

96 Ibid., 292.

97 L. Clayton Dubois, "The Sniper," 70.

98 Laurence Zuckerman, "The Debate is Done for 'Firing Line,'" *San Diego Union Tribune*, January 4, 2000, sec. E.

99 George Will, "A Farewell to Firing Line," *National Review*, December 31, 1999, 16.

100 Rusher, *The Rise of the Right*, 81.

101 Dan Flynn, "National Review Turns Fifty," *Flynn Files*, November 19, 2005, http://www.flynnfiles.com/archives/2005_11.php.

102 Arnold Forster and Benjamin Epstein, *Danger on the Right* (New York: Random House, 1964), 240.

103 Will, "Thankful Praise," sec. A.

104 Hillel Italie, "William F. Buckley, Jr. dies at 82," *USA Today*, February 27, 2008.

Chapter 4

1 Barry Goldwater, *The Conscience of a Conservative* (New York: McFadden Capitol Hill Books, 1964), 11–12.

2 Clarence Manion to R. B. Snowden, May 27, 1959, box 69, folder 1, Manion Papers, Chicago Historical Society [CHS from here forward]; *Our Sunday Visitor*, "Right or Wrong," Huntington, Indiana, May 8, 1960, 2.

3 Carolyn Manion, "A Life Worth Living," (Georgetown Visitation Junior College: Unpublished assignment, 1957), box 74, folder 11, Manion Papers, CHS, 1.

4 Ibid., 2.

5 Ibid., 1.

6 Ibid., 2.

7 Ibid., 3.

8 Ibid., 4.

9 Ibid., 5–6.

10 Ibid., 6.

11 Ibid., 8.

12 Chris Manion, personal interview with author Ron Robinson, June 20, 2006.

13 Ibid.

14 *Augusta (GA) Bulletin*, "Dr. Manion Speaker at C.L.A. Meeting," October 28, 1939, 1.

15 *New York Sun*, "Manion on Liberty," November 11, 1939, 1.

16 Carolyn Manion, "A Life Worth Living," 10.

17 Ibid., 11.

18 *Columbus (GA) Ledger*, "Walker Flays Foreign Isms in Talk Here," October 31, 1939, 10.

19 Chris Manion, personal interview with author Ron Robinson, June 20, 2006.

20 Rick Perlstein, interview by Brian Lamb, *Booknotes*, C-SPAN, June 3, 2001.

21 Clarence Manion, interview by David Tudor, 73–17, Oral History Program, Indiana University Center for the Study of History and Memory, May 31, 1973, 3.

22 Ibid., 3.

23 Clarence Manion, "The Election," 1960, box 68, folder 7, Manion Papers, CHS, 1.

24 Dwight D. Eisenhower to Alexander Wiley, June 8, 1953, In *The Papers of Dwight David Eisenhower*, eds. L. Galambos and D. Van, doc. 233, World Wide Web facsimile by The Dwight D. Eisenhower Memorial Commission of the print edition; Baltimore, MD: The Johns Hopkins University Press, 1996, http://www.eisenhowermemorial.org/presidential-papers/first-term/documents/233.cfm.

25 Stephen E. Ambrose, *Eisenhower the President* (New York: Simon and Schuster, 1984), 68.

26 Clarence Manion, interview by David Tudor, 14.

27 Ibid., 4.

28 Ibid., 5.

29 Ibid.,, 7.

30 Chris Manion, personal interview with author Ron Robinson, June 20, 2006.

31 Ibid.

32 *New York Times*, "Manion Ousted by White House As Head of Governmental Survey," February 18, 1954, 1.

33 Clarence Manion to President Dwight Eisenhower, February 17, 1954, box 74, folder 11, Manion Papers, CHS.

34 Clarence Manion, interview by David Tudor, 7.

35 Ambrose, *Eisenhower*, 155.

36 Clarence Manion, interview by David Tudor, 2.

37 "Clarence Manion Biography," (South Bend, Indiana: The Manion Forum, September 1973) box 74, folder 12, Manion Papers, CHS, 1.

38 *Wall Street Journal*, Advertisement, March 17, 1958, 15.

39 Mark Sherwin, *The Extremists* (New York: St. Martin's Press, 1963), 90.

40 Fred J. Cook, "Hate Clubs of the Air," *Nation*, May 25, 1964, 524.

41 Chris Manion, personal interview with author Ron Robinson, June 20, 2006.

42 Ibid.

43 Ibid.

44 Clarence Manion to C. S. Hallauer, May 25, 1959, box 69, folder 1, Manion Papers, CHS.

45 Bonner Fellers to Clarence Manion, April 13, 1959, box 69, folder 1, Manion Papers, CHS.

46 Clarence Manion, "The Election," 1.

47 Ibid.

48 Clarence Manion to Henry Loeb, July 2, 1959, box 69, folder 1, Manion Papers, CHS.

49 Clarence Manion to the Honorable Barry Goldwater, July 21, 1959, Arizona Historical Foundation, Personal and Political Papers of Barry M. Goldwater, MSS #1, Personal Writings 1955–1959, box 1.

50 Jonathan Martin Kolkey, *The New Right, 1960–1968* (Lanham, Maryland: University Press of America, 1983), 33.

51 Clarence Manion to General Robert E. Wood, April 20, 1959, box 69, folder 1, Manion Papers, CHS.

52 Clarence Manion to Earl Platt, August 11, 1959, box 70, folder 1, Manion Papers, CHS.

53 Clarence Manion to Frank Brophy, July 28, 1959, box 70, folder 11, Manion Papers, CHS.

54 "List of Those who have Accepted Membership on Goldwater Committee," *Confidential Memorandum*, July 31, 1959, box 74, folder 14, Manion Papers, CHS.

55 Clarence Manion to M. Stanton Evans, November 30, 1959, box 70, folder 3, Manion Papers, CHS.

56 Clarence Manion to the Honorable Barry Goldwater, July 27, 1959, Arizona Historical Foundation, Personal and Political Papers of Barry M. Goldwater, MSS #1, Personal Writings 1955–1959, box 1.

57 Clarence Manion to the Honorable Barry Goldwater, July 27, 1959, Arizona Historical Foundation, Personal and Political Papers of Barry M. Goldwater, MSS #1, Personal Writings 1955–1959, box 1.

58 Clarence Manion to Frank Brophy, October 23, 1959, box 68, folder 4, Manion Papers, CHS.

59 Clarence Manion to Roger Milliken, January 29, 1960, box 68, folder 4, Manion Papers, CHS.

60 Clarence Manion to the Honorable Barry Goldwater, July 27, 1959,

Notes

folder: Goldwater: Personal Writings 1955–1959, Personal and Political Papers of Senator Barry M. Goldwater, Arizona Historical Foundation.

61 Peter Edson, "Goldwater Books Reaps Financial, Political Hay," New-York World-Telegram, April 26, 1960.

62 Clarence Manion to the Honorable Barry Goldwater, July 27, 1959, Arizona Historical Foundation, Personal and Political Papers of Barry M. Goldwater, MSS #1, Personal Writings 1955–1959, box 1.

63 Rick Perlstein, Before the Storm (New York: Hill and Wang, 2001), 62.

64 Harry Crocker, interview with author Nicole Hoplin, August 4, 2005.

65 Chicago Daily Tribune, "Nixon Defends Bid to Nikita to Visit U.S.," Sept. 21, 1959, 3.

66 Denver Post, "So the People May Know," August 30, 1959, sec. AA.

67 Lee Edwards, Goldwater, The Man Who Made a Revolution (Washington, D.C.: Regnery Publishing, 1997), 114.

68 Clarence Manion to George Montgomery Jr., November 25, 1959, box 70, folder 3, Manion Papers, CHS.

69 Edwards, Goldwater, 115.

70 Ibid., 115.

71 Virginia Manion to the Honorable Barry Goldwater, June 7, 1989, Young America's Foundation files.

72 Goldwater, Conscience, 23.

73 Ibid., 126–127.

74 Chris Manion, personal interview with author Ron Robinson, June 20, 2006.

75 Edwards, Goldwater, 119.

76 Ibid., 113.

77 Clarence Manion, "April 12 and 13, 1960," box 68, folder 5, Manion Papers, CHS, 1.

78 Ibid., 2.

79 Edwards, Goldwater, 119–120.

80 R. L. Duffus, "One Senator's Manifesto," New York Times, June 26, 1960, sec. BR.

81 Ralph Holsinger, "Is There Really Gold in That Water?" Cincinnati Enquirer, June 12, 1960, sec. G.

82 Newsweek, "Week's Top Bestsellers," August 22, 1960, 91.

83 Lee Edwards, "A Modern Don Quixote Fought the Good Fight," Insight on the News 13, no. 21 (June 9, 1997), 30.

84 Edwards, Goldwater, 115.

85 Perlstein, Before the Storm, 63.

86 Edwards, Goldwater, 139.

87 Time, "Salesman for a Cause," June 23, 1961, 12–13.

88 Edwards, Goldwater, 150.

89 Time, "Salesman," 12–13.

90 John Micklethwait and Adrian Wooldridge, The Right Nation (New York: The Penguin Press, 2004), 59; Rick Perlstein, interview by Brian Lamb, Booknotes, C-SPAN, June 3, 2001.

91 William F. Buckley Jr., "L. Brent Bozell, RIP," National Review 49, no. 9 (May 19, 1997): 22.

92 Rick Perlstein, interview by Brian Lamb, Booknotes, C-SPAN, June 3, 2001.

93 William Rusher, The Rise of the Right, 161.

94 George Will, "Goldwater: A Man Who Won the Future," Washington Post, March 27, 1994, sec. C.

95 Perlstein, Before the Storm, 107.

96 David M. Shribman, "Visionary Saw Future of Politics," Boston Globe, May 30, 1998, sec. A.

97 Chicago Daily Tribune, "Conservative Comeback," Nov. 7, 1959, 12.

98 Dan Manion, "In Conclusion," The Manion Forum Broadcast 1293, August 12, 1979, box 75, folder 4, Manion Papers, CHS, 1.

99 Rick Perlstein, interview by Brian Lamb, Booknotes, C-SPAN, June 3, 2001.

100 Goldwater, Conscience, 11–12.

101 Ibid.

Chapter 5

1 Ronald Reagan, An American Life (New York: Simon and Schuster, 1990), 143.

2 Lou Cannon, Ronnie & Jessie: A Political Odyssey (New York: Doubleday & Company, Inc., 1969), 72.

3 Holmes Tuttle, interview by Steven Edgington, The Kitchen Cabinet, Oral History Program, California State University–Fullerton, June 9, 1981, 114.

4 Los Angeles Times, "Holmes Tuttle, a Force in Reagan Political Rise, Dies," June 17, 1989, sec. 1.

5 Ibid.

6 Jody Jacobs, "This-Is-Your-Life Tribute for Holmes Tuttle," Los Angeles Times, October 8, 1973, sec. C.

7 Tuttle, The Kitchen Cabinet, 109; Kenneth Reich, "Holmes Tuttle, Key Reagan Backer, Honored by Friends," Los Angeles Times, October 6, 1973, sec. 2; Jacobs, "This-Is-Your-Life Tribute."

8 Tuttle, The Kitchen Cabinet, 109.

9 Robert Tuttle Interview, Miller Center, University of Virginia, Ronald Reagan Presidential Oral History Project, December 12, 2003.

10 Ibid.

11 Bob Colacello, Ronnie & Nancy (New York: Warner Books, 2004): 326.

12 Ibid.

13 Ibid.

14 Tuttle, The Kitchen Cabinet, 111.

15 Los Angeles Times, "Holmes Tuttle."

16 Bill and Nancy Boyarsky, "Take Me to Your Power Structure," Los Angeles Times, October 4, 1970, sec. O.

17 Ibid.

18 Henry Salvatori, interview by Steven Edgington, The Kitchen Cabinet, Oral History Program, California State University–Fullerton, April 24, 1981, 1.

19 Delores Proubasta, "Henry Salvatori," Geophysics: The Leading Edge of Exploration 2, no. 8 (August 1983): 14.

20 Ibid.

21 Ibid.

22 Ibid.

23 Ibid.

24 Proubasta, "Henry Salvatori"; Colacello, Ronnie & Nancy, 328.

25 Proubasta, "Henry Salvatori."

26 Salvatori, The Kitchen Cabinet, 4.

27 Joel Kotkin and Paul Grabowicz, California, INC., (New York: Avon Books, 1982), 52.

28 Salvatori, The Kitchen Cabinet, 3.

29 Ibid.

30 Ibid.

31 Larry Arnn, Claremont Institute Bulletin (California: July 1997), quoted in William F. Buckley, "Henry Salvatori, RIP," National Review, August 11, 1997, 18.

32 Kotkin, California, INC., 50–51.

33 Los Angeles Times, "County Mourns Death of Oilman A. C. Rubel," June 2, 1967, sec. 1.

34 Los Angeles Times, "New Position Won by Rubel," March 16, 1931, 14.

35 Los Angeles Times, "A. C. Rubel, Miss Blomquist Win Awards," April 29, 1963, sec. B.

36 Los Angeles Times, "County Mourns Death," 30.

37 Salvatori, The Kitchen Cabinet, 25.

38 Peter van Wyk, "Courting Union Oil Co. of California," http://abc-books.pacificblog.com/blog/MajorBurnham/_archives/2004/10/30/171394.html.

39 Los Angeles Times, "County Mourns Death," 30.

40 Ibid.

41 Los Angeles Times, "A Deserved Ovation for 'Cy' Rubel," June 5, 1967, sec. A.

42 Tuttle, The Kitchen Cabinet, 123.

43 Salvatori, The Kitchen Cabinet, 25.

44 Kotkin, California, INC., 52.

45 Ibid.

46 Cannon, Ronnie & Jessie, 70.

47 Ibid., 76.

48 Ibid., 71.

49 Ibid.

50 Kurt Ritter, "Ronald Reagan and 'The Speech': The Rhetoric of Public Relations Politics," Western Speech 32, no. 1 (1968), 52.

51 Ibid.

52 Thomas W. Evans, The Education of Ronald Reagan (New York: Columbia University Press, 2006), 57.

53 Helene Von Damm, Sincerely, Ronald Reagan (Ottawa, Illinois: Green Hills Publishers, Inc., 1976), 69.

54 Reagan, An American Life, 140.

55 Jonathan M. Schoenwald, A Time for Choosing (New York: Oxford University Press, 2001), 195.

56 Reagan, An American Life, 140.

57 Ibid.

58 Ibid., 141.

59 Ronald Reagan, "A Time for Choosing," October 27, 1964, Reagan Foundation, http://www.reaganfoundation.org/reagan/speeches/speech.asp?pid=1.

60 Herbert M. Baus and William B. Ross, Politics Battle Plan (New York: Macmillan Company, 1968), 77.

61 Ibid., 76.

62 Ibid., 91.

63 F. Clifton White and William J. Gill, Why Reagan Won (Chicago: Regnery Gateway, 1981), 24.

64 Lou Cannon, Reagan (New York: Perigee Books, 1982), 13.

65 Ibid., 13.

Notes

66 Kurt Ritter and David Henry, *Ronald Reagan: The Great Communicator* (New York: Greenwood Press, 1992), 24.

67 T. R. Reid, "Reagan: A Life Built on Performing," *Washington Post*, October 22, 1980, sec. A.

68 *Time*, "Stage to Sacramento?" July 30, 1965, 14.

69 Ritter, *Ronald Reagan*, 24; William Pemberton, *Exit with Honor: The Life and Presidency of Ronald Reagan* (Armonk, New York: M. E. Sharpe, 1998), 54.

70 Walter Pincus, "The Fight Over Money," *Atlantic Monthly* 217, no. 4 (April 1966): 73.

71 David S. Broder and Stephen Hess, *The Republican Establishment* (New York: Harper & Row Publishers, 1967), 253–254.

72 *Time*, "Stage to Sacramento?" 13.

73 Salvatori, *The Kitchen Cabinet*, 14.

74 White, *Why Reagan Won*, 27.

75 Reagan, *An American Life*, 144.

76 Ibid., 146.

77 Tuttle, *The Kitchen Cabinet*, 124.

78 Ritter, "Ronald Reagan and 'The Speech,'" 51.

79 Ibid.

80 Ritter, "Ronald Reagan and 'The Speech,'" 57; *Time*, "The Milkman Cometh," November 5, 1965, 38; *Time*, "Stage to Sacramento?" 14.

81 Edward Mills, interview by Lawrence de Graaf, *The Kitchen Cabinet*, Oral History Program, California State University–Fullerton, June 23 and July 8, 1981, 67.

82 Lee Edwards, "Why Californians Look to Ronald Reagan," *Human Events* 26, no. 8 (February 19, 1966): 9.

83 Lee Edwards, *Goldwater The Man Who Made a Revolution* (Washington, D.C.: Regnery Publishing, Inc., 1997), 337.

84 Reagan, *An American Life*, 143.

85 Reid, "Reagan: A Life Built on Performing."

86 Ronald Reagan, "On Becoming Governor," an oral history conducted by Gabrielle Morris and Sarah Sharp in 1979 in *Governor Reagan and His Cabinet: An Introduction*, Regional Oral History Office, University of California, Berkeley, 1986, 3. Courtesy, Bancroft Library.

87 Reagan, *An American Life*, 199.

88 Peter B. Sperry, "The Real Reagan Economic Record: Responsible and Successful Fiscal Policy," *Backgrounder* 1414 (Washington, D.C.: Heritage Foundation, March 1, 2006), 3.

89 Joint Economic Committee, *The 2000 Joint Economic Report* (Washington, D.C.: GPO, April 2000), 6.

90 Ronald Reagan, "Message on the Management of the United States Government," January 18, 1989, *The Public Papers of President Ronald W. Reagan*, Ronald Reagan Presidential Library, http://www.reagan.utexas.edu/archives/speeches/1989/011889a.htm.

91 Ritter, *Ronald Reagan*, 25.

92 John Fund, "'A Time for Choosing,'" *Wall Street Journal*, October 27, 1994, sec. A.

93 Dick Armey, "Reagan: Strength to Rise Above Undaring Advisors," *Post-Tribune* (Gary, Indiana), June 11, 2004, sec. B.

94 Henry Lowman, "'The Speech' Is Relevant for State GOP," *Patriot-News*, July 13, 2004, sec. A.

95 William French Smith, *Evolution of the Kitchen Cabinet, 1965–1973*, an oral history conducted by Gabrielle Morris in 1988, Regional Oral History Office, University of California, Berkeley, 1989, 8–9. Courtesy, Bancroft Library.

96 Robert Lindsey, "Reagan's Inner Circle of Self-Made Men," *New York Times*, May 31, 1980, sec. 1.

97 Kotkin, *California, INC.*, 52.

98 Robert L Bartley, "Money and Politics: A Better Way to Make a Mark," *Wall Street Journal*, November 20, 2000, sec. A.

99 Cannon, *Reagan*, 13.

100 Reagan, *An American Life*, 142.

101 *New York Times*, January 5, 1989.

Chapter 6

1 Antony Fisher, *Fisher's Concise History of Economic Bungling* (Ottawa, Illinois: Caroline House Books, 1978), x.

2 Gerald Frost, *Antony Fisher: Champion of Liberty* (London: Profile Books, 2002), 8.

3 Frost, *Antony Fisher*, 7.

4 Ralph Harris, "The Monday Book; The Chicken Farmer Who Changed the World," *Independent* (London), December 16, 2002, 12.

5 Antony Fisher, *Must History Repeat Itself?* (Middlesex, England: Churchill Press Limited, 1974), xv.

6 Frost, *Antony Fisher*, 28.

7 Ibid., 31.

8 Linda Whetstone, "Sir Antony Fisher," *Tanker Talk* (1989), quoted in Gerald Frost, *Antony Fisher: Champion of Liberty* (London: Profile Books, 2002), 5–6.

9 Frost, *Antony Fisher*, 39.

10 Ibid., 36–37.

11 Ibid., 39.

12 Richard Cockett, *Thinking the Unthinkable, Think-Tanks and the Economic Counter-Revolution 1931–1983* (London: Fontana Press, 1995), 123.

13 Fisher, *Must History Repeat Itself?* 103–104.

14 John Hyde, "Tomorrow's Reform," *IPA Review*, March 2003, 16.

15 Frost, *Antony Fisher*, 21.

16 Ibid., 33.

17 Ibid., 46.

18 Ibid.

19 Ibid., 49.

20 *Times* (London), "Sir Antony Fisher: Obituary," July 12, 1988.

21 Frost, *Antony Fisher*, 51.

22 Gerald Frost, "Consequences of a 'Chicken Farmer's' Ideas," *Forbes Global*, February 3, 2003, 25.

23 Antony Fisher, *City Press* (April 1948), quoted in Gerald Frost, *Antony Fisher: Champion of Liberty* (London: Profile Books, 2002), 38.

24 Simon Heffer, "Politics: The Man who Took on Socialism and Won," *Daily Telegraph* (London), January 11, 2006, 019.

25 Digby Anderson, "Fighting for Freedom," *Asian Wall Street Journal*, September 24, 2002, sec. A.

26 Ibid.

27 Institute of Economic Affairs, "About the IEA," http://iea.org.uk/record.jsp?type=page&ID=23.

28 Antony Fisher to Oliver Smedley, personal letter (1956), quoted in Richard Cockett, *Thinking the Unthinkable, Think-Tanks and the Economic Counter-Revolution 1931–1983* (London: Fontana Press, 1995), 130–131.

29 Cockett, *Thinking the Unthinkable*, 133.

30 Frost, *Antony Fisher*, 44.

31 Ralph Harris, interview with Gerald Frost (March 2001), quoted in Gerald Frost, *Antony Fisher: Champion of Liberty* (London: Profile Books, 2002), 44.

32 Harris, "The Monday Book," 12.

33 Dennis Kavanagh, *The Reordering of British Politics* (Oxford: Oxford University Press, 1997), 96.

34 David Warsh, "Think-Tank Approach Helped Fuel America's Turn to the Right," *Washington Post*, September 5, 1990, sec. F.

35 Cockett, *Thinking the Unthinkable*, 146.

36 Alan Peacock to Arthur Seldon, personal letter (July 1975), quoted in Richard Cockett, *Thinking the Unthinkable, Think-Tanks and the Economic Counter-Revolution 1931–1983* (London: Fontana Press, 1995), 156.

37 Kavanagh, *The Reordering of British Politics*, 99.

38 Ibid.

39 Cockett, *Thinking the Unthinkable*, 157.

40 F. A. Hayek, interviewed by Cato Institute, *Cato Policy Report*, (February 1983), quoted in David Boaz, *Toward Liberty: The Idea That Is Changing the World 25 Years of Public Policy from the Cato Institute* (Washington, D.C.: Cato Institute: 2002), 17.

41 Kavanagh, *The Reordering of British Politics*, 97.

42 Cockett, *Thinking the Unthinkable*, 156.

43 Peter Botsman, "Thatcher's Politicisation of Ideas," *Courier Mail* (Queensland, Australia), May 4, 1999, 13.

44 Margaret Thatcher, *The Path to Power* (Norwalk, Connecticut: Easton Press, 1995), 254.

45 Frost, *Antony Fisher*, 106.

46 Kavanagh, *The Reordering of British Politics*, 97.

47 John Chamberlain, "All Eyes on Britain," *National Review* 31, no. 47 (November 23, 1979): 1499.

48 Daniel Yergin and Joseph Stanislaw, *The Commanding Heights* (New York: Simon and Schuster, 1998), 124.

49 Frost, *Antony Fisher*, 109.

50 Cockett, *Thinking the Unthinkable*, 122.

51 Milton Friedman, "Principles of Freedom," *Times* (London), October 7, 1991.

52 Ralph Harris, "The Plan to End Planning," *National Review* 49, no. 11 (June 16, 1997): 24.

53 Gerald Frost, "Consequences of a 'Chicken Farmer's' Ideas," 25.

54 Frost, *Antony Fisher*, 103–104.

55 Ibid., 104.

56 Cockett, *Thinking the Unthinkable*, 132.

57 Arthur Seldon, *Capitalism* (Cambridge, Massachusetts: Basil Blackwell, Inc., 1990), 41.

58 Friedman, "Principles of Freedom."

59 Warsh, "Think-Tank Approach," F3.

60 Fred Kaplan, "Conservatives Plant a Seed in NYC; Think Tank Helps Giuliani Set His Agenda," *Boston Globe*, February 22, 1998, sec. A.

61 Steven Schwalm, "Pacific Research Institute," *Human Events* 53,

no. 5 (February 7, 1997): 20.
62 *Times* (London), "Sir Antony Fisher: Obituary."
63 J.A.S.H., "Sir Antony Fisher," *Times* (London), July 23, 1988.
64 Frost, *Antony Fisher*, 21.

Chapter 7

1   Ronald Reagan, "Tribute to Ambassador Jeane Kirkpatrick," *Imprimis*, Hillsdale College Online Archive, May 1984, http://www.hillsdale.edu/news/imprimis/archive/issue.asp?year=1984&month=05.
2   Julie Nicklin, "Defiantly Independent," *Chronicle of Higher Education* 42, no. 25 (March 1, 1996): A30.
3   PR Newswire, "Princeton Review Names Top 10 'Best Value' Colleges—Private & Public," (New York: March 28, 2006); Philip Rosenbaum, "Rice Again Rated Best College Buy," *Buffalo News*, September 2, 1992, sec. A.
4   Jennifer Holmes, "At Hillsdale College, Kilts Are In; Kennedy Is Out," *Detroit Free Press*, January 25, 1981, 18.
5   Gilbert, *The Permanent Things*, 62–63.
6   Hillsdale College, *Winona* (Hillsdale, Michigan: Hillsdale College, 1926), 124.
7   Elli Leutheuser, personal e-mail interview with author Nicole Hoplin, April 26, 2006.
8   Hillsdale College, "Mission Statement," http://www.hillsdale.edu/collegehistory/missionstatement.htm.
9   Clarence Thomas, "Friends' Voices," Hillsdale College, http://www.hillsdale.edu/admissions/about/voices/friends.asp.
10 Arlan Gilbert, *The Permanent Things* (Hillsdale, Michigan: Hillsdale College Press, 1998), 15–21; John Seiler, "What Makes Hillsdale Special?" *Orange County Register*, May 21, 2000, sec. G.
11 Annette Kirk, personal telephone interview with author Nicole Hoplin, May 15, 2006.
12 Michael Catanzaro, "Hillsdale College," *Human Events* 53, no. 17 (May 2, 1997): 14.
13 Willfred Otto Mauck, *Hillsdale Alumnus* (July 1975), quoted in Arlan K. Gilbert, *The Permanent Things* (Hillsdale, Michigan: Hillsdale College Press, 1998), 78.
14 Vivian Lyon Moore, *The First Hundred Years of Hillsdale College* (Ann Arbor, Michigan: Vivian Lyon Moore, 1943), 218.
15 Gilbert, *The Permanent Things*, 91.
16 John Chamberlain, *Freedom and Independence: The Hillsdale Story* (Hillsdale, Michigan: Hillsdale College Press, 1979), 24.
17 Dr. Harvey Turner, *Hillsdale Alumnus* (February 1951), quoted in Arlan K. Gilbert, *The Permanent Things* (Hillsdale, Michigan: Hillsdale College Press, 1998), 123.
18 Gilbert, *The Permanent Things*, 164.
19 Lamar "Tony" Fowler, personal interview with author Nicole Hoplin, April 19, 2006.
20 John Muller, memorandum to faculty, May 10, 1982, Hillsdale College Archives.
21 Larry Arnn, *Liberty and Learning* (Hillsdale, Michigan: Hillsdale College Press, 2004), 43–44.
22 Arnn, *Liberty and Learning*, 45.
23 Hillsdale College Board of Trustees, "Hillsdale College Declaration of Independence," February 16, 1962, quoted in Larry Arnn, *Liberty and Learning* (Hillsdale, Michigan: Hillsdale College Press, 2004), 99–100.
24 Fowler, personal interview.
25 Arnn, *Liberty and Learning*, 47.
26 Roger Kimball, "In Defense of Hypocrisy," *Wall Street Journal*, November 22, 1999, sec. A.
27 Chamberlain, *Freedom and Independence*, 1.
28 Seiler, "What Makes Hillsdale Special?"
29 Chamberlain, *Freedom and Independence*, 5.
30 Ibid., 19.
31 Arnn, *Liberty and Learning*, 48.
32 Gilbert, *The Permanent Things*, 248.
33 Chamberlain, *Freedom and Independence*, xi.
34 Arnn, *Liberty and Learning*, 52.
35 *Grand Rapids Press News Service*, "Hillsdale College Flourishes Without Student Aid Programs," October 20, 1994, sec. B.
36 Associated Press, "D'oh! More Know Simpsons than Constitution," MSNBC, March 1, 2006, http://www.msnbc.msn.com.
37 David J. Bobb, "Scholarly Mesearch," *American Spectator* 39, no. 3 (April 2006): 50.
38 Don Mossey, personal interview with author Nicole Hoplin, April 26, 2006.
39 Hillsdale College Board of Trustees, minutes, October 15, 1966, Hillsdale College Archives.
40 Hillsdale College Board of Trustees, minutes, October 11, 1968, Hillsdale College Archives.

41 Gerald D. "Spike" Hennessy, letter to Hillsdale College Board of Trustees, May 4, 1982, Hillsdale College Archives.
42 Gerald and Helen Hennessy Record of Gifts and Donations, Institutional Advancement, Hillsdale College Archives.
43 Source: www.hillsdale.edu/about/default.asp

Chapter 8

1   Edwin Feulner, "Salute to a Visionary Founder," *Washington Times*, March 19, 2003, sec. A.
2   Dan Baum, *Citizen Coors An American Dynasty* (New York: William Morrow, 2000), 8.
3   Ibid., 9.
4   Ibid., 23.
5   Ibid., 13.
6   Ibid.
7   Marshall B. Paisner, *Sustaining the Family Business: An Insider's Guide to Managing Across Generations* (Reading, Massachusetts: Perseus Books, 1999), 159.
8   Baum, *Citizen Coors*, 31.
9   William Bulkeley, "The Brewmasters," *Wall Street Journal*, October 26, 1973, sec. 1.
10 *Time*, "The Beer that Won the West," February 11, 1974, 11.
11 Ibid.
12 Grace Lichtenstein, "Rocky Mountain High," *New York Times*, December 28, 1975, 152; Feulner, "Coors, R.I.P."
13 Steven Greenhouse, "The Coors Boys Stick to Business," *New York Times*, November 30, 1986, sec. 3.
14 Adam Bernstein, "Joseph Coors Sr., 85, Dies," *Washington Post*, March 18, 2003, sec. B.
15 Baum, *Citizen Coors*, 49.
16 Bulkeley, "The Brewmasters," 22.
17 Ibid.
18 *Time*, "Bitter Beercott," December 26, 1977, 15.
19 Louis Aguilar and Jim Kirksey, "Joseph Coors—1917–2003," *Denver Post*, March 17, 2003, sec. A.
20 Baum, *Citizen Coors*, 70.
21 Eric Morgenthaler, "Reagan Makes Joseph Coors a Happy Fellow," *Wall Street Journal*, June 4, 1981, sec. 1.
22 Ibid., 84–85.
23 Ibid., 86.
24 Ibid., 89.
25 Ibid., 13.
26 Ibid., 90.
27 Ibid.
28 Lee Edwards, *The Power of Ideas* (Ottawa, Illinois: Jameson Books, Inc., 1997), 7.
29 Paul Weyrich, "The Most Important Legacy of Joseph Coors," March 24, 2003, http://www.enterstateright.com/archive/articles/0303/0303coors.txt.
30 Ibid.
31 Ibid.
32 Edwards, *The Power of Ideas*, 6.
33 Baum, *Citizen Coors*, 105.
34 Edwards, *The Power of Ideas*, 10.
35 Ibid.
36 Ibid.
37 Bernard Weinraub, "Heritage Foundation 10 Years Later," *New York Times*, September 30, 1983, sec. A.
38 Amy Wilentz, "On the Intellectual Ramparts," *Time*, September 1, 1986, 23.
39 Edwards, *The Power of Ideas*, 44.
40 Ibid., 47.
41 Ibid.
42 Ibid., 49.
43 Ibid., 67.
44 William Farrell and Warren Weaver, "Mandate and the Sequel," *New York Times*, December 5, 1984, sec. A.
45 Mark Muro, "The Right House," *Boston Globe*, February 4, 1986, 11.
46 Boffey, "Heritage Foundation," 62.
47 Edwards, *The Power of Ideas*, 71.
48 Philip Boffey, "Heritage Foundation: Success in Obscurity," *New York Times*, November 17, 1985, sec. 1.
49 John McCaslin, "Moment of Truth," *Washington Times*, March 20, 2003, sec. A.
50 George Nash, *The Conservative Intellectual Movement in America* (Wilmington, Delaware: Intercollegiate Studies Institute, 1998), 334.
51 Paul Richter, "Coors' New Brew: Taking out the Political Aftertaste," *Los Angeles Times*, September 27, 1987, sec. 4.
52 John J. Miller, "Joseph Coors, RIP," *Wall Street Journal*, March 20, 2003, http://www.opinionjournal.com/extra/?id=110003221.
53 John Micklethwait and Adrian Wooldridge, *The Right Nation* (New

Notes

York: The Penguin Press, 2004), 167.
54 Ibid., 167–168.
55 Jane Mayer, "Politics '84—Heritage Foundation: Right-Wing Thinkers Push Ideas," *Wall Street Journal*, December 7, 1984, sec. 1.
56 Muro, "Right House."
57 Margaret Rankin, "Heritage Foundation Counts Its Blessings," *Washington Times*, December 10, 1999, 12.
58 Edwards, *The Power of Ideas*, 212.
59 Rankin, "Heritage Foundation," 12.
60 *New York Times*, "Senate Unit Sets Coors Vote Delay," September 12, 1975, sec. 2.
61 Stanhope Gould, "Coors Brews the News," *Columbia Journalism Review* 13, no. 6 (March/April 1975): 18.
62 Gould, "Coors Brews," 18.
63 Lichtenstein, "Rocky Mountain High," 152.
64 Baum, *Citizen Coors*, 113.
65 *Nation*, "Editorials," November 15, 1975, 485.
66 *New York Times*, "Senate Unit," 66.
67 *New York Times*, "No Birch Member, Coors Maintains," September 11, 1975, sec. 2.
68 Baum, *Citizen Coors*, 103.
69 *New York Times*, "Senate Unit," 66.
70 Lichtenstein, "Rocky Mountain High," 152.
71 Gould, "Coors Brews," 28.
72 Jennifer Harper, "Fox to Air more than 'Just the Facts': Murdoch's New News Channel Takes on Rivals with Analysis Emphasis," *Washington Times*, October 4, 1996, 10.
73 Micklethwait, 163.
74 Ibid.
75 Morgenthaler, "Reagan Makes," 26.
76 Baum, *Citizen Coors*, 237.
77 Ibid., 235.
78 Lichtenstein, "Rocky Mountain High," 152.
79 Baum, *Citizen Coors*, 236.
80 Lichtenstein, "Rocky Mountain High," 152.
81 Warren Weaver, "Coors Said to Aid Reagan Campaign," *New York Times*, March 31, 1976, 25.
82 Feulner, "Salute to a Visionary Founder."
83 Ronald Reagan, "Remarks at a White House Ceremony Commemorating the Bicentennial Year of Air and Space Flight," February 7, 1983, *The Public Papers of President Ronald W. Reagan*, Ronald Reagan Presidential Library, http://www.reagan.utexas.edu/archives/speeches/1983/20783b.htm.
84 Ibid., 666.
85 Ibid., 677.
86 Ronald Reagan, *An American Life* (New York: Simon & Schuster, 1990), 548.
87 William Schmidt, "The 'Colorado Mafia' Puts Its Stamp on the Government," *New York Times*, September 6, 1981, sec. A.
88 Bertram Wolfe to Joseph Coors, July 18, 1975, box 4, folder 70, Bertram David Wolfe Papers, Hoover Institution Archives.
89 Joseph Coors to Bertram Wolfe, August 6, 1975, box 4, folder 70, Bertram David Wolfe Papers, HIA.
90 *San Francisco Chronicle*, "Wright's Accuser/Gingrich Defends His Own Book Deal," April 26, 1989, sec. A.
91 Jim Sanders, "Deal in Lawsuit Reveals Donors," *Sacramento Bee*, May 19, 2005, sec. A.
92 Baum, *Citizen Coors*, 8.

Chapter 9

1 John Engalitcheff to the Honorable Harry Hull, June 4, 1930, Baltimore Aircoil Company's John Engalitcheff Display, Dorsey, Maryland.
2 Richard Pipes, *Russia Under the Bolshevik Regime* (New York: Alfred A. Knopf, 1993), 9.
3 Frederick M. Long, personal interview with authors Ron Robinson and Nicole Hoplin, September 2, 2005.
4 *New York Times*, "Capt. Cyril Engalitcheff," August 29, 1933, 17.
5 Georgana Long, personal interview with authors Ron Robinson and Nicole Hoplin, September 2, 2005.
6 *Washington Post*, "Russian Exiles, Other Lands Barred, Told to Quit Baltimore," May 16, 1934, 15.
7 John Engalitcheff, "If I were 21," *Refrigerating Engineering* (American Society of Refrigerating Engineers, October 1958).

8 Frederick M. Long, "Speech to BAC Employees," Frederick M. Long personal files, Nov. 21, 1984.
9 Frederick M. Long, personal interview with authors Ron Robinson and Nicole Hoplin, September 2, 2005.
10 John Engalitcheff to the Honorable Harry Hull, June 4, 1930, Baltimore Aircoil Company's John Engalitcheff Display, Dorsey, Maryland.
11 Ibid.
12 Ibid.
13 Scott Moore, "Tight Times and Nostalgic Tales," *Washington Post*, November 14, 1993, sec. Y.
14 Ralph Simpson, "Engineer Started in Depression," *Baltimore Sun*, July 16, 1972.
15 *New York Times*, "Son of Ex-Prince Weds Mrs. Rogow," November 11, 1935, 26.
16 Ellison Moss, "Founder of Honored 'Firm' Recalls Flight from Russia," *Baltimore Sun*, November 14, 1967.
17 Susan Irving-Monshaw, *John Engalitcheff, Jr.* (Fund For American Studies: Washington, D.C., 1994), 9.
18 Simpson, "Engineer Started in Depression."
19 *Washington Post*, "Baltimore Struck by 10-Alarm Fire," Feb. 3, 1956, 26; Moss, "Founder of Honored 'Firm.'"
20 Moss, "Founder of Honored 'Firm.'"
21 Edward Schinner, personal interview with author Nicole Hoplin, August 2, 2005.
22 Ibid.
23 Norva Pope, personal interview with author Nicole Hoplin, September 2, 2005.
24 Spiro T. Agnew, Executive Records, Governor Spiro T. Agnew, 1967–1969, *Archives of Maryland Online*, vol. 83, November 16, 1967, 518.
25 Ibid.
26 Simpson, "Engineer Started in Depression."
27 *Wall Street Journal*, "Amsted Completes Purchase," May 21, 1985, sec. 2.
28 John Engalitcheff Retirement Brochure, Baltimore Aircoil Company's John Engalitcheff Display, Dorsey, Maryland.
29 Norva Pope, personal interview with author Nicole Hoplin, September 2, 2005.
30 John Fisher, personal telephone interview with author Nicole Hoplin, July 21, 2005.
31 Aljean Harmetz, "A Growth of Issues-Oriented Advocacy Programs and Commercials on TV," *New York Times*, November 25, 1984, sec. C.
32 Bruce Kennedy, "War Games," CNN Perspectives Series, episode 22, http://www.cnn.com/SPECIALS/cold.war/episodes/22/spotlight/.
33 Robert Timberg and Jesse Glasgow, "Retired Head of Baltimore Firm Dies After Collapsing at White House Affair," *Baltimore Sun*, November 20, 1984, sec A.
34 Edward Schinner, personal interview with author Nicole Hoplin, August 2, 2005.
35 John Engalitcheff Jr. to Ron Robinson, March 25, 1981, Young America's Foundation files.
36 Ronald Reagan, "Radio Address to the Nation on Foreign Policy," September 24, 1988, *The Public Papers of President Ronald W. Reagan*, Ronald Reagan Presidential Library, http://www.reagan.utexas.edu/archives/speeches/1988/092488a.htm.
37 Frederick M. Long, personal interview with authors Ron Robinson and Nicole Hoplin, September 2, 2005.
38 C-SPAN, "Ronald Reagan," *American Presidents: Life Portraits*, 1999.
39 Ronald Reagan, "President Reagan Addresses 15th Anniversary Student Conference," 1993, Young America's Foundation files.
40 Ronald Reagan, "Farewell Address to the Nation," Reagan Foundation, January 11, 1989, http://www.reaganfoundation.org/reagan/speeches/farewell.asp.
41 Frederick M. Long, personal interview with authors Ron Robinson and Nicole Hoplin, September 2, 2005.
42 Will Lester, "Americans Agree Washington Not 1 of Top Presidents," *Advocate*, February 21, 2005, sec. C.
43 Edward Schinner, personal interview with author Nicole Hoplin, August 2, 2005.
44 Norva Pope, personal interview with author Nicole Hoplin, September 2, 2005.